Basic Social Statistics and Quantitative Research Methods

Basic Social Statistics and Quantitative Research Methods

A Computer-Assisted Introduction

James W. Grimm & Paul R. Wozniak

Western Kentucky University

Wadsworth Publishing Company
Belmont, California
A Division of Wadsworth, Inc.

Sociology Editor: Serina Beauparlant

Editorial Assistant: Marla Nowick

Production Editors: Gary Mcdonald and Angela Mann

Managing Designer: James Chadwick

Print Buyer: Barbara Britton

Designer: Rick Chafian

Copy Editor: Tom Briggs

Technical Illustrator: Alexander Teshin Associates

Compositor: TypeLink, Inc.

Cover: Harry Voigt

Signing Representative: Mark Francisco

© 1990 by Wadsworth, Inc. All rights reserved. No part of this book may be reproduced, stored in a retrieval system, or transcribed, in any form or by any means, electronic, mechanical, photocopying, recording, or otherwise, without the prior written permission of the publisher, Wadsworth Publishing Company, Belmont, California 94002, a division of Wadsworth, Inc.

Printed in the United States of America   19

1 2 3 4 5 6 7 8 9 10—94 93 92 91 90

Library of Congress Cataloging in Publication Data

Grimm, James W.
    Basic social statistics and quantitative research methods : a
computer-assisted introduction / James W. Grimm. Paul R. Wozniak.
        p.   cm.
    ISBN 0-534-12594-8
    1. Social sciences—Data processing—Study and teaching.
I. Wozniak, Paul R.   II. Title.
HA35.G69   1990
300'.72—dc20   89-28592
                                                                CIP

We would like to dedicate this book to the members of our families who have supported us so faithfully, not only in this project but throughout our professional careers and personal lives.

To our families with love and thanks.

Contents

Section 5   Forming and Testing Hypotheses

Section 6   Measurement

Preface

The purpose of this text is to provide an effective means for the teaching and learning of social statistical techniques and quantitative research methods. Our approach emphasizes understanding and applying such techniques, rather than simply reading about and memorizing them. Each of the 15 sections in the text explains the reasoning behind and the analytic steps involved in statistical and related methodological procedures that are employed to answer important research questions in sociology and the social sciences. The examples and illustrations in each section encourage active involvement in thinking about and seeing how various procedures address statistical and quantitative methodological problems. And the exercises that conclude each section engage students in actually doing what was discussed and illustrated in the text. Furthermore, both the illustrations and the exercises enable instructors and students to conduct statistical and methodological activities in noncomputerized and/or computerized ways. No prior knowledge of or familiarity with computerized statistical programs on the part of the students or faculty is needed to do the computer exercises.

Each section contains discussion, illustrations, and exercises covering an important aspect of statistics and quantitative research methodology. Our approach combines basic topics usually included in statistics books and in the quantitative parts of methods books into one volume. Throughout the text we have sought to provide the following:

1. concise and logically organized discussions of both basic social statistics and quantitative research methods

2. clear and meaningful illustrations that enable students to understand how and why procedures are done

3. examples of how to interpret statistical and other quantitative techniques in research reports

4. exercises that are directly related to text material and that give students an opportunity to actually *do* statistical and quantitative research

5. the means by which both computer users and nonusers can benefit from the text and the exercises

6. an interesting real-world dataset, the CPS (Community Preference Survey), which is easy to use and which integrates text material, illustrations, and exercises

The CPS study that we conducted (along with our students in a Survey Applications course) has played an important role not only in our teaching but also in this text and exercises. The CPS study provides a dataset that allows instructors to discuss and do state-of-the-art research and represents a practical, on-going vehicle for discussing, illustrating, and applying a wide range of basic statistical and quantitative research procedures. The CPS codebook, the CPS datafile, and the CPS questionnaire are all clear and useful resources that will be used throughout the text and exercises.

In the CPS, 611 adult residents of a county (18 years of age or older) were interviewed by telephone using random digit dialing and random household respondent selection techniques. The responses to over 80 questions asked in the interview provided information on the concerns and attitudes of county residents on a wide range of community issues and problems. The types of questions included involve issues that are applicable and that have relevance to communities throughout the country; many questions are similar to those typically asked in community issues surveys. Above all, the CPS dataset and the SPSS/PC+ and STATPAC statistical programs provide a "user friendly" tool with which to integrate computer usage into the teaching and learning of methodology and statistics. We have found the CPS dataset to be very appropriate for many of the statistical and methodological procedures discussed in this text, as well as more usable than many other datasets.

We want to emphasize that the text and exercises not only represent the outgrowth of many years of teaching but also reflect our experiences over the past several years in leading groups of students through both basic statistics and quantitative methods courses with a "hands on" approach. Our students have benefited much more from this latter approach than from traditional methods. We are convinced that instructors and students who use our text and exercises will become more involved in statistics and quantitative methods, for several reasons:

1. Students are better able to follow and comprehend these short, pointed discussions of statistical and quantitative research topics than they are the generally wordier discussions found in traditional texts.

2. Many students enjoy actually *doing* the statistical and methodological exercises.

3. Students get more involved with a dataset that offers interesting variables and is easy to use.

4. Students with no computer literacy can easily run the SPSS/PC+ or STATPAC routines on IBM, or IBM-compatible, personal computers by following the instructions we have provided. The CPS file and data also can be uploaded, with minimal modifications, for use on SPSS[x] by mainframe users.

5. Students learn more and retain more by completing the written assignments in the exercises than they would by merely reading and memorizing points about statistics and quantitative methods.

Because student enthusiasm for and involvement in basic statistics and quantitative research methods is increased, the instructor's job becomes both easier and more rewarding. Professors will enjoy teaching more because statistics and research techniques will become vehicles for understanding and conducting social analyses. Even professors who dread and dislike teaching statistics and quantitative research methods courses or who have not taught this material before will find the effort spent in this approach to be workable and worthwhile.

The sections are organized on the basis of our classroom experiences in teaching both quantitative methods and statistics courses and are arranged in the following manner: In Sections 1–3 we cover topics that introduce students to the basic steps and objectives of quantitative research and descriptive statistics. In Sections 4 and 5 we discuss cross-tabulation, or bivariate analysis, and hypothesis formulation. In Sections 6–9 we deal with various aspects of quantitative methods, each of which represents an area where statistical procedures come into play. In Sections 10–15 we present numerous statistical principles and procedures that serve as the major means by which quantitative researchers analyze and interpret data, test hypotheses, and reach conclusions.

Our text is integrated enough in content and in structure that it can be used in a course that includes both statistical and quantitative methodological topics. However, the text is also flexible enough that specific sections can be used in either statistics or quantitative methods courses. Because each section has been developed as a self-contained module of textual material, examples, illustrations, and exercises (usually including options for both noncomputerized and computerized learning activities), we encourage instructors to use this text in a variety of ways, including choosing selected sections and reordering the sections. We hope that those who use our text view it as a wide-ranging and adaptable device rather than a fixed blueprint.

The overall goal of this text is to promote an understanding of what the research process entails and of how statistical techniques and quantitative research methods fit together as research is conducted. The exercises provide an opportunity to learn basic statistics and quantitative research methods by actually doing them. We hope that this kind of learning experience increases interest in, and confidence in doing, research and in analyzing and interpreting the results.

ACKNOWLEDGMENTS

We wish to acknowledge the contributions and assistance of a number of people at Wadsworth Publishing Company. Sheryl Fullerton initiated this project and Mark Francisco was instrumental in getting us started. Their suggestions and skillful guidance were very helpful in the early and formative stages. Serina Beauparlant has worked with us to complete the book, and her dedication to this innovative project, as well as her encouragement to "hang in there," kept the book on schedule. The assistance of Karen Rovens and Marla Nowick is also appreciated. Gratitude is also extended to the superb production staff. Angela Mann ably guided the production process. Gary Mcdonald and Tom Briggs performed a careful and conscientious line-by-line critique and editing of the final manuscript, correcting, improving, and adding organization, coherence, and style to the book. Stacey Pollard did a masterful job of producing the Instructor's Manual that contains the solutions to all the exercises in the book.

Also, we wish to acknowledge and thank the many colleagues who reviewed the manuscript in its many stages of preparation. All of their suggestions, criticisms, and evaluations were helpful, and many of their suggestions were incorporated into the final manuscript. The reviewers are: Francesca Alexander, California State University, L.A.; Robert Bendiksen, University of Wisconsin, La Crosse; Jerry Bode, Ball State University; Daniel M. Cherwin, Cumberland County College; Barbara Finlay, Texas A & M; Charles F. Holm, San Diego State University; Jean Schurz Huryn, Neuse Mental Hospital; Michael B. Kleiman, University of South Florida; Stephen Kulis, Arizona State University; Larry M. Lance, University of North Carolina; Jon Lorence, University of Houston; Thomas D. Meyers, Albright College; Kenneth J. Mietus, Western Illinois University; Steven L. Nock, University of Virginia; H. Wesley Perkins, Hobart and William Smith Colleges; Josephine Ruggiero, Providence College; Steven Stack, Auburn University; Arthur St. George, University of New Mexico; Robert W. Suckner, Northern Illinois University; Ann R. Tickamyer, University of Kentucky; and Gayle Wyckle, University of Alabama.

Special thanks are also extended to our colleagues Aaron Podolefsky, who provided support and equipment necessary for this project, and John Faine, who generously provided computer assistance whenever needed. The typing and word-processing assistance of Elashia Martin, Rachel Jones, and Michael Hanner also are greatly appreciated.

Finally, and very importantly, we are grateful to our many students in statistics and methods courses who have helped us develop and revise this book and its exercises. We especially wish to recognize the students in the Survey Applications course who conducted the CPS study that is used so extensively in the book and exercises: Beth Bayens, Theresa Burks, Timothy Fowlkes, Vickie Golden, Vicki Gregory, Susan Griffith, Nicholas Hicks, Lisa Norman, Brian Pickerill, Neil Quisenberry, and Kimberly Raybourne.

Introduction
Basic Math Review

> *"I hate math."*
> *"I'm no good at math."*
> *"I have always had difficulty with math."*
> *"I have _____ (a fear of math) (math anxiety) (a math phobia) (math avoidance) (a math attack)."*

Do any of the above sound familiar? Do they apply to you? Often students worry about, dread taking, and postpone taking as long as possible research methods and statistics courses because they believe the "math" will do them in.

The math review contained in this section will show you how elementary the math skills required for successful completion of statistics and research methods are. The math you need to learn or refamiliarize yourself with involves little more than basic arithmetic, squares, square roots, negative numbers, and formulas involving the order of operations and basic algebra.

Although most books ignore this topic or put a math review in an appendix at the end of the book, we have found this topic to be so important to student confidence and success that we begin the text with it. It helps to know right at the start what math skills are needed. And, once most students see that they possess or can easily acquire these basic skills, a lot of their worries and apprehensions disappear.

Those who are deficient in these basic arithmetic and math skills frequently encounter problems, become frustrated, and perform poorly in research methods and statistics courses simply because they cannot solve the problems and compute the formulas correctly. In contrast, those who are proficient in these basic skills can easily learn, and enjoy learning and applying, the subject matter. And most do. The few failures here result from lack of effort, not lack of ability.

After you finish the review, complete one of the diagnostic Math Review quizzes in the Exercise section. If you can satisfactorily complete the quiz, then you have the skills needed to successfully compute statistics and do research.

ARITHMETIC WITH POSITIVE AND NEGATIVE NUMBERS

When adding numbers with positive and negative signs, add up all the positive numbers and add up all the negative numbers. Then subtract the smaller total from the larger and use the sign of the larger.

When multiplying or dividing two numbers with different signs, remember that the product or quotient is negative.

Examples

$$3 - 8 = -5 \qquad -3 + 8 = 5$$

$$3 - (8) = -5 \qquad 3(-8) = -24$$

$$-3 - (8) = -11 \qquad (-3)(-8) = +24$$

$$-3 + (-8) = -11 \qquad -3/8 = -.375$$

ROUNDING

For the sake of greater accuracy only the final answer in a series of calculations should be rounded. All decimal places should be maintained in intermediate calculations. In most cases it is customary to round final answers to two decimal places. The following rounding rules will prevent any systematic rounding bias from occurring:

1. If the remaining decimal fraction to the right of the second decimal place is:
   a. greater than (>) .50, round up.
   b. less than (<) .50, round down.

   Examples

   8.578 = 8.58

   8.574 = 8.57

2. If the remaining fraction to the right of the second decimal place is exactly .50:
   a. round up to the next even number if the number in the second decimal place is odd.
   b. round down to the next even number if the number in the second decimal place is even.

   Examples

   8.575 = 8.58 (because 7 is odd)
   8.585 = 8.58 (because 8 is even)

   8.565 = 8.56 (because 6 is even)
   8.5851 = 8.59 (because .51 > .50)

ORDER OF OPERATIONS

An inexpensive calculator is a necessity—with a calculator you can easily solve all the formulas used in this text. In addition to the basic arithmetic functions, make sure your calculator has the square root ($\sqrt{\ }$) function. A memory for storage of intermediate results is also helpful.

In order to obtain the answer to an expression or formula that involves more than one operation, you must follow the order of operations. Failure to adhere to the order of operations is probably the main reason why errors in computation occur (aside from faulty or incomplete entering of numbers into the calculator).

Operations *must* be performed in the following order:

1. Do what is indicated within parentheses or brackets.

2. Square numbers and take square roots.

3. Multiply and divide.

4. Add and subtract.

   Examples

$$20 - 1.64 \left[\frac{-40}{\sqrt{74}} \right] = 20 - 1.64 \left[\frac{-40}{8.6023252} \right]$$

$$= 20 - 1.64(-4.6499055)$$

$$= 20 + 7.625845$$

$$= 27.625845$$

$$= 27.63$$

$$4(6 - 2) - \left[1.96 \left(\frac{.22}{\sqrt{88}} \right) \right] 2 + 3(-.02)^2 = 4(4) - \left[1.96 \left(\frac{.22}{9.3808315} \right) \right] 2 + 3(.0004)$$

$$= 16 - (.045966)2 + .0012$$

$$= 16 - .091932 + .0012$$

$$= 15.909268$$

$$= 15.91$$

ALGEBRA

Remember these two rules and the order of operations:

1. When you add/subtract a value or term on one side of the equation, you must also add/subtract the value or term on the other side. (Shortcut procedure: When you move an added or subtracted term or value from one side of the equation to the other side, its sign changes.)

   Example

$$x - 4 = y + 7$$

   To solve for x:

Add $+4$ to each side	or	Move -4 to other side and change sign
$x - 4 + 4 = y + 7 + 4$		$x = y + 7 + 4$
$x = y + 11$		$x = y + 11$

2. When you multiply/divide a value or term on one side of the equation, you must also multiply/divide the value or term on the other side. (Short-cut procedure: If a term is multiplied on one side of the equation, when moved to the other side it will be divided; and, if a

term is divided on one side of the equation, it will be multiplied when moved to the other side.)

Examples

$$z = x(y)$$

To solve for x:

Divide each side by y   or   Move y to the other side; because it multiplies on one side, it will divide on the other

$$\frac{z}{y} = \frac{x(y)}{y} \qquad\qquad x = \frac{z}{y}$$

$$x = z/y$$

$$x - 8 = 3/4y - 6$$

To solve for y:

$$x - 2 = 3/4y$$

$$4/3(x - 2) = y \quad \text{or} \quad y = 1.33x - 2.67 \quad \text{or} \quad y = \frac{x - 2}{3/4}$$

THE SUMMATION SIGN

The Greek letter Σ (capital sigma) means to sum or add. Whenever Σ appears it means that all values of the variable appearing to the right of it should be summed or added together.

Consider the following distributions of variables x and y for five cases or individuals.

Case or Individual	Value of x	Value of y
A	1	2
B	2	4
C	3	6
D	4	8
E	5	10

1. Σx means add all the values of x: $1 + 2 + 3 + 4 + 5$. Therefore, $\Sigma x = 15$.

2. Σy means add all the values of y: $2 + 4 + 6 + 8 + 10$. Therefore, $\Sigma y = 30$.

3. $\Sigma(x + y)$ means add values of x and y for each case together and then sum.

x	y	x + y
1	2	3
2	4	6
3	6	9
4	8	12
5	10	15
$\Sigma x = 15$	$\Sigma y = 30$	$\Sigma(x + y) = 45$

Note: $\Sigma(x + y) = \Sigma x + \Sigma y = 15 + 30 = 45$

4. $\Sigma(xy)$ means multiply values of x and y for each case together and sum the products.

x	y	xy
1	2	2
2	4	8
3	6	18
4	8	32
5	10	50
$\Sigma x = 15$	$\Sigma y = 30$	$\Sigma(xy) = 110$

Note: $\Sigma(xy) \neq$ (is not equal to) $(\Sigma x)(\Sigma y)$

5. $(\Sigma x)(\Sigma y) = (15)(30) = 450$

6. Σx^2 means square each value of x and then sum.

x	x²
1	1
2	4
3	9
4	16
5	25
$\Sigma x = 15$	$\Sigma x^2 = 55$

7. $(\Sigma x)^2$ means sum all values of x and then square the total: $(\Sigma x)^2 = (15)^2 = 225$.

Exercise A:
Math Review Quiz

Perform the following calculations:

1. $-2 + 3 + 5 - 4 + 2 + 1 - 18 =$
2. $(59)^2 =$
3. $\sqrt{180} =$
4. $2(4) + 7(2 + 1) - 15 =$
5. $3^5 =$
6. $(1/3)^4 =$
7. $(\sqrt{15} + 6)^2 =$
8. $-99/11 =$
9. $(-9)(-6) =$
10. $2.58 + 4/9(77) =$
11. $\dfrac{\sqrt{25}}{\sqrt{5}} =$
12. $\dfrac{18}{\dfrac{3(.40)}{\sqrt{16}}} =$
13. If $a + b = c$, then $b =$
14. If $b = a/x$, then $x =$
15. If $x = 2/5(y) + 7$, then $y =$

Round the following numbers to two decimal places:

16. 88.435
17. 33.445
18. 88.437

For the following values of x

$$1, 2, 3, 3, 5, -5, 7, -9, 9, 10$$

calculate:

19. Σx
20. $(\Sigma x)^2$
21. Σx^2
22. $\Sigma (2x)^2$

Exercise B:
Math Review Quiz

Perform the following calculations:

1. $-3 + 14 + 6 - 5 + 3 + 2 - 9 =$
2. $(49)^2 =$
3. $\sqrt{280} =$
4. $2(5) + 7(3 + 1) - 16 =$
5. $4^5 =$
6. $(1/4)^4 =$
7. $(\sqrt{17} + 6)^2 =$
8. $88/-12 =$
9. $(-8)(-9) =$
10. $1.96 + 4/9(77) =$
11. $\dfrac{\sqrt{49}}{\sqrt{7}} =$
12. $\dfrac{20}{\dfrac{4(.50)}{\sqrt{25}}} =$
13. If $x + y = z$, then $y =$
14. If $y = x/z$, then $z =$
15. If $a = 3/4(b) + 6$, then $b =$

Round the following numbers to two decimal places:

16. 32.875
17. 32.864
18. 32.865

For the following values of x

$$1, 2, -3, 3, 4, 5, 7, 9, 9, -10$$

calculate:

19. Σx
20. $(\Sigma x)^2$
21. Σx^2
22. $\Sigma (2x)^2$

Overview

This book and exercises depart in several ways from traditional statistics and methods books. For one, because we believe it is essential to communicate the logic and substance of basic social statistical and quantitative research methods with an economy of words, we have attempted to write concise and focused treatments of the topics we cover. Furthermore, we believe students should engage in learning activities that systematically apply and reinforce concepts and procedures discussed and illustrated in textual material. Therefore, we have tried to provide a wide variety of thoughtfully constructed exercises. In the exercises *learning takes place through doing* and is more effective and enjoyable than merely reading about the subjects.

We believe you will learn more about statistical procedures and quantitative techniques when these areas are integrated with one another—our viewpoint is that statistical and methodological areas should not be treated as completely separate specialties. Our book thus includes material that allows your instructors the option of integrating statistics and methods in a variety of ways and to varying degrees. In doing so, they can realistically and meaningfully convey to you how statistical procedures and methodological procedures fit together in the quantitative research process.

This text, and the accompanying exercises, also reflect our belief that computerized analyses can and should be integrated into both the scope and content of textual material. Students gain more experience in using computers and thereby have a better chance to overcome their hesitancies about computers when computing is dealt with throughout a text rather than only in certain sections or in appendices. Our class-room experiences with students who have had little or no computer experience suggests that, whatever your knowledge of computers, you should have no trouble learning and applying the techniques we present in this text. The detailed step-by-step instructions for each procedure covered also allow instructors who are computer illiterate to use computers in their classes even if they have not done so previously. We have included computerized illustrations and sample computer output throughout the book. We have explained why computers are used and how computer output is interpreted. Answers to selected exercises appear in Appendix F. It is important to stress that the statistical software packages that we use (SPSS/PC+ and STATPAC) do *not* require that either students or instructors be sophisticated in the use of computers or in any programming language.

For instructors who do not have access to computers or who do not use them, our book includes a full complement of noncomputerized exercises. Our goal has been to develop a text that can be applied to both computerized and noncomputerized learning experiences.

The text and exercises have been developed with systematic reference to a dataset obtained through an actual community survey conducted by the authors and their students (the CPS, or Community Preference Survey, dataset). It is our experience that the CPS's wide-ranging set of topics and variables enhances students' interest in doing statistical and methodological exercises (see the CPS Questionnaire in Appendix E). The dataset can serve a variety of functions: (1) as a source of illustrations and examples; (2) as a means of assigning exercises; and (3) as a model for discussing or conducting various aspects of survey research such as interviewing, sampling, and coding, as well as doing an actual community survey. We have found the CPS to be an invaluable aid in our teaching.

Our approach results from many years of teaching both statistics and quantitative methods courses and from experimenting with a variety of teaching methods. Using this approach we have found our most recent years of teaching to be our most gratifying. We hope that our readers will also find that this approach increases both the quality of and the satisfaction from their classroom experiences.

The continuing process by which theory, measurement, sampling, research design, data collection, statistical testing, and presentation of research results are interrelated is depicted in the following diagram. Various sections of this text and the exercises deal with the linkages between theory, research, and statistics. The diagram shows how the interrelationships between theory, research methods, and statistics fuel the research process.

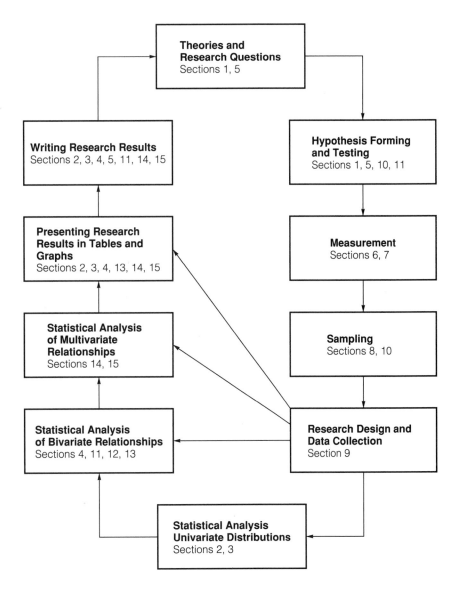

How theory, research methods, and statistics interrelate

Through this approach we hope to introduce you to the exciting world of social research, where you will learn how to conduct various aspects of quantitative research and to apply statistics to answer important theoretical and practical questions. In this text and exercises we will show you how to use methodological and statistical procedures to do research. Though they are based upon numbers, and though they are conducted using technical procedures, quantitative methods and statistics are means by which researchers and those who are made aware of research results experience the genuine excitement of sharing an enhanced understanding of the world.

1

Variables and the Research Process

Variables are necessary and important in describing and measuring the world. A *variable* is something that has two or more meaningful and useful divisions, categories, characteristics, or values. When we assign names, numerals, and numbers to things that change in the real world, we have variables. In fact, we would find it impossible to understand the world without variables.

For example, do you buy a pizza or sweatshirt without specifying the size (small, medium, large)? Do you buy a house without knowing how many bedrooms it has? Do you understand "temperature" without a thermometer or "speed" without a speedometer? Do you understand "social class" without the categories of upper, middle, and lower class or "religion" without the categories of Protestant, Catholic, and Jew? Variables allow us to purchase goods, to travel, to be aware of our environment, and to understand people and society in efficient ways. Variables are essential to our description and understanding of one another and the real world.

TYPES OF VARIABLES

The social world would be impossible to understand if the characteristics of people and their social lives could not be classified and compared by type (kind) and by amount (degree). Social researchers generally divide variables into three classifications: nominal, ordinal, and interval/ratio. These classifications represent both types of variables and levels of measurement.

Nominal Variables

Social researchers call variables that classify people or things into types or kinds *nominal variables*. The categories of nominal variables do not differ by quantity, degree, or amount, but only by kind. Nominal categories or classes are distinct, mutually exclusive, exhaustive, and non-orderable. For example, the two categories of the nominal variable "gender" (male and female) are distinct, do not overlap, include all possible sexes, and cannot be ordered or ranked. The same would be true of the nominal variable "region," which might be broken into the categories of East, West, North, and South.

Nominal variables represent the lowest level of measurement because they allow you only to count and compare the number of cases in each category.

Ordinal Variables

Like nominal variables, *ordinal variables* also classify people or things into types or kinds, but with one additional feature: Here the classes or categories can be ranked. Ordinal categories are distinct, mutually exclusive, and exhaustive, but they are also orderable in terms of quantity, magnitude, or some other criteria. For example, the three categories of the ordinal variable "social class" (upper, middle, and lower) are distinct, do not overlap, include the entire range of social class, and can be ranked: The upper class is higher than the middle class and the middle class is higher than the lower class. No statement can be made, however, about the amount of difference between categories. The differences between upper and middle and between middle and lower are not calculable.

Ordinal variables also provide a more specific and higher level of measurement than do nominal variables. Not only can the number of cases in each category be counted and the size of categories compared, but conclusions about "more than" and "less than" can be made about the categories.

Interval/Ratio Variables

Although the categories of nominal and ordinal variables cannot be further subdivided on a measurement scale, the values of *interval/ratio variables* permit distances and differences between values on a scale to be considered or measured. Some social researchers even distinguish between interval and ratio variables. In both cases scale intervals are of equal size. Whereas with interval variables there is an arbitrary zero point, however, with ratio variables there is a true zero point where zero is equivalent to a total absence of the variable. For example, time measured by calendars, temperature on the Fahrenheit scale, and intelligence by IQ scores are interval variables because zero values do not mean the total absence of time, temperature, or intelligence, respectively. In contrast, age, income, and urbanization (percent of a population living in urban places) are ratio variables because zero values do indicate a total absence of those attributes.

For most statistical purposes interval and ratio variables are treated as a similar type of variable. Note, however, that a major difference is the fact that one cannot form ratios with the values of interval variables. For example, it is incorrect to say that 60° is twice as hot as 30°; but it is correct to say that $60,000 is twice as much as $30,000. Because of the scarcity of interval variables, the ambiguity concerning the differences between interval and ratio variables, and their similar statistical treatment, it makes sense to treat these two types of variables as one type.

Interval/ratio variables have all the features of ordinal variables; in addition, there are equal units of difference—years of age, dollars of income, points of IQ—throughout the full range of the measurement scale. This represents the highest level of measurement. Different points on the scale may be compared by addition, subtraction, multiplication, and division. Some interval/ratio variables are *continuous* in nature, meaning that the values used in the scale have intermediate values and that the values can be subdivided infinitely into values that lie between any two adjacent values (e.g., age, time, percent urban). Other interval/ratio variables have values that are *discrete*—that is, that are distinct with no value falling between adjacent values on the scale (e.g., number of children in a family or family income). Even though the number of children in a family is discrete, when numbers of children in families of different groups are compared through the use of a summary measure, such as an average, the variable is appropriately treated as continuous. Here it is possible and meaningful for the variable to have fractional values, for example, an average of 3.5 children in one group compared to an average of 1.8 for another.

USING VARIABLES IN RESEARCH

Several important points need to be made in order to clarify how variables are used in research. First, traits or characteristics that describe or pertain to individuals, such as being male, belonging to the middle class, and earning $20,000, cannot be used in research until they are grouped as variables. "Gender" is the variable consisting of the traits male and female. The variable "social class" may result from distinguishing and grouping the categories of upper, middle, and lower class (or some other set of categories). "Income" is the variable made up of all the values of the number of dollars earned from a job. Although these examples concern variables dealing with traits or characteristics of persons, it should be noted that traits or characteristics of other social units of analysis also need to be grouped as variables. For example, a private, for-profit organization is not a variable, but the variable "organizational type" consists of several groupings: private, for-profit organizations; private, nonprofit organizations; and public, nonprofit organizations. Through the use of variables the traits or characteristics of people or things can be grouped and arranged by type, by rank, or by amount. Table 1.1 shows some potential relationships between traits of persons and variables.

Second, social researchers are not interested in describing or explaining people or things as individual cases, but rather in describing and explaining variables and the relationship among variables. It is not the people per se who are being examined in social research; it is the classification, ranks, or values of variables that are of interest. (See the groupings of individuals according to variables in Table 1.1.)

Examination of single-variable, or univariate, distributions is one type of description social researchers are interested in. Sections 2 and 3 cover the construction and analysis of univariate frequency distributions; Sections 6–9 discuss the gathering of data on variables in survey research, sampling procedures, and basic methodological and statistical considerations in measuring variables, including variable construction, operationalization, indicators, index construction, and issues of validity and reliability.

Another type of description and explanation that is of interest to social researchers involves two variables, or bivariate analysis. The construction and analysis of bivariate tables to determine how nominal and ordinal variables are related to one another is presented in Section 4. Relationships between two interval/ratio–level variables are covered in Section 13 with an examination of regression and correlation. Section 5

Table 1.1 Relationships Between Traits or Characteristics
of Persons and Variables

Traits	Variable	Type of Variable	Examples of Traits of 10 Individuals Grouped According to the Variable							
male (M)	gender	nominal (classification only)	M	M	M	M	M	M	=	6
female (F)			F	F	F	F			=	4
upper class (U)	social class	ordinal	U	U					=	2
middle class (M)		(classifications can be ranked)	M	M	M	M	M	M	=	6
lower class (L)			L	L					=	2

number of dollars earned	income	interval/ratio (values represent equal amounts of difference)	——— $50,000
			——— 43,000
			——— 37,000
			——— 29,000
			——— 24,000
			23,000
			——— 20,000
			19,000
			18,000
			——— 14,000
			———
			———

deals with forming and testing hypotheses about variables; and tests of hypotheses for data on variables obtained from samples are covered in Sections 10–12.

Researchers also are involved in more complex studies involving variables. A basic introduction to analyses of more than two variables, or multivariate analysis, is covered in Sections 14 and 15 dealing with bivariate table elaboration and multiple regression.

VARIABLES AND THE STEPS OF RESEARCH

Social researchers use variables at every stage of the research process. Though the steps of the research process are not always completed in exactly this order, researchers can logically discuss what they will do or have done based on the following stages: (1) asking a research question, (2) formulating hypotheses, (3) constructing a research design, (4) developing measures, (5) collecting data, (6) analyzing results, and (7) drawing conclusions.

1. Asking Research Questions

The questions that researchers typically ask and seek to answer are questions about one or more variables. For example, questions about one variable are answered by examining how that variable is distributed (see Sections 1 and 2). Questions about how two variables are related to each other are answered by research that deals with bivariate relationships (see Sections 4 and 11–13). Still other research questions and types of research deal with how three or more variables are interrelated (see Sections 14 and 15). The nature and scope of a research project depends upon the type and number of variables in the research question.

2. Formulating Hypotheses

Researchers usually formulate hypotheses or statements of how one or more variables are expected to be distributed or interrelated. Such hypotheses are compared to the results obtained after the research is completed. The purpose of having hypotheses is not to predetermine research outcomes but to provide baselines against which to compare actual results (see Sections 5 and 10). Hypotheses are formulated on the basis of researchers' understandings of or theories about the research topic (see Section 5). Whether or not results support hypotheses is how research contributes to an increased understanding of the social world (see Sections 10 and 11). Such understanding is increased regardless of whether variables operate as researchers expected them to (see step 7).

3. Constructing Research Designs

Before research can begin, researchers must select and develop a research design. Social researchers can choose from among a variety of research strategies—observation, experimentation, survey research, and use of documents, among others. Because the various types of survey research are widely used by social researchers, we focus on them in the text and exercises. The basic aspects of survey research include sampling the population being studied (see Section 8) and identifying methods by which to obtain information from the sample, such as interviews or questionnaires (see Section 9). An emphasis on survey research is appropriate because much academic research, as well as research done by government agencies and private businesses, involves surveys. Survey research is a major way in which researchers discover how variables are distributed and interrelated and make inferences about larger populations.

4. Developing Measures

Social reseachers deal with variables that involve the different levels of measurement defined and illustrated in previous parts of this section. No matter what level of measurement is used, researchers must answer important questions about the measurement of the variables they are studying. Will a single indicator or a trait or concept be used? Or will more than one indicator be employed? If a variable is measured using several indicators, how will they be combined and scored to form an index or a scale? What techniques will be used to determine if the ways in which variables have been measured are reliable and valid? Construction and evaluation of measures is crucial for successful research (see Sections 6 and 7).

5. Collecting Data

A major part of any research project is the actual process by which evidence is gathered. As was mentioned previously, considerable attention is given in the text and exercises to how researchers actually select samples and use interviews or questionnaires (see Sections 8 and 9). Careful sampling is essential if variables are to be studied meaningfully. Different ways to conduct survey research are used depending upon the types of research questions and hypotheses researchers have.

6. Analyzing Results

Social researchers use different statistical techniques to analyze their results, depending on the type(s) and number of variables being studied. Certain techniques are appropriate for describing and summarizing single variables (see Sections 1 and 2). Some statistical and methodological techniques are appropriate for nominal or ordinal variables (see Sections 3, 4, and 14). Other techniques are appropriate for studying bivariate relationships between interval/ratio variables (see Section 13); and still others must be used to analyze relationships between more than two interval/ratio variables (see Section 15). The principles behind inferential statistical analyses (see Section 10) and the different statistical tests available to analyze data (see Sections 11–15) require that researchers use techniques appropriate for the types of variables they are studying. Illustrations and exercises are provided to help you understand and apply these basic principles and procedures in actual analyses of survey data involving different types of variables and their relationships.

7. Drawing Conclusions

The basic conclusions of the typical research project involve a discussion that addresses whether the evidence analyzed supports the hypothesis. Do the results support the expectations about how variables will be distributed or interrelated? If so, it may be desirable to replicate the research project—that is, repeat it to see if similar findings can be obtained again. Replication of results increases confidence in explanations and enhances their generalizability. Even if results do not support expectations about variables, researchers still learn how variables actually *are* distributed or interrelated in the real world. How research results are written and how findings are used to draw conclusions and make generalizations about variables are illustrated throughout this book. Being able to communicate research results is a particularly valuable skill useful in many different types of careers.

Exercise 1A:
Types of Variables in Everyday Life

Identify each of the following as either a nominal, an ordinal, or an interval/ratio variable.

1. paint color (red, blue, etc.) _____

2. miles (per hour) _____

3. weight (in pounds) _____

4. weight (underweight, appropriate, overweight) _____

5. shirt/blouse size (small, medium, large) _____

6. air pressure (pounds per square inch) _____

7. players' uniform numbers (00, 15, etc.) _____

8. signs of the zodiac (Aries, etc.) _____

9. undergraduate major (Soc, Eng, etc.) _____

10. political party preference (Dem, etc.) _____

11. brands of light beer (Bud, Miller, etc.) _____

12. movie ratings (G, PG, R, X) _____

Exercise 1B:
Types of Variables in Social Research

Identify each of the following as either a nominal, an ordinal, or an interval/ratio variable.

1. education: illiterate or literate   _____

2. occupation: type of industry (agriculture, construction, etc.)   _____

3. education: years of schooling completed   _____

4. occupation: white-collar or blue-collar   _____

5. schooling: private or public   _____

6. occupation: NORC prestige scores   _____

7. schooling: type of diploma (elementary, high school, college)   _____

8. race: white or nonwhite   _____

9. organizations: for-profit or nonprofit   _____

10. size of organizations: by numbers of employees   _____

11. type of workers: "line" or "staff"   _____

12. marital status: married or not married   _____

Exercise 1C:
Types of Variables on a Questionnaire

The ways questions on a questionnaire are asked illustrate different types of variables. Identify whether each of the questions below results in a nominal, an ordinal, or an interval/ratio variable.

Type of Variable

_____

_____

_____

Question

1. What is your age? _____ years

2. What is your marital status?

   (1) _____ never married

   (2) _____ married

   (3) _____ divorced

   (4) _____ separated

   (5) _____ widowed

3. What is the size of your home community?

   (1) _____ rural or farm area

   (2) _____ small town (under 10,000)

   (3) _____ small city (10,000–49,999)

   (4) _____ medium city (50,000–249,999)

   (5) _____ large city (over 250,000)

_____

4. What is your social security number?

_____ _____ _____

Do you receive any of the following forms
of financial aid?

_____

5. Loan   (1) _____ yes   (2) _____ no

_____

6. Grant   (1) _____ yes   (2) _____ no

7. How many hours did you transfer to State
    U. from another college or university?

_____ hours

_____

8. What is your overall grade point average?

(1) _____ under 2.00

(2) _____ 2.00–2.49

(3) _____ 2.50–2.99

(4) _____ 3.00–3.49

(5) _____ 3.50–4.00

_____

9. What is your major? _____

_____

10. Where do you live?

(1) _____ residence hall

(2) _____ fraternity/sorority house

(3) _____ off-campus

2
Univariate Frequency Distributions

This section examines the ways in which information gathered on a variable is summarized and displayed in a table. It is important to understand something about survey research in order to comprehend how information on variables is collected by survey researchers (survey research is discussed further in Section 9).

THE COMMUNITY PREFERENCE SURVEY (CPS)

Survey research involves asking questions of or obtaining information from a carefully chosen sample of people, households, or other social units. There are several ways to draw samples and several ways to ask survey questions. As mentioned previously, the Community Preference Survey (CPS) is a survey of 611 adult residents (18 years of age or older) of a county who were interviewed by telephone using random digit dialing (RDD) techniques. *RDD* is a procedure by which telephone numbers are sampled and people are interviewed without the need to know their names. Such a technique has many advantages with respect to sampling and to interviewing. (See Sections 8 and 9 for detailed discussions of sampling and surveying, respectively.)

CPS *respondents*—people who give answers to survey questions—were asked over 80 questions during the telephone interview on a variety of community issues and problems, as well as questions about their social backgrounds. (A copy of the CPS interview schedule appears in Appendix E.) Respondents' answers were recorded on an interview schedule, and code numbers were assigned to the answers so that responses could be entered into and then counted and compared by the SPSS/PC+ and STATPAC computer programs. Assigning numbers to survey responses is called *coding*, and the document that describes how numbers are assigned to survey responses is called a *codebook*. (A copy of the CPS Codebook appears in Appendix B.)

The remainder of this section discusses how survey responses are summarized and reported in tables. The overall pattern of responses to a particular survey question is called a *univariate frequency distribution*. Univariate frequency tables thus show the type and number of responses to each survey question. Because each question relates to a particular type of variable, the pattern of responses to a question indicates the distribution of a variable. Constructing and discussing univariate frequency tables is often the first step by which researchers summarize their results.

TABLE CONSTRUCTION FOR UNIVARIATE FREQUENCY DISTRIBUTIONS

Suppose you conducted a small-scale survey using three variables from the CPS: Political Party, a nominal variable; Perception of the Seriousness of Unemployment, an ordinal variable; and Age of the Respondent, an interval/ratio variable. You collected data from 30 individuals ($N = 30$) and arranged the ungrouped distribution of the results as in Table 2.1. Unfortunately, in this form the data are unmanageable and not very informative. Therefore, your next step might be to group these data in a systematic fashion into tables displaying univariate frequency distributions.

Nominal and Ordinal Variables

In the case of the nominal (Political Party) and ordinal (Seriousness of Unemployment) variables, the task of creating a univariate table is a straightforward task: Simply tally each time a category or value of the variable occurs and present it in a table as shown in Tables 2.2 and 2.3. Be sure to title the table appropriately; in addition, it is customary to indicate not only the frequency with which each response occurred but also the relative frequency or percentage in each category. A percentage is calculated by dividing the number in a category by the total number of cases and then multiplying by 100. For example, the percentage of Republicans in Table 2.2 is $(7/30)100 = 23.3$ percent.

Table 2.1 Data on Political Party, View of the Seriousness of Unemployment and Age for a Sample of 30 Respondents

#	Pol Party	Unemploy	Age	#	Pol Party	Unemploy	Age
1	Rep	slight	45	16	Dem	serious	21
2	Dem	serious	19	17	Dem	slight	64
3	Dem	no prob	91	18	Ind	slight	27
4	Rep	serious	47	19	Dem	serious	63
5	Rep	no prob	20	20	Ind	serious	70
6	Dem	slight	30	21	Dem	slight	35
7	Ind	serious	29	22	Ind	no prob	72
8	Dem	serious	56	23	Dem	serious	42
9	Rep	no prob	23	24	Rep	no prob	80
10	Dem	slight	62	25	Ind	serious	40
11	Ind	serious	31	26	Dem	serious	87
12	Dem	slight	65	27	Ind	slight	23
13	Rep	no prob	36	28	Dem	serious	48
14	Rep	slight	36	29	Ind	slight	41
15	Dem	serious	50	30	Ind	slight	47

Table 2.2 Frequency Distribution of Political Party Affiliation

Political Party	Frequency	Percentage	Cumulative Percentage
Republican	7	23.3	23.3
Democrat	14	46.7	70.0
Independent	9	30.0	100.0
Totals	30	100.0	

Table 2.3 Frequency Distribution of Perception of Seriousness of Unemployment

Seriousness of Unemployment	Frequency	Percentage	Cumulative Percentage
Serious	13	43.3	43.3
Slight	11	36.7	80.0
No problem	6	20.0	100.0
Totals	30	100.0	

Table 2.4   Frequency Distribution of Age of Respondents

Age Category	Frequency	Percentage	Cumulative Percentage
Under 25	5	16.7	16.7
25–44	10	33.3	50.0
45–64	9	30.0	80.0
65 and over	6	20.0	100.0
Totals	30	100.0	

Cumulative percentages are optional but may be useful in some cases. Percentages in the cumulative percentage column represent the increase in the percentage of total cases as each succeeding category of a variable is added. For example, in Table 2.4 the cumulative percentage for the under-25 age category is 16.7 percent. When the percentage of the 25–44 age group is added to the previous 16.7 percent, the cumulative percentage is 50.0 percent, which means that 50 percent of the respondents are under 45 years of age. The cumulative percentage for the final category should of course be 100.0 percent.

Interval/Ratio Variables

In the case of the interval/ratio variable of age, the researcher must decide how many categories or age intervals are desired or necessary before frequencies can be displayed in a table such as Table 2.4. The number of categories is arbitrary but should realistically divide the distribution into a manageable number of meaningful categories. In Table 2.4 age has been divided into these categories: "under 25" (young), "25–44" (early midlife), "45–64" (older midlife), and "65 and over" (later life). Then, the number of people in each category, and the relative frequency or percentage of the respondents in each age grouping, is counted and reported in the table.

Larger datasets are handled in a similar fashion, except that computers are used to store and process information obtained from all the people studied. In SPSS/PC + the FREQUENCIES command is a statistical procedure that produces univariate frequency distributions for variables. Output includes frequencies, percentages, and cumulative percentages in "on screen" and/or "printed" tables. In STATPAC the "Frequency distribution" analysis control file is used to produce univariate frequency distributions. STATPAC does not display tables on screen; rather, all STATPAC output is in printed hard copy tables.

FREQUENCY DISTRIBUTIONS:
SPSS/PC+ AND STATPAC OUTPUTS

In the following pages are examples of printed output displaying the univariate distributions for the nominal variable Political Party and the ordinal variable Seriousness of Unemployment from the CPS dataset (N = 611). Instructions for and examples from both SPSS/PC+ and STATPAC are provided (SPSS^x users see Appendix A). SPSS/PC+ output includes two sets of percentages. Those in the "Percent" column are calculated with the missing cases included in the total, while those in the "Valid Percent" column are figured with the missing cases excluded. Missing cases refer to the number of people who did not answer a question (e.g., the 27 people who did not answer the political party preference question). Valid percentages are usually used in research reports. STATPAC reports only the valid percentages, with missing cases excluded.

A. "Political Party" Using SPSS/PC+

Instructions:

```
SPSS/PC: GET FILE='SPSSCPS'. [Enter]
       : SET PRINTER=ON. [Enter]
       : FREQUENCIES VARIABLES=POLPARTY. [Enter]
```

Table 2.5   SPSS/PC+ POLPARTY Political Party Preference

Value Label	Value	Frequency	Percent	Valid Percent	Cum Percent
republican	1	154	25.2	26.4	26.4
democratic	2	291	47.6	49.8	76.2
independent	3	134	21.9	22.9	99.1
other	4	5	.8	.9	100.0
	.	27	4.4	MISSING	
	TOTAL	611	100.0	100.0	
Valid Cases 584	Missing Cases 27				

B. "Political Party" Using STATPAC

Instructions:

- If STATPAC is on hard disk, store analysis file on floppy disk in Drive A. If using STATPAC with two disk drives, store analysis file on disk containing files CPSCODE and CPSDATA in Drive B.

- Follow steps 1–10 in STATPAC ANALYSIS MANAGEMENT PROGRAMS in Appendix C
- Analysis type #2, "Frequency Distribution"
- Variable number = 86 for "Political Party"
- Select #6, "End task and write to disk"
- Execute now and start with Task 1

Table 2.6 STATPAC Frequency Distribution Political Party

POLITICAL PARTY	Number	Percent	Cumulative
1 = REPUBLICAN	154	26.4%	26.4%
2 = DEMOCRAT	291	49.8%	76.2%
3 = INDEPENDENT	134	22.9%	99.1%
4 = OTHER	5	0.9%	100.0%
5 = DK	0	0.0%	100.0%
Total	584	100.0%	100.0%
Missing cases	= 27	Response percent = 95.6%	

C. "Seriousness of Unemployment" Using SPSS/PC+

Instructions:

```
SPSS/PC: GET FILE='SPSSCPS'. [Enter]
        : SET PRINTER=ON. [ENTER]
        : FREQUENCIES VARIABLES=UNEMP. [Enter]
```

Table 2.7 SPSS/PC+ UNEMP Seriousness of Unemployment

Value Label		Value	Frequency	Percent	Valid Percent	Cum Percent
serious		1	286	46.8	47.4	47.4
slight		2	251	41.1	41.6	89.1
no problem		3	27	4.4	4.5	93.5
dk		4	39	6.4	6.5	100.0
		.	8	1.3	MISSING	
		TOTAL	611	100.0	100.0	
Valid Cases	603	Missing Cases	8			

D. *"Seriousness of Unemployment" Using STATPAC*

Instructions:

- Follow steps 1–10 in STATPAC ANALYSIS MANAGEMENT PROGRAMS in Appendix C
- Analysis type #2, "Frequency Distribution"
- Variable Number = #55 for "Unemployment"
- Select #6, "End task and write to disk"
- Execute now and start with Task 1

Table 2.8 STATPAC Frequency Distribution Seriousness Unemploy

SERIOUSNESS OF UNEMPLOYMENT	Number	Percent	Cumulative
1 = SERIOUS	286	47.4%	47.4%
2 = SLIGHT	251	41.6%	89.1%
3 = NO PROBLEM	27	4.5%	93.5%
4 = DK	39	6.5%	100.0%
Total	603	100.0%	100.0%

Missing cases = 8
Response percent = 98.7%

The frequency distribution for interval/ratio variables that contain many values looks very different from the previous tables. The SPSS/PC+ univariate frequency distribution for all the values of the interval/ratio variable age is presented below.

E. *"Age" Using SPSS/PC+*

Instructions:

```
SPSSPC: GET FILE='SPSSCPS'. [Enter]
      : SET PRINTER=ON. [Enter]
      : FREQUENCIES VARIABLES=AGE. [Enter]
```

Table 2.9 SPSS/PC+ AGE Age of Respondent

Value Label	Value	Frequency	Percent	Valid Percent	Cum Percent
	18	14	2.3	2.3	2.3
	19	7	1.1	1.2	3.5
	20	2	.3	.3	3.8
	21	18	2.9	3.0	6.8
	22	13	2.1	2.2	8.9
	23	13	2.1	2.2	11.1
	24	10	1.6	1.7	12.7
	25	17	2.8	2.8	15.6
	26	11	1.8	1.8	17.4
	27	5	.8	.8	18.2
	28	13	2.1	2.2	20.4
	29	16	2.6	2.6	23.0
	30	18	2.9	3.0	26.0
	31	19	3.1	3.1	29.1
	32	11	1.8	1.8	31.0
	33	23	3.8	3.8	34.8
	34	14	2.3	2.3	37.1
	35	11	1.8	1.8	38.9
	36	16	2.6	2.6	41.6
	37	11	1.8	1.8	43.4
	38	14	2.3	2.3	45.7
	39	14	2.3	2.3	48.0
	40	18	2.9	3.0	51.0
	41	7	1.1	1.2	52.2
	42	18	2.9	3.0	55.1
	43	13	2.1	2.2	57.3
	44	12	2.0	2.0	59.3
	45	8	1.3	1.3	60.6
	46	9	1.5	1.5	62.1
	47	10	1.6	1.7	63.7
	48	8	1.3	1.3	65.1
	49	4	.7	.7	65.7
	50	2	.3	.3	66.1
	51	11	1.8	1.8	67.9
	52	7	1.1	1.2	69.0
	53	3	.5	.5	69.5
	54	7	1.1	1.2	70.7

Table 2.9 continued

Value Label	Value	Frequency	Percent	Valid Percent	Cum Percent
	55	10	1.6	1.7	72.4
	56	11	1.8	1.8	74.2
	57	4	.7	.7	74.8
	58	7	1.1	1.2	76.0
	59	12	2.0	2.0	78.0
	60	6	1.0	1.0	79.0
	61	9	1.5	1.5	80.5
	62	10	1.6	1.7	82.1
	63	7	1.1	1.2	83.3
	64	7	1.1	1.2	84.4
	65	9	1.5	1.5	85.9
	66	5	.8	.8	86.8
	67	10	1.6	1.7	88.4
	68	5	.8	.8	89.2
	69	4	.7	.7	89.9
	70	8	1.3	1.3	91.2
	71	3	.5	.5	91.7
	72	6	1.0	1.0	92.7
	73	9	1.5	1.5	94.2
	74	2	.3	.3	94.5
	75	6	1.0	1.0	95.5
	76	5	.8	.8	96.4
	77	5	.8	.8	97.2
	78	3	.5	.5	97.7
	79	2	.3	.3	98.0
	80	2	.3	.3	98.3
	81	3	.5	.5	98.8
	82	1	.2	.2	99.0
	84	1	.2	.2	99.2
	86	1	.2	.2	99.3
	87	1	.2	.2	99.5
	89	2	.3	.3	99.8
	91	1	.2	.2	100.0
	.	7	1.1	MISSING	
	TOTAL	611	100.0	100.0	
	Valid Cases	604	Missing Cases	7	

Obviously, information in such a long table is neither very useful nor understandable. This distribution needs to be presented in a much more compact form, and examining a long table such as this may help a researcher decide how to meaningfully collapse the values of an interval/ratio variable into fewer categories. After deciding on the number of desired categories, recoding options in SPSS/PC + and STATPAC allows you to combine original values of an interval/ratio variable into fewer categories. SPSS/PC + and STATPAC tables presenting the same four age categories that were used in Table 2.4 are presented below:

F. *"Four Age Groups" Using SPSS/PC +*

Instructions:

```
SPSS/PC: GET FILE='SPSSCPS'.[Enter]
       : SET PRINTER=ON.[Enter]
       : RECODE AGE (18 THRU 24=1) (25 THRU 44=2)
         [Enter]
       : (45 THRU 64=3) (65 THRU HI=4).[Enter]
       : VALUE LABELS AGE 1 'UNDER 25' 2 '25-44' [Enter]
       : 3 '45-64' 4 '65 and over'.[Enter]
       : FREQUENCIES VARIABLES=AGE.[Enter]
```

Table 2.10   SPSS/PC + AGE Age of Respondent

Value Label		Value	Frequency	Percent	Valid Percent	Cum Percent
UNDER 25		1	77	12.6	12.7	12.7
25-44		2	281	46.0	46.5	59.3
45-64		3	152	24.9	25.2	84.4
65 AND OVER		4	94	15.4	15.6	100.0
		.	7	1.1	MISSING	
		TOTAL	611	100.0	100.0	
Valid Cases	604	Missing Cases	7			

G. *"Four Age Groups" Using STATPAC*

Instructions:

- Follow steps 1–10 in STATPAC ANALYSIS
- MANAGEMENT PROGRAMS in Appendix C
- Analysis type #2, "Frequency Distribution"
- Variable number = 75 for "Age"
- Option 1: Recode Variable 75
- Recode statement $(18 - 24 = 01)(25 - 44 = 02)(45 - 64 = 03)$ $(65 - 91 = 04)$
- Select #6, "End task and write to disk"
- Execute now and start with Task 1

Table 2.11   STATPAC AGE OF RESPONDENT

AGE	Number	Percent	Cumulative
01 =	77	12.7%	12.7%
02 =	281	46.5%	59.3%
03 =	152	25.2%	84.4%
04 =	94	15.6%	100.0%
Total	604	100.0%	100.0%

Missing cases = 7
Response percent = 98.9%

Note: STATPAC does not produce new value labels unless changes are made to the variable in the codebook. 01 = under 25, 02 = 25-44, 03 = 45-64, 04 = 65 and over.

Computer output should not appear in a research report. The computer output from SPSS/PC+ or STATPAC on age is used to construct a table, such as Table 2.12. Analysis of the results of univariate tables is covered in Section 3.

Table 2.12 Frequency Distribution of Age of CPS
Respondents

Age Group	Frequency	Percentage	Cum. Percentage
Under 25	77	12.7	12.7
25–44	281	46.5	59.3
45–64	152	25.2	84.4
65 and over	94	15.6	100.0
Totals	604	100.0	

Exercise 2A:
Univariate Frequency Distribution Tables

In the spaces below construct univariate frequency distribution tables for Marital Status, Level of Education, and Income for the 20 respondents in Table 2.13. Include proper table titles, the meaningful categories, frequencies, category percentages* (to one decimal point, for example 45.3), and the cumulative percentages** following the format of tables presented in Section 2.

Table 2.13. Data on Marital Status, Level of Education, and Income for a Sample of 20 Respondents

	Marital Status	Level of Education	Income
1.	Never married	some college	$18,000
2.	Married	less than high school	21,000
3.	Married	high school graduate	23,000
4.	Widowed	high school graduate	22,000
5.	Married	high school graduate	25,000
6.	Divorced	less than high school	14,000
7.	Never married	college graduate	23,000
8.	Never married	college graduate	46,000
9.	Widowed	less than high school	15,000
10.	Separated	less than high school	17,000
11.	Married	some college	24,000
12.	Divorced	high school graduate	18,000
13.	Married	some college	21,000
14.	Divorced	some college	31,000
15.	Married	college graduate	52,000
16.	Widowed	high school	21,000
17.	Never married	high school	17,000
18.	Divorced	college graduate	48,000
19.	Married	college graduate	45,000
20.	Never married	high school graduate	19,000

*Percentages are calculated by dividing the number of cases in a category (e.g., 10) by the total sample size (e.g., 20) and multiplying the result by 100 (e.g., 50.0 percent).

**Cumulative percentages are calculated by adding the percentage of the category to the sum of the percentages of all the preceding categories.

MARITAL STATUS

Table 2.14 _____

_____ _____ _____ _____

_____ _____ _____ _____

Totals

_____

LEVEL OF EDUCATION

Table 2.15 _____

_____ _____ _____ _____

_____ _____ _____ _____

Totals

_____

INCOME

Group the data into three meaningful categories

Table 2.16 _____

_____ _____ _____ _____

1.

2.

3.

_____ _____ _____ _____

Totals

Exercise 2B:
Computer Applications

Use SPSS/PC+ or STATPAC to obtain the frequency distribution of marital status for the CPS respondents. Obtain a printed copy of the table or fill in the information in the table below. (Remember, STATPAC only gives printed copies.)

Table 2.17 _____

_____   _____   _____   _____

_____   _____   _____   _____
_____

Construct another table that reports marital status by combining the five original categories into three meaningful categories. Use the space below to construct your table. Remember to calculate appropriate percentages.

Table 2.18 _____

_____ _____ _____ _____

1.

2.

3.

_____ _____ _____ _____

Totals

_____

Note: Many other CPS variables could be used for Exercise 2B. For example, if a nominal variable is desired: Sex, Race, or Political Party. If an ordinal variable is desired: Diploma, Grades Given to a Community Agency or Service, or Perceived Seriousness of Various Community Problems. See the CPS CODEBOOK in Appendix B.

Exercise 2C:
Computer Applications

1. Use SPSS/PC + or STATPAC to obtain a frequency distribution for the income of CPS respondents using the following six categories: "less than $10,000;" "10,000–$19,999;" "$20,000–$29,999;" "$30,000–$39,999;" "40,000–$49,999;" and "$50,000 or more." Present the table in the space provided below.

Table 2.19 _____

_____ _____ _____ _____

1.

2.

3.

4.

5.

6.

_____ _____ _____ _____

Totals

2. Construct another table that reports income by collapsing the six income categories from the previous table into three categories. Construct your table in the space below. Remember to calculate appropriate percentages.

Table 2.20 _____

_____   _____   _____   _____

1.

2.

3.

_____   _____   _____   _____

    Totals
_____

Note: Other variables from the CPS that could be used for exercise 2C include Years Lived in County, Grade Level, Number of People in Household, Number of People Under 18 in Household.

3

Statistical Measures and Descriptions of Univariate Frequency Distributions

Data presented in a univariate frequency distribution table are neither obvious nor self-explanatory. In addition to properly constructing tables for univariate variables (see Section 2), it is also necessary to describe and interpret the meaning of the distribution. Various statistical tools are available to assist you in summarizing results. Some of the more common statistics that can be used to characterize a distribution are proportions, percentages, and ratios.

PROPORTIONS, PERCENTAGES, AND RATIOS

Formulas   *Proportion*

$$p = f/n$$

where f = frequency or number in a category

n = total number in all categories

A proportion is always expressed in decimal form.

Percentage

$$\% = (f/n)100$$

Table 3.1   Age of Respondents

Age Group	f	Proportion (p)	Percentage (%)
Under 25	77	.127	12.7
25–44	281	.465	46.5
45–64	152	.252	25.2
65 and over	94	.156	15.6
Totals	$N = 604$	1.000	100.0

A percentage is a proportion multiplied by 100.

Ratio

$$\text{ratio} = f_1/f_2$$

where f_1 = frequency or number in one category

f_2 = frequency or number in another category

As an illustration of the computation and use of proportions, percentages, and ratios, look at the data on the distribution of CPS respondents in Table 3.1.

To calculate the proportion (p) in the under-25 age group, divide the number of respondents in the age group ($f = 77$) by the total in the sample ($N = 604$): $p = 77/604 = .127$. Multiplied by 100, this proportion yields the percentage in that age group: $\% = .127 \times 100 = 12.7$ percent. The same procedures are used to calculate the proportions and percentages for the other three age groups. Note that the total of all proportions in a distribution should equal 1.0 and the total of all percentages should equal 100 percent.

A discussion of data in terms of percentages and proportions is much more useful and understandable than the reporting of frequencies in each category. Instead of saying, "94 of the 604 respondents were in the 65-and-over age category and the largest number of respondents (281) were in the 25–44 age group," it makes more sense and is more informative to say, "The 65-and-over age group contained 15.6 percent of the respondents; the largest percentage of respondents, 46.5 percent, were aged 25–44." Proportions can also be used in discussing distributions, but their use is less common than that of percentages.

Table 3.2   Respondents 65 and over in Two Surveys

Age Group	CPS Survey		Survey X (Hypothetical)	
	f	%	f	%
65 and over	94	15.6	80	26.7
Totals	$N = 604$		$N = 300$	

The following is an example of how the information on the entire age distribution in Table 3.1 might be discussed:

Example   The age distribution of CPS respondents is presented in Table 3.1. Nearly one-half of the respondents (46.5 percent) are aged 25–44 and another one-fourth (25.2 percent) are in the 45–64 age group. The remaining quarter of the sample is nearly equally divided between the under-25 (12.7 percent) and the 65-and-over age group (15.6 percent).

Ratios are also useful when making statements about the relative sizes of various categories of a variable. A ratio results when the number in a category (f_1) is divided by the number in another category (f_2). In Table 3.1 the ratio of respondents aged 25–44 to those aged 45–64 is 281 (f_1) divided by 152 (f_2), or 1.85. This tells you that for every person aged 45–64 there are 1.85 persons aged 25–44, or that the age group 25–44 is 1.85 times as large or 85 percent greater than the 45–64 age group. Use of multipliers, such as 100, is common to avoid "decimal persons." The ratio of 1.85 also can be expressed as 185 per 100 persons. Using ratios, you might describe the age distribution in Table 3.1 as follows:

Example   For every 100 persons aged 45–64 there are 185 persons aged 25–44. There are 299 persons aged 25–44 for every 100 persons 65 and over, and 365 persons aged 25–44 for every 100 persons 25 years of age or younger. The 25–44 age group is nearly twice as large as the 45–64 age group, three times as large as the oldest age group, and over three and one-half times larger than the youngest age group.

Not only is the use of percentages rather than frequencies to describe distributions helpful, it is also necessary when comparing distributions of different sizes in order to avoid drawing erroneous conclusions. For example, consider the data in Table 3.2. If we merely compared the frequencies of those 65 and over in both surveys, we might mistakenly conclude that because there are 94 people in the 65-and-over category in the CPS and 80 people in the 65-and-over category in Survey

X, there is a greater representation of elderly people in the CPS than in Survey X. However, the percentages indicate that there is a considerably higher representation of those 65 and over in Survey X (26.7 percent compared to 15.6 percent). Because the sample sizes are different, comparisons cannot be made from the frequencies. Percentages standardize for size differences and allow us to make appropriate comparisons.

MEASURES OF CENTRAL TENDENCY

Measures of *central tendency* are summary single values that can be calculated to show the most typical or average value representing the distribution of a variable. The most commonly used statistical measures of central tendency are the mode, median, and mean.

Mode

The *mode* is the value that occurs most frequently in a distribution. Used most often with nominal and ordinal variable distributions, it identifies the category to which the greatest number of cases belong. In the distribution of the nominal variable Political Party in Table 2.2, the largest category, with a frequency of 14, was Democrat. Therefore, the modal category of this distribution is Democrat.

The mode also is used, though less frequently, with interval/ratio variables. For example, in the following set of ungrouped data:

87, 92, 47, 58, 87, 62, 73, 87, 61

the mode is 87 because it occurs more frequently—three times—than any other value.

It is possible to have two modes in a distribution if two values occur with equal maximum frequency. If there are two modes, such distributions are called *bimodal*. It is also possible for a distribution to have no mode if no value occurs more than once or if all values occur with equal frequency. If a distribution has three or more modes, however, the mode is not useful as an indicator of central tendency. Furthermore, even if there is only one mode, that value may not necessarily reflect the middle or center of the distribution of ordinal- or interval/ratio–level data. For a set of grouped data the mode is the category, or midpoint of the interval (for interval/ratio data), that contains the largest frequency. In the distribution of the interval/ratio variable Age in Table 3.1, the largest category was the 25–44 age group. Therefore, the mode can be identified either as that age group or as its midpoint of 34.5.

Median

The *median* is the exact midpoint of a distribution of ordered values: One-half of the values in a distribution are larger than the median (or are above it), and one-half are smaller than the median (or are below it). The median is the 50th percentile, the point that exceeds 50 percent of the values and that is exceeded by 50 percent of the values.

The method of calculating the median depends on whether there are an odd or an even number of values. For ungrouped data when there are an *odd* number of values, the median is the *middle value* when all the values have been arranged in order from high to low. In this case the following formula applies:

Formula
$$\text{median value} = (N + 1)/2$$

where N = the number of cases or values

Example Consider the following 9 values:

$$87, 92, 47, 58, 87, 62, 73, 73, 61$$

Arrange the values in order:

$$92, 87, 87, 73, 73, 62, 61, 58, 47$$

Because there are nine values, the median value = $(9 + 1)/2$ = the value of the fifth case (four values are larger than it and four values are smaller). Therefore, the median = 73.

For ungrouped data when there are an *even* number of values, the median is the *average of the two middle values* when all the values have been arranged in order from high to low. The first middle value is $N/2$ and the second middle value is $N/2 + 1$.

Example Consider these 10 ordered values:

$$92, 87, 87, 73, 73, 62, 61, 58, 47, 46$$

The first middle value = $10/2$ = fifth value and the second middle value = $10/2 + 1$ = sixth value. The fifth value is 73 and the sixth value is 62. Therefore, the median = $(73 + 62)/2 = 67.5$.

A *percentile* is a measure of location in a distribution. Percentiles, other than the median or 50th percentile, are calculated as follows: Multiply the number of values in the distribution by the proportion corresponding to the desired percentile to determine what ordered value is the percentile.

Example   For the same 10 values as ordered previously:

$$92, 87, 87, 73, 73, 62, 61, 58, 47, 46$$

the 90th percentile, P_{90}, is .90(10) = the ninth value, counting up starting with the smallest of the ordered values; thus, P_{90} = 87. The 20th percentile, or the value that exceeds 20 percent of the values in the distribution, is .20(10) = the second value, so P_{20} = 47.

The median can be calculated for ordinal and interval/ratio variables. Given the abundance of ordinal variables that social researchers examine, the median is widely used in social science research. The median is also appropriate for and preferred as a measure of the center of an interval/ratio variable distribution when the distribution of the variable is skewed. *Skewed distributions* are not balanced or symmetric, but have more values toward one end of the distribution than the other. A positively skewed distribution has more high values and a negatively skewed distribution has more low values. Because the distribution of the variable "income" is skewed, the measure of central tendency most often used to describe it is median income. The median, unlike the mean, is not affected by extreme values; therefore, in such cases it is a better indicator of the middle of a distribution.

Mean

The *mean* is the arithmetic average of all the values in a distribution—the sum of all the values in a distribution divided by the total number of values in that distribution. The formula for the mean is

Formula   *Mean*

$$\mu = \frac{\Sigma x}{N} \quad \text{or} \quad \bar{x} = \frac{\Sigma x}{N}$$

where μ = the mean of a population (μ is pronounced "mew")

$\bar{x}$ = the mean of a sample ($\bar{x}$ is stated as "x bar")

Σx = the sum of all the values in a distribution

N = the number of values in the distribution

Example   To calculate the mean of the following nine values:

$$87, 92, 47, 58, 87, 62, 73, 73, 61$$

we add all of the values ($\Sigma x = 640$) and divide by the number of values ($N = 9$). The result is the mean of the distribution:

$$\mu = \frac{640}{9} = 71.11$$

The mean is appropriate for interval/ratio data, but not for ordinal or nominal data. The mean is undoubtedly the most widely used measure of central tendency for interval/ratio–level variables. Not only is it easy to calculate, but it is also the basis of numerous other statistical measures and techniques that are used in descriptive and inferential studies.

MEASURES OF DISPERSION

In addition to measures of central tendency, which provide information on the typical or central value of a distribution, it is sometimes helpful to know how spread out from or clustered around the central value the values in a distribution are. Measures of *dispersion* tell us how narrow or wide the spread of values around the central value is. The most common measures are the range, the interquartile range, the variance, and the standard deviation.

Range

The *range* is the difference between the highest and lowest values in a distribution. For example, for the following nine values:

$$87, 92, 47, 58, 87, 62, 73, 73, 61$$

$$\text{range} = 92 \text{ (highest value)} - 47 \text{ (lowest value)} = 45$$

Because the range is affected by extreme high or low values in a distribution, which may be atypical of the entire distribution, it only gives a general indication of the variability of values in a distribution.

Interquartile Range

The interquartile range avoids the problem of extreme values by examining only the middle 50 percent of a distribution. The *interquartile range* is the difference between the third quartile and the first quartile:

$$IQR = Q_1 - Q_3$$

Example Consider the following 12 values:

16, 81, 32, 97, 83, 36, 44, 56, 71, 73, 14, 41

To calculate the IQR, first arrange the values in order from high to low:

97, 83, 81, 73, 71, 56, 44, 41, 36, 32, 16, 14

Q_1 is the first quartile, the value that exceeds one-fourth or 25 percent of the values. $Q_1 = $ the value of the $N(1/4)$ case; here, $12(1/4) = $ the third value counting up from the lowest score, so $Q_1 = 32$. Q_3 is the third quartile, the value that exceeds three-fourths or 75 percent of the values. $Q_3 = $ the value of the $N(3/4)$ case; here, $12(3/4) = $ the ninth value counting up from the lowest score, so $Q^3 = 73$.

$$IQR = 73 - 32 = 41$$

When N multiplied by 1/4 or 3/4 does not result in a whole number, Q_1 and Q_3 can be approximated by taking the value of the case that is closest to the number. For example, if $N = 15$, then $Q_1 = 15(1/4) = 3.75$ or the value of the fourth case; $Q_3 = 15(3/4) = 11.25$ or the value of the eleventh case.

Variance and Standard Deviation

Both the range and the IQR are crude measures of dispersion used for ordered ordinal- and interval/ratio–level data. More useful, and therefore more widely used, measures of dispersion for interval/ratio variables that indicate the average deviation of scores around the mean are the variance and standard deviation. Both of these measures are based on the following properties of the mean: (1) The sum of the differences of each value in a distribution from the mean of the distribution equals 0, or $\Sigma(x - \mu) = 0$; and (2) the sum of the squared differences of each value in a distribution from the mean of the distribution yields the minimum value, or $\Sigma(x - \mu)^2$ = the minimum value. The squared differences of each value from any value other than the mean will yield a higher number than if the mean had been used.

Both the variance and standard deviation are based on differences (deviations) from the mean. Theoretically, the *variance* (σ^2 for *populations*, where data are collected from all the eligible cases or individuals; s^2 for *samples*, where data are collected from a representative portion of a population) is the sum of the squared differences of each value from the mean, divided by N for populations or N − 1 for samples; more simply stated, the variance is the average squared deviation from the mean.

Formulas

Populations *Samples*

$$\sigma^2 = \frac{\Sigma(x - \mu)^2}{N} \qquad s^2 = \frac{\Sigma(x - \bar{x})^2}{N - 1}$$

Although the above formulas can be used to calculate the variance, the easier-to-use computational formulas are:

Formulas

$$\sigma^2 = \frac{\Sigma x^2}{N} - \mu^2 \qquad s^2 = \frac{\Sigma x^2 - \frac{(\Sigma x)^2}{N}}{N - 1}$$

The *standard deviation* is simply the square root of the variance. So whereas the variance shows the average dispersion in a distribution in squared units, the standard deviation (σ for populations, s for samples) shows the average dispersion in a distribution in the original units of measurement:

Formulas

$$\sigma = \sqrt{\sigma^2} \qquad s = \sqrt{s^2}$$

Example To calculate the variance and standard deviation of the following nine values:

$$87, 92, 47, 58, 87, 62, 73, 73, 61$$

proceed as follows if you are dealing with population values: Square each value, sum the squared values, and divide the total by N. Then, subtract the mean squared from $\Sigma x^2 / N$. Use the computational formula as illustrated below.

X	x^2
87	7,569
92	8,464
47	2,209
58	3,364
87	7,569
62	3,844
73	5,329
73	5,329
61	3,721
$\Sigma x = 640$	$\Sigma x^2 = 47,398$

$$\mu = \frac{\Sigma x}{N} = \frac{640}{9} = 71.11$$

$$\sigma^2 = \frac{\Sigma x^2}{N} - \mu^2 = \frac{47,398}{9} - (71.11)^2$$

$$= 5,266.444 - 5,056.790 = 209.654$$

$$\sigma = \sqrt{\sigma^2} = \sqrt{209.654} = 14.48$$

If the nine values are from a sample, $\bar{x} = 71.11$, and the variance and standard deviation are calculated as follows:

$$s^2 = \frac{\Sigma x^2 - \frac{(\Sigma x)^2}{N}}{N - 1} = \frac{47,398 - \frac{(640)^2}{9}}{9 - 1} = 235.86$$

$$s = \sqrt{s^2} = 15.36$$

MEASURES OF CENTRAL TENDENCY AND DISPERSION: SPSS/PC+ AND STATPAC OUTPUT

The following are examples of printed output displaying the mode, median, mode, variance, and standard deviation for the interval/ratio variable AGE from the ungrouped data in the CPS. Estimates of *skewness* (the departure of the distribution from symmetry) and *kurtosis* (the peakedness of the distribution, an indication of whether the values are clustered close to the mean or located further away) also are provided. Instructions for and examples from both SPSS/PC+ and STATPAC are also given. In SPSS/PC+ the formulas for sample variance and sample standard deviation are used. In STATPAC the formulas for both population and sample variances and standard deviations are used.

A. *Measures of Central Tendency and Dispersion for "Age" (Ungrouped) Using SPSS/PC+*

Instructions:

```
SPSS/PC: GET FILE='SPSSCPS', [Enter]
        : SET PRINTER=ON, [Enter]
        : FREQUENCIES VARIABLES=AGE [Enter]
        : /STATISTICS=ALL,
```

The output will contain the same long table with all age values, as found in Table 2.9, and the following statistics will be printed:

Table 3.3 SPSS/PC+

Mean	43.800	Std Err	.699	Median	40.000
Mode	33.000	Std Dev	17.183	Variance	295.255
Kurtosis	−.722	S E Kurt	.199	Skewness	.507
S E Skew	.099	Range	73.000	Minimum	18.000
Maximum	91.000	Sum	26455.000		
Valid Cases	604	Missing Cases	7		

In this distribution the most frequent age value was age 33, with a frequency of 23. Therefore, the mode = 33. The median = 40.0 and the mean = 43.8. The sample variance = 295.255 and the sample standard deviation = 17.183. As is seen next, STATPAC output, under the heading "Unbiased estimates of population," has the same results for the sample variance and standard deviation. STATPAC also shows the population variance = 294.766 and population standard deviation = 17.169.

B. *Measures of Central Tendency and Dispersion for "Age" (Ungrouped) Using STATPAC*

Instructions:
* Follow steps 1–10 in STATPAC ANALYSIS MANAGEMENT PROGRAMS in Appendix C
* Analysis type #3, "Descriptive Statistics"
* Variable number = 75 for "Age"
* Select #6, "End task and write to disk"
* Execute now and start with Task 1

Table 3.4 STATPAC DESCRIPTIVE STATISTICS ON AGE

	AGE
Minimum	= 18
Maximum	= 91
Range	= 73
Sum	= 26455
Mean	= 43.800
Median	= 40
Mode	= 33
Variance	= 294.766
Standard deviation	= 17.169
Standard error of the mean	= 0.699
95 Percent confidence interval around the mean	= 42.429 − 45.170
99 Percent confidence interval around the mean	= 41.999 − 45.600
Unbiased estimates of population	
Variance	= 295.255
Standard deviation	= 17.183
Data distribution coefficients	
Skewness	= 0.506
Kurtosis	= 2.274
Valid cases	= 604
Missing cases	= 7
Response percent	= 98.9%

The meaning of ungrouped distributions for interval/ratio variables comes from a discussion of the values of relevant measures of central tendency and dispersion. In the case of the CPS variable AGE, it would be appropriate and meaningful to discuss the values of the median, mean, range, and standard deviation as follows:

Example   The median age of CPS respondents is 40 and the mean or average age of the CPS sample is 43.8. The mean is higher because of the presence of several very elderly respondents. The CPS respondents range in age from 18 to 91. The standard deviation for the age of CPS respondents is approximately 17, indicating that the average dispersion of age among members of the CPS sample is considerable. Ages do not cluster closely around the average value.

MEASURES OF CENTRAL TENDENCY FOR GROUPED DATA

When data are available in ungrouped or raw form (which is most often the case today), it is not necessary to use the grouped data formulas that are covered here. However, there are occasions when only tables of grouped data are published or presented. In these cases the grouped formulas need to be used to estimate measures of central tendency and dispersion.

Establishing Equal-Sized Intervals

In order to calculate the median and mean for interval/ratio data grouped in a univariate table, you must first have or create a table in which the *intervals are all of equal width*. When data are grouped, we make the assumption that values in each category are evenly distributed within the interval and that the midpoint of the interval represents all the cases in it. Therefore, it is necessary that each interval be the same size. Because exact values are not used here, calculations of the median and mean from grouped data should be regarded as approximations of the actual median and mean calculated from ungrouped data.

The distribution of age in Table 3.1 should not be used for the calculation of the median and mean because the intervals are not of equal width. However, a table with equal-sized intervals can be constructed. The procedure for determining the size of the intervals needed is as follows:

1. Decide on the number of intervals desired.
2. Determine the minimum width necessary for each interval by
   a. finding the range of the distribution (the highest value − the lowest value = the range)
   b. adding 1 to the range to obtain the total number of values that must be contained in all the intervals
   c. dividing the range plus 1 by the number of intervals desired.
   The result is the minimum width necessary for each interval.
3. If the minimum width is not a whole number, round up to the next whole number.

Example For the variable Age four intervals are desired. The highest age is 91 and the lowest age is 18. Therefore, the range = 91 − 18 = 73; 73 + 1 = 74, and 74/4 = 18.5, which, rounded to the next whole number, is 19. Therefore, the minimum width needed for each interval is 19. The width of

Table 3.5   Age of Respondents—Equal-Sized Intervals

Age Interval	Real Limits	Frequency	Cumulative Frequency
18–37	17.5–37.5	262	262
38–57	37.5–57.5	190	452
58–77	57.5–77.5	135	587
78–97	77.5–97.5	17	604
Total		604	

intervals can be larger than 19, but needs to be at least 19 to include all the values of the distribution in four intervals.

It is necessary only that the intervals be of equal width for the calculation of the mean. The median can be found regardless of whether intervals are all equal and can usually be found even when the top and bottom intervals are open. However, because both measures are usually computed, it is good practice to construct intervals of equal width.

In Table 3.5 the variable Age has been grouped into four equal-sized intervals, each with a width of 20. The real limits of each interval as well as frequencies and cumulative frequencies, which are necessary for the calculation of the median, have been included in the table. Because many interval/ratio data are considered to be continuous in nature, .5 is subtracted from each lower interval boundary and .5 is added to each upper interval boundary so that the real limits reflect the continuous nature of such variables.

Calculating the Median

The median for grouped data is calculated with the following formula:

Formula   *Median (Grouped Data)*

$$Md = L_m + \left[\frac{.5N - cf_{bm}}{f_m} \right] i$$

where L_m = the lower real limit of the interval that contains the median value

N = the total number of values

cf_{bm} = the cumulative frequency of the interval that is below the interval that contains the median value

f_m = the frequency of the interval that contains the median value

i = the width of the interval

To determine what interval contains the median, divide N by 2 and look down the cumulative frequency column until you find the first number that exceeds $N/2$. That is the interval that contains the median. In the example above, $N/2 = 604/2 = 302$.

Looking down the cumulative frequency column, the first number that exceeds 302 is 452. Therefore, the median will fall in the interval 38–57, which has real limits of 37.5–57.5. $L = 37.5$, $cf_{bm} = 262$, $f_m = 190$, and $i = 20$. Applying the formula presented before, we find:

$$Md = 37.5 + \left[\frac{.5(604) - 262}{190} \right] 20 = 37.5 + 4.21 = 41.71$$

When the median is calculated in SPSS/PC+ or STATPAC, however, the above formula is not used. Both statistical packages use the midpoint of the interval that contains the median value as the median. The midpoint of the interval 38–57 is 47.5; therefore, in output provided by SPSS/PC+ and STATPAC, the median = 47.5. If you need more exact values of central tendency than computer programs provide, you must be able to calculate the values yourself or use the ungrouped data.

Calculating Percentiles

Recall that the percentile is the value that exceeds X percent of the values in the distribution. For example, the 90th percentile is the value that exceeds 90 percent of the values in a distribution; the 25th percentile exceeds 25 percent of the values. Because the median is the 50th percentile, the same general formula that was used to calculate the median can be used, with some modifications, to calculate any percentile.

Formula   *Percentile*

$$P_x = L_p + \left[\frac{.x(N) - cf_{bp}}{f_p} \right] i$$

where P_x = percentile (e.g., P_{90} = 90th percentile, P_{25} = 25th percentile)

L_p = the lower real limit of the interval that contains the percentile value

$.x =$ the proportion corresponding to the percentile being calculated (e.g., for 90th percentile, $.x =$ .90; for 25th percentile, $.x =$ .25)

$cf_{bp} =$ the cumulative frequency of the interval that is below the interval that contains the percentile value. The first number in the cumulative frequency column that exceeds $.x(N)$ is the interval that contains the percentile.

$f_p =$ the frequency of the interval that contains the percentile

$i =$ the width of the interval

The calculation of the 90th percentile for the variable Age in Table 3.5 is as follows: To determine what interval contains the 90th percentile, multiply N by .90 and look down the cumulative frequency column until you find the first number that exceeds $.90(N)$. Here, $.90(604) = 543.6$. The first cumulative frequency that exceeds it is 587, which is the cumulative frequency of the age interval 58–77. So, the lower real limit of the interval that contains the 90th percentile is 57.5. Applying the formula presented above, we find:

$$P_{90} = 57.5 + \left[\frac{.9(604) - 452}{135} \right] 20 = 57.5 + 13.57 = 71.07$$

In Table 3.6 the variable Age is grouped into four equal-sized intervals, each with a width of 20. Midpoints and a column that shows the product of the midpoint multiplied by the frequency of the interval have been included so that the calculation of the mean for grouped data can be illustrated.

Table 3.6 Age of Respondents Grouped for Calculation of the Mean

Age Interval	Midpoints(x)	Frequency(f)	fx (Frequency × Midpoints)
18–37	27.5	262	7,205.0
38–57	47.5	190	9,025.0
58–77	67.5	135	9,112.5
78–97	87.5	17	1,487.5
Totals		604	26,830.0

Calculating the Mean

The mean for grouped data is calculated with the following formula:

Formulas

Populations   *Samples*

$$\mu = \frac{\Sigma f x}{N} \qquad \text{or} \qquad \bar{x} = \frac{\Sigma f x}{N}$$

where $\Sigma f x$ = the sum of the frequencies (f) in each interval
multiplied by the midpoint (x) of each
interval

Thus, for the sample data in Table 3.6, the mean is:

$$\bar{x} = \frac{26,830}{604} = 44.42$$

Again, if ungrouped data are used, somewhat different values for means will be obtained. Remember, calculations from ungrouped data give exact values; calculations from grouped data give estimates.

MEASURES OF DISPERSION FOR GROUPED DATA

When data are grouped, as in Table 3.6 (and also Table 3.7), the variance and standard deviation are calculated with the following formulas:

Formulas

Population Data   *Sample Data*

$$\sigma^2 = \frac{\Sigma f x^2}{N} - \mu^2 \qquad\qquad s^2 = \frac{\Sigma f x^2 - \frac{(\Sigma f x)^2}{N}}{N-1}$$

$$\sigma = \sqrt{\sigma^2} \qquad\qquad\qquad s = \sqrt{s^2}$$

where $\Sigma f x^2$ = the sum of the frequencies (f) in each interval
multiplied by the squared midpoint of each
interval

μ^2 = the mean squared

Table 3.7 Age of Respondents Grouped for Calculation of σ^2 and σ

Age Interval	Midpoints(x)	Frequency(f)	fx*	fx²**
18–37	27.5	262	7,205	198,137.50
38–57	47.5	190	9,025	428,687.50
58–77	67.5	135	9,112.5	615,093.75
78–97	87.5	17	1,487.5	130,156.25
Totals		604	26,830.0	1,372,075.00

*fx = frequency multiplied by midpoint (x) in each interval
**fx^2 = the value of fx multiplied by x (e.g., for 1st interval $fx^2 = 7205 \times 27.5 = 198{,}137.5$)
or by squaring each value of x and multiplying by f (e.g., $fx^2 = (27.5)^2 \times 262 = 198{,}137.5$)

The data in Table 3.7 above illustrate the procedure for the calculation of the variance and standard deviation.

Because the data in the CPS are from a sample, s^2 and s should be calculated as follows:

Variance

$$s^2 = \frac{1372075 - \frac{(26830)^2}{604}}{603}$$

$$= 298.959$$

Standard Deviation

$$s = \sqrt{s^2}$$

$$= 17.29$$

If the data had been from a population, σ^2 and σ would have been calculated as follows:

$$\sigma^2 = \frac{1372075}{604} - (44.42053)^2$$

$$= 2271.647 - 1973.183$$

$$= 298.464$$

$$\sigma = \sqrt{\sigma^2}$$

$$= 17.28$$

MEASURES OF CENTRAL TENDENCY AND DISPERSION FOR GROUPED DATA: SPSS/PC+ AND STATPAC OUTPUTS

The following examples of printed output display the measures of central tendency and dispersion for the variable Age from grouped data in the CPS. Instructions for and examples from both SPSS/PC+ and STATPAC are provided.

C. Measures of Central Tendency and Dispersion for "Age" (Grouped) Using SPSS/PC+

Instructions:

```
SPSS/PC+: GET FILE='SPSSCPS', [Enter]
        : SET PRINTER=ON, [Enter]
        : RECODE AGE (18 THRU 37=27,5) (38 THRU 57=47,5)
          [Enter]
        : (58 THRU 77 = 67,5) (78 THRU 97 = 87,5), [Enter]
        : VALUE LABELS AGE 27,5 '18-37' 47,5 '38-57'
          [Enter]
        : 67,5 '58-77' 87,5 '78-97', [Enter]
        : FREQUENCIES VARIABLES=AGE [Enter]
        : /STATISTICS=ALL, [Enter]
```

Table 3.8   SPSS/PC+ AGE   Age of Respondent

Value Label	Value*	Frequency	Percent	Valid Percent	Cum Percent
18-37	28	262	42,9	43,4	43,4
38-57	48	190	31,1	31,5	74,8
58-77	68	135	22,1	22,4	97,2
78-97	88	17	2,8	2,8	100,0
	.	7	1,1	MISSING	
	TOTAL	611	100,0	100,0	

Mean	44,421	Std Err	,704	Median	47,500
Mode	27,500	Std Dev	17,290	Variance	298,959
Kurtosis	−,797	SE Kurt	,199	Skewness	,565
S E Skew	,099	Range	60,000	Minimum	27,500
Maximum	87,500	Sum	26830,000		
Valid Cases	604	Missing Cases	7		

*Note: Even though the SPSS output shows midpoints of 28, the value 27,5, which was used in the recode statement, is used in the calculation of the mean, SPSS/PC+ has rounded the midpoint values in the printed output, but has used the values specified in the recode statement in the calculations.

D. Measures of Central Tendency and Dispersion for "Age" (Grouped) Using STATPAC

Instructions:

- Follow steps 1–10 in STATPAC ANALYSIS MANAGEMENT PROGRAMS in Appendix C
- Analysis type #3, "Descriptive Statistics"
- Variable number = 75 for "Age"
- Option #1: Recode Variable 75
- Recode statement: $(18 - 36 = 27)$ $(37 - 55 = 46)$ $(56 - 74 = 65)$ $(75 - 93 = 84)$
- Select #6, "End task and write to disk"
- Execute now and start with Task 1

    In the STATPAC example we will use an interval width of 19, instead of the width of 20 that was used in the previous examples. As you will see, this will produce different results for all measures of central tendency than when the width is 20. To obtain the table displaying these age intervals, you need to run analysis type #2, "Frequency Distribution." Shown below are the mean, median, mode, variance, and standard deviation from the descriptive statistics analysis.

Table 3.9 STATPAC AGE DISTRIBUTION

Minimum	= 27
Maximum	= 84
Range	= 57
Sum	= 26815
Mean	= 44.396
Median	= 46
Mode	= 27
Variance	= 306.428
Standard deviation	= 17.505
Standard error of the mean	= 0.713
95 Percent confidence interval around the mean	= 42.998 − 45.793
99 Percent confidence interval around the mean	= 42.560 − 46.231
Unbiased estimates of population	
Variance	= 306.936
Standard deviation	= 17.520
Valid cases	= 604
Missing cases	= 7
Response percent	= 98.9%

Remember that the values of measures of central tendency and dispersion will differ depending upon whether ungrouped or grouped data are used in the calculation. Computer programs and calculations done by hand provide approximations when using grouped data. If more exact values are necessary, then the ungrouped data have to be used. Datasets processed by computers are easily handled without grouping data.

GRAPHIC REPRESENTATIONS OF FREQUENCY DISTRIBUTIONS

Sometimes researchers feel that graphic representations of the data in a frequency table are more effective ways to present the data than just reporting the numbers. The most commonly used graphic techniques and the types of variables for which they are appropriate are:

Nominal and Ordinal Variables	*Interval/Ratio Variables*
bar chart	histogram
pie chart	frequency polygon

Bar Charts

In a *bar chart* the categories of the variable are usually arranged along the horizontal axis of the chart, and percentages or frequencies are scaled on the vertical axis. Separate, equal-width vertical bars are used to represent the number or percentage of each category. Figure 3.1 depicts a bar chart for the data on the nominal variable Political Party from the CPS.

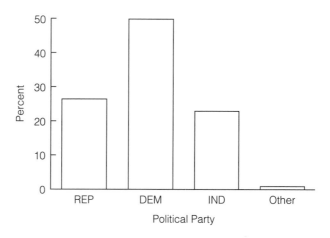

Figure 3.1 Bar chart, "Political Party"

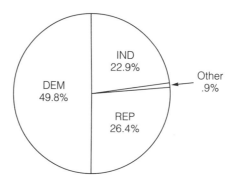

Figure 3.2 Pie chart, "Political Party"

Bar charts can also be constructed with the percentages or frequencies on the horizontal axis and the categories of the variable arranged on the vertical axis with the bars extending across the chart.

Pie Charts

Pie charts contain the same information as bar charts, but display the categories of the variable as segments of a circle. Starting with the percentage distribution of the variable, each category of the variable is allocated a percentage of 360° (the total number of degrees in a circle) that is proportional to its percentage of the entire distribution. Figure 3.2 shows a pie chart for the data on Political Party from the CPS. Because 26.4 percent of the respondents are Republicans, 95° (360° × .264) of the circle are allocated for the Republican category; Democrats get 179° (360° × .498), Independents 82° (360° × .229), and other 3° (360° × .009). A compass and protractor can then be used to draw the circle.

Histograms

A *histogram* presents the frequency distribution of an interval/ratio variable in graphic form. It is similar to a bar chart, but here the bars are connected. In a histogram the real limits of the intervals of the variable are arranged on the horizontal axis, and the percentages or frequencies are scaled on the vertical axis. Contiguous, equal-width vertical bars are used to represent the percentage or frequency of values in each interval. Figure 3.3 shows a histogram for the data on Age from the CPS.

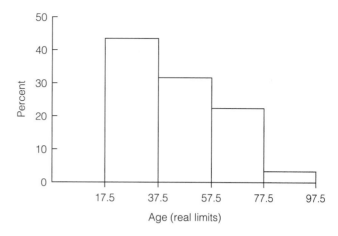

Figure 3.3   Histogram of "Age"

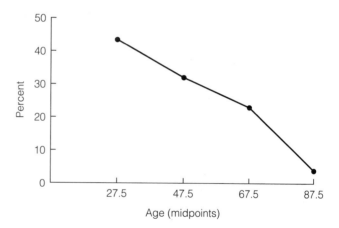

Figure 3.4   Frequency polygon of "Age"

Frequency Polygons

An alternative to the histogram is the frequency polygon. In a *frequency polygon* the midpoints of the intervals of the variable are arranged on the horizontal axis, and the percentages or frequencies are scaled on the vertical axis. Dots representing the percentages or frequencies of values in the intervals are placed above the midpoints of the intervals, and then straight lines are drawn to connect the dots. Figure 3.4 shows a frequency polygon for the data on Age from the CPS.

There are several software packages that will produce charts. The bar chart, pie chart, histogram, and frequency polygon shown in Figures 3.5–3.8, respectively, are similar to those depicted earlier in this section. They were made with one of the software programs for personal computers.

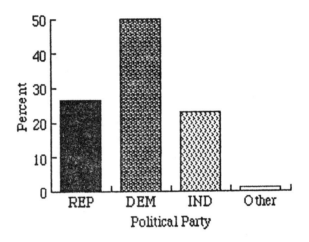

Figure 3.5   Bar chart, POLPARTY

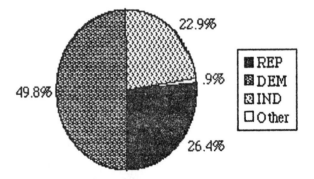

Figure 3.6   Pie chart, POLPARTY

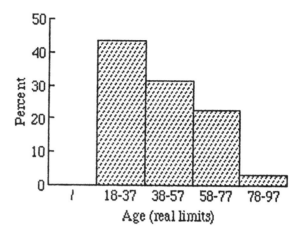

Figure 3.7   Histogram, AGE

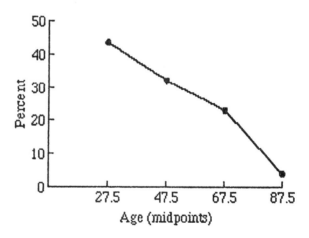

Figure 3.8   Frequency polygon, AGE

Exercise 3A:
Proportions, Percentages, and Ratios

For the CPS data presented below, answer the accompanying questions.

1. In the CPS there were 252 males and 359 females.
   a. What is the ratio of males to females?

   b. Males constitute what percentage of respondents in the survey?

   c. What is the proportion of females in the survey?

2. In the CPS there were 340 city residents and 256 county residents.
   a. What is the proportion of county residents in the survey?

b. What is the ratio of city residents to county residents?

c. City residents constitute what percentage of respondents in the survey?

Exercise 3B:
Distribution of Variables

Examine the tables that were constructed for the variables Marital Status, Education, and Income in Exercise 2A. In the spaces below write a paragraph using percentages, proportions, and ratios that describes and summarizes the distribution of each variable; then, construct charts for the variables as indicated.

1. Marital Status:

2. Education:

3. Income:

4. Construct a pie chart for each of the three variables.

5. Construct a bar chart for each of the three variables.

Exercise 3C:
Measures of Central Tendency and
Dispersion for Ungrouped Data

An "adjustment to prison" test was given to 10 inmates six months after they entered prison. Their scores were:

89, 22, 97, 58, 47, 61, 62, 84, 73, 79

For this set of ungrouped data calculate or answer the following:

1. Mode =

2. Median =

3. Mean =

4. Select the most appropriate measure of central tendency in this case, and explain the reason(s) for your choice.

5. Range =

6. What happens to the mean if you add 3 to each score?

7. What happens to the mean if you multiply each score by 3?

8. Interquartile range =

9. Variance =

10. Standard deviation =

Exercise 3D:
Measures of Central Tendency, Location, and Dispersion for Ungrouped Data

For the ungrouped data on Income in Table 2.13, calculate or answer the following:

1. Mode =   21 000

2. Median =   21,500

3. Mean =   26000

4. Which is the most appropriate measure of central tendency in this case? Why?

5. Range = 38000

6. Interquartile range = ~~7000~~   13 000

7. Variance = 140,210,526.3

8. Standard deviation = 11,841.05

Exercise 3E:
Measures of Central Tendency, Location, and Dispersion for Grouped Data

Group the data on Income in Table 2.13 into four equal-sized intervals. Present the grouped table on Income with intervals below, including information in all the columns as indicated. Then, calculate, answer, or draw graphs for the items below (show work).

Table 3.10 Grouped Income Data from Table 2.13

Intervals	Real Limits	Midpoints(x)	Frequency	Cumulative Frequency	fx	fx^2
14-23	13.5-23.5	18.5	13	13	240S	4444.2S
		28.5	3	16	8S.S	2436.7S
24-33				16	0	0
34-43		38.5	6			
44-53		48.5	4	20	194.0	9409.0
Totals					520	16295

$^2S = 14605263.6$

$S = 12065$

$median = 21192$

$mean = 26000$

1. Minimum width necessary for each interval =

2. Mode =

3. Median =

4. Mean =

5. 75th percentile =

6. Variance =

7. Standard deviation =

8. Draw a histogram of the data.

9. Draw a frequency polygon of the data.

NAME _____   DATE _____

Exercise 3F:
Measures of Central Tendency, Location, and
Dispersion for Grouped Data

Complete the following table, and then calculate the statistics or draw the graphs as indicated.

Table 3.11 Anxiety Scores of Students Taking a Statistics Course

Intervals	Real Limits	Midpoints(x)	f	cf	fx	fx^2
1–10	0.5 – 10.5	5.5	8	8		
11–20	10.5 – 20.5	15.5	15	23		
21–30	20.5 – 30.5	25.5	20	43		
31–40	30.5 – 40.5	35.5	21	64		
41–50	40.5 – 50.5	45.5	10	74		
51–60	50.5 – 60.5	55.5	6	80	—	—
Totals						

1. Mode =

2. Median =

87

3. Mean =

4. 25th percentile =

5. Variance =

6. Standard deviation =

7. Draw a histogram of the data.

8. Draw a frequency polygon of the data.

Exercise 3G:
Computer Applications

In this exercise you will examine frequency distributions for a number of variables contained in the CPS. Your tasks are to (1) use SPSS/PC+ or STATPAC to obtain the necessary computer printouts of the frequency analyses for each of the variables, and (2) provide succinct, understandable, and compelling typewritten paragraphs analyzing each of the issues presented below. Be sure to utilize and cite appropriate descriptive and summary statistics from your output to support the discussions in your written analyses. Turn in your computer printouts of the frequency tables with your typewritten analyses.

1. Local officials think the public is in favor of a new 18-hole golf course. Do data from the CPS support their position? (#65, GOLF.)

2. How serious are illiteracy and pornography considered to be in the community, and which one is perceived to be the more serious problem? (#52, ILLIT, and #53, PORN.)

3. a. The average educational attainment of adults nationally is 11.0 years. Is the educational attainment of county respondents higher or lower?

   b. Also, determine if the following statement is true: "Less than 50 percent of the CPS respondents have completed high school (12 years)." (#79, GRADE.)

4. Which was graded higher, the local newspaper or the local TV station? (#36, NEWSPAP, and #37, CH 13.)

5. Run a frequency analysis for variable #____ (your choice), and describe what the frequency distribution and statistics show.

4

Bivariate Frequency Distributions: Tables and Statistical Procedures

A *bivariate table* displays the joint or simultaneous frequencies of two variables. *Bivariate analysis, crosstabulation, joint frequency analysis,* and *contingency table analysis* are all commonly encountered and interchangeable terms used to describe one of the most common forms of analysis in the social sciences for categorical data (variables measured at the nominal and ordinal level). What is involved here is an analysis of the relationship between two variables or an analysis of the differences between categories of one variable as they relate to categories of a second variable.

NOMINAL BIVARIATE DISTRIBUTIONS

In Table 2.1 data for the two variables, Political Party, (nominal) and Perception of Seriousness of Unemployment (ordinal) were presented. In Section 2 univariate frequency distribution tables were constructed for each of these variables. Suppose you are now interested in determining whether there is a relationship between these two variables. Or, to be more precise, in this case you are interested in knowing whether there is any difference between the political parties in their perception of the seriousness of unemployment. You hypothesize that Democrats are more likely to see unemployment as a serious problem than are Republicans or Independents. (See Section 5 for a fuller discussion of hypotheses.) A nominal bivariate table is appropriate to examine this issue. If one or both of the variables are nominal, then the table is considered to be nominal. A 2 × 2 (two rows and two columns) table is the smallest bivariate table and will be examined first.

NOMINAL BIVARIATE TABLE CONSTRUCTION

In the construction of a nominal bivariate table, you should arrange your table according to the following order: (1) writing a title, (2) forming columns, (3) forming rows, and (4) sorting, tallying, and percentaging data.

1. Title

The title should contain the name of the dependent variable (Y) and the name of the independent variable (X). In this case Political Party is presumed to affect Perception of Seriousness of Unemployment. Therefore, Political Party is the independent variable (X) and Perception of Seriousness of Unemployment is the dependent variable (Y). (Independent and dependent variables are discussed in detail in Section 5.) The title thus should read:

> Table 4.1 Perception of Seriousness of Unemployment by Political Party

2. Columns

Categories or values of the independent variable (X) form the *columns* of the table; that is, categories of the independent variable are the headings for the columns of the table.

3. Rows

Categories or values of the dependent variable (Y) form the *rows* of the table; that is, categories of the dependent variable are the labels to the left of each row.*

4. Sorting, Tallying, and Percentaging

Once the number of categories for each variable has been determined, sort and tally each case according to its value on both variables. For example, in Table 4.1 Dem and Rep/Ind will be the two categories of

---

*Note: It is the convention and is most convenient for the independent variable to be the column variable and for the dependent variable to be the row variable. However, this arrangement can be reversed.

Table 4.1 Perception of Seriousness of Unemployment by Political Party

Seriousness of Unemployment	Political Party		
	Dem	Rep/Ind	Total
Serious	8	5	13
Slight/No Prob	6	11	17
Totals	14	16	30

Political Party (Rep and Ind are collapsed or combined to form one category). Serious and Slight/No Prob will be the two categories of Seriousness of Unemployment (Slight and No Prob are combined to form one category). To complete such a 2 × 2 table, tally up each time a respondent chooses either Dem and Serious, Dem and Slight or No Prob, Rep/Ind and Serious, or Rep/Ind and Slight/No Prob.

Using data from Table 2.1, the bivariate table is presented in Table 4.1. The row and column totals are called the *marginals* and reflect the univariate distribution of each variable.

One of the first steps taken in order to determine whether the independent variable is related to the dependent variable is to percentage the table properly. To assess the impact of the independent variable on the dependent variable, column percentages should be calculated. Bivariate tables should be percentaged down the columns (in the direction of the independent variable). Divide each cell frequency in the table by its column total and multiply by 100. A properly percentaged table for the data in Table 4.1 is shown in Table 4.2.* This bivariate percentage distribution allows an examination of the percentage distribution of the dependent variable within each category of the independent variable.

1. *Percentaging down* allows us to see the influence Political Party may have on Seriousness of Unemployment.

2. *Percentaging across* shows how each category of unemployment is distributed by Political Party.

3. *Percentaging to the grand or overall total* shows the joint percentage distribution of Political Party and Seriousness of Unemployment (or

*Note: In this type of table percentages customarily are carried out to one decimal place, all column percentages add up to 100.0 percent, and the N for each column is presented in parentheses ( ) so that any cell frequency can be determined if needed.

Table 4.2 Perception of Seriousness of Unemployment by Political Party (%)

Seriousness of Unemployment	Political Party		
	Dem	Rep/Ind	Total
Serious	57.1	31.2	43.3
Slight/No Prob	42.9	68.8	56.7
Totals	100.	100.0	100.0
(N)	(14)	(16)	(30)

what percentage of the total was both Democrat and saw unemployment as serious).

All types of percentages (column, row, and total) are included in STATPAC output. They are options on SPSS/PC+. For most analyses column percentages are sufficient.

DESCRIBING NOMINAL BIVARIATE TABLE PERCENTAGE RESULTS

It is clear from Table 4.2 that, as hypothesized, Political Party is related to Perception of Seriousness of Unemployment. Overall, 43.3 percent see unemployment as a serious problem. However, Democrats are more likely than Republicans or Independents to see unemployment as a serious problem: Over 57 percent of Democrats regard it as a serious problem, compared to 31 percent of Republicans/Independents. In other words over 26 percent more Democrats see unemployment as a serious problem than do Republicans/Independents.

When the distribution of one variable differs in at least some of the categories of the other variable, then an association exists between the two variables. The greater the differences, the greater the association. We can see this when we compare column percentages across the rows of the table. In Table 4.2 the percentage distributions of Democrats and Republicans/Independents differ with regard to Perception of Seriousness of Unemployment. One way of summarizing this is to report "epsilon"—the difference between percentages "serious" on perception of unemployment between Democrats and Republican/Independents. Here epsilon = 57.1 − 31.2 = 25.9 percentage points. Thus, roughly 26 percent more Democrats see unemployment as a serious problem than do Republicans/Independents (57.1 versus 31.2 percent). In tables that are larger than the 2 × 2, epsilon is the difference between the largest and smallest percentages in a row, and a number of percentage contrasts may be computed and discussed. Remember: Bivariate tables are analyzed and discussed by examining differences between or among the column percentages in a particular row. The rule in examining bivariate tables is to *percentage down the columns* and *compare percentages across the rows*.

TESTING HYPOTHESES WITH NOMINAL BIVARIATE TABLES

When data from samples are examined, bivariate tables are used in tests of hypotheses. *Hypotheses* are predictions about how two or more variables are related (Sections 5 and 11 discuss hypotheses in more detail). As hypotheses are tested, information in bivariate tables is used to address these questions:

1. Does a significant association or relationship exist between the variables (a determination based on the chi-square test of significance)?
2. If so, what is the strength of the association (based on measures of categorical association), and what is the nature of the relationship?

The Chi-Square Test for the Existence of a Relationship

The *chi-square* test of independence is used to answer the question of whether a relationship exists between two variables in a nominal bivariate table. The *null hypothesis, H_0,* states that there is no relationship between the two variables (they are independent). The *alternative hypothesis, H_1,* states that there is a relationship between the two variables. (See sections 5 and 11 on hypotheses).

The calculated or obtained value of the chi-square (χ^2) statistic is compared to a critical chi-square value corresponding to a specific probability that the differences in a table could have occurred by chance or sampling variability. If the obtained chi-square value is greater than the critical value, which usually corresponds to a probability of .05 or .01, then the null hypothesis can be rejected and the conclusion reached that there is a statistically significant relationship between the two variables. If the obtained chi-square value is less than the critical value, then the probability of such differences occurring by chance or sampling variability is greater than the probability level chosen. If, for example, the obtained value is less than the critical value for the .05 level, the null hypothesis of no relationship cannot be rejected because such differences might occur by chance more than 5 out of 100 times; the conclusion therefore is that the two variables are independent or that there is no relationship between the two variables. (Refer to Sections 10 and 11 for discussions of probability levels and hypothesis tests.)

Chi-square is calculated as follows:

Formula   *Chi-Square*

$$\chi^2 = \Sigma \left[\frac{(O - E)^2}{E} \right] \quad \text{or} \quad \Sigma \left[\frac{O^2}{E} \right] - N_T$$

where O = the observed frequency in the cell of a table

E = the expected frequency in the cell if no relationship exists

N_T = total sample size

Expected frequencies are calculated for each cell as follows:

$$E = \frac{(\text{row marginal})(\text{column marginal})}{N}$$

From the data in Table 4.1 we can set up the following table:

Expected Frequencies (E)

	Dem	Rep/Ind	
Serious	$O = 8$ $E = \dfrac{13 \times 14}{30} = 6.07$	$O = 5$ $E = \dfrac{13 \times 16}{30} = 6.93$	13
Slight/ No Prob	$O = 6$ $E = \dfrac{17 \times 14}{30} = 7.93$	$O = 11$ $E = \dfrac{17 \times 16}{30} = 9.07$	17
	14	16	30

Using the first formula for chi-square:

$$\chi^2 = \frac{(8 - 6.066)^2}{6.066} + \frac{(5 - 6.933)^2}{6.933} + \frac{(6 - 7.933)^2}{7.933} + \frac{(11 - 9.066)^2}{9.066}$$

$$= .62 + .54 + .47 + .41$$

$$= 2.04$$

Or, using the second formula:

$$\chi^2 = \frac{8^2}{6.066} + \frac{5^2}{6.933} + \frac{6^2}{7.933} + \frac{11^2}{9.066} - 30$$

$$= 10.55 + 3.61 + 4.54 + 13.34 - 30$$

$$= 32.04 - 30$$

$$= 2.04$$

In a chi-square test of independence there are $(r - 1)(c - 1)$ degrees of freedom (d.f.), where r = the number of row categories and c = the number of column categories. There is $(2 - 1)(2 - 1) = 1$ d.f. for Table 4.1. Using Table IV in Appendix D, if we had selected a probability level of .05 ($\alpha = .05$), the critical value of χ^2 at $\alpha = .05$, for 1 d.f. is 3.841. Because our obtained value is less than the critical value, we would fail to reject the null hypothesis of no relationship and would conclude that there is not a statistically significant relationship between political party preference and perception of the seriousness of unemployment. The small observed differences could have occurred by chance more than 5 percent of the time with a sample size that small.

With 2×2 tables where the cells are labeled:

a	b
c	d

Chi-square can also be calculated as follows:

Formula *Chi-Square*

$$\chi^2 = \frac{N(ad - bc)^2}{(a + b)(c + d)(a + c)(b + d)}$$

Using the data from Table 4.1, we can calculate the following:

$$\chi^2 = \frac{30[8(11) - 5(6)]^2}{(13)(17)(14)(16)}$$

$$= \frac{30(58)^2}{49,504} = \frac{100,920}{49,504} = 2.039$$

$$= 2.04$$

Note that chi-square should only be used in cases where you have a sufficiently large sample to yield expected frequencies of at least five in each of the cells of the table. In 2 × 2 tables the value of chi-square is often adjusted by applying Yates' correction for continuity. Yates' correction will lower the obtained chi-square value and make it more difficult to reject the null hypothesis of no relationship or no difference. Originally, Yates' correction was applied for 2 × 2 tables when one or more expected frequencies were less than 10, but some statisticians always recommend its use in a 2 × 2 table.

Chi-square with Yates' correction for continuity is calculated as follows:

Formula *Chi-Square with Yates' Correction*

$$\chi_c^2 = \Sigma \left[\frac{(|O - E| - .5)^2}{E} \right]$$

where $|O - E|$ = the absolute difference between the observed and expected in each cell. Ignore the signs of O and E and subtract the smaller number from the larger one.

Using the data from Table 4.1, we can set up the following equation:

$$\chi_c^2 = \frac{(|8 - 6.066| - .5)^2}{6.066} + \frac{(|5 - 6.933| - .5)^2}{6.933} + \frac{(|6 - 7.933| - .5)^2}{7.933} + \frac{(|11 - 9.066| - .5)^2}{9.066}$$

$$= \frac{(1.934 - .5)^2}{6.066} + \frac{(1.933 - .5)^2}{6.933} + \frac{(1.933 - .5)^2}{7.933} + \frac{(1.934 - .5)^2}{9.066}$$

$$= \frac{2.056}{6.066} + \frac{2.053}{6.933} + \frac{2.053}{7.933} + \frac{2.056}{9.066}$$

$$= .339 + .296 + .259 + .227$$

$$= 1.12$$

Chi-square with Yates' correction can also be calculated using another formula (with the a, b, c, d cell designations) as follows:

Formula *Chi-square with Yates' Correction (alternate method)*

$$\chi_c^2 = \frac{N(|ad - bc| - N/2)^2}{(a + b)(c + d)(a + c)(b + d)}$$

where $|ad - bc|$ = the absolute difference between ad and bc

Again, using the data from Table 4.1, we calculate the following:

$$\chi_c^2 = \frac{30(|88 - 30| - 30/2)^2}{(13)(17)(14)(16)}$$

$$= \frac{30(58 - 15)^2}{(13)(17)(14)(16)} = \frac{30(43)^2}{49{,}504} = \frac{55{,}470}{49{,}504}$$

$$= 1.12$$

In reports, articles, and papers chi-square results might be reported as follows:

Results of the chi-square test indicate that no statistically significant relationship exists between political party preference and perception of the seriousness of unemployment ($\chi_c^2 = 1.12$ (1 d.f., n.s.*)). Democrats are no more or less likely to see unemployment as a serious problem than are respondents of other party preferences.

In cases where there is a significant relationship, report the value of chi-square, the degrees of freedom, and the probability (e.g., $p < 0.05$ or $p < 0.01$).

Nominal Measures of the Strength of an Association

Measures of association tell how weak or strong an association is between two variables. There are several commonly used measures that should be used as indicators of the strength of the association between variables if one or both variables are nominal. The values of these measures are expressed as proportions and range between 0 and +1. The higher the value, the stronger the association.

Formulas for the Calculation of Phi, Cramer's V, Contingency Coefficient, and Lambda

Phi (Φ)—for 2×2 nominal table—is calculated with the following formula:

Formula   Phi

$$\Phi = \sqrt{\frac{\chi^2}{N}}$$

where χ^2 = corrected chi-square

N = sample size

*"n.s." means not significant.

Therefore, in the example above,

$$\Phi = \sqrt{\frac{1.12}{30}} = .19$$

indicating a somewhat weak association between political party and perception of the seriousness of unemployment.

Cramer's V, a modified version of Φ for nominal tables larger than 2×2, is calculated with the following formula:

Formula *Cramer's V*

$$V = \sqrt{\frac{\chi^2}{N(K - 1)}}$$

where K = the smaller of the number of rows and columns

Phi and Cramer's V are chi-square-based measures. If table size is 2×2, phi can be calculated. If table size is larger than 2×2 (e.g., 2×3, 3×2, 3×3), Cramer's V is appropriate. As the two formulas above show, Cramer's V, if computed for a 2×2 table, would be the same as phi.

Contingency coefficient (c)—for nominal tables with the same number of rows and columns (e.g., 2×2, 3×3)—is calculated with the following formula:

Formula *Contingency Coefficient*

$$C = \sqrt{\frac{\chi^2}{\chi^2 + N}}$$

Therefore,

$$C = \sqrt{\frac{1.12}{1.12 + 30}} = .19$$

Lambda (λ)—for any sized table—is what is known as a Proportional Reduction of Error (PRE) measure of association. What this means is that, in addition to interpreting the value of lambda as a measure of the strength of the association on a scale of 0 to 1, you can also interpret the value of λ as an indication of how much error is reduced when a value of variable X is used to predict the value of variable Y, as opposed to predicting Y without the use of X.

Lambda asymmetric* (where the independent variable is specified) is calculated as follows:

Formula *Lambda*

$$\lambda = \frac{E_1 - E_2}{E_1}$$

where E_1 = errors made ignoring the independent variable

E_2 = errors made using the independent variable

E_1 = N minus the largest row total

E_2 = the sum of each column total minus the largest cell frequency in each column

Thus, in our example:

$$E_1 = 30 - 17 = 13$$

$$E_2 = (14 - 8) + (16 - 11) = 6 + 5 = 11$$

$$\lambda = \frac{13 - 11}{13} = \frac{2}{13} = .15$$

This can be interpreted as a weak association, but also, because of the PRE property of lambda, we can say that we would make .15, or 15 percent, fewer errors predicting views on the seriousness of unemployment when using Political Party than we would without it.

Because of its PRE quality and its use with any size table, lambda is often the preferred nominal measure of association. However, sometimes lambda can have a value of 0 even when there is an association. This will happen when the largest frequencies in each column lie in the same row of the table. In such cases Cramer's V should be used.

In situations where more than one nominal measure could be used, remember that, despite being calculated differently, each measure indicates roughly the same strength of association between the two variables. In the example above $\Phi = .19$, $C = .19$, and asymmetric $\lambda = .15$. All measures indicate a weak association.

---

*There is also lambda symmetric (where no independent variable is specified). Its calculation is not discussed here.

Crosstab of UNEMP BY POLPARTY

The following are examples of printed output of the crosstabulation of perception of the seriousness of unemployment by political party from the CPS dataset, using SPSS/PC+ and STATPAC procedures. Statistics on and discussion of the chi-square test of significance and nominal measures of association appropriate for this table are also provided.

A. Crosstab of UNEMP BY POLPARTY Using SPSS/PC+

Instructions:

```
SPSS/PC: GET FILE='SPSSCPS', [Enter]
       : SET PRINTER=ON, [Enter]
       : SELECT IF (UNEMP LT 4), [Enter]
       : SELECT IF (POLPARTY LT 4), [Enter]
       : RECODE UNEMP (1=1)(2,3=2), [Enter]
       : RECODE POLPARTY (1,3=1)(2=2), [Enter]
       : VALUE LABELS UNEMP 1 'SERIOUS' 2 'SLIGHT/
         NO PROB' [Enter]
       : /POLPARTY 1 'Rep/Ind' 2 'DEM', [Enter]
       : CROSSTABS TABLES=UNEMP BY POLPARTY [Enter]
       : /OPTIONS=4 [Enter]
       : /STATISTICS=1,2,3,4, [Enter]
```

Note: OPTIONS = 4 displays column percentages only.
STATISTICS: 1 = chi-square, 2 = phi for 2 × 2 tables, or Cramer's V for larger tables, 3 = contingency coefficient, 4 = lambda.

Table 4.3 SPSS/PC+

| Crosstabulation: | UNEMP | Seriousness of Unemployment |
| | By POLPARTY | Political Party Preference |

POLPARTY→	Count Col Pct	Rep/Ind 1	Dem 2	Row Total
UNEMP serious	1	118 44.2	157 57.3	275 50.8
slight/no prob	2	149 55.8	117 42.7	266 49.2
	Column Total	267 49.4	274 50.6	541 100.0

Continued

Chi-Square	D.F.	Significance	Min E.F.	Cells with E.F. <5
8.77459	1	.0031	131.279	None
9.29151	1	.0023	(Before Yates Correction)	

Page 5   SPSS/PC+

Statistic	Symmetric	With UNEMP Dependent	With POLPARTY Dependent
Lambda	.11820	.11654	.11985

Statistic	Value	Significance
Phi	.13105	
Contingency Coefficient	.12994	

Number of Missing Observations = 0

B. Crosstab of UNEMP BY POLPARTY Using STATPAC

Instructions:

- Follow steps 1–10 in STATPAC ANALYSIS MANAGEMENT PROGRAMS in Appendix C
- Analysis type #4, "Crosstabs + Chi-Square Analysis"
- First Variable (X) = #86 for "Political Party"
- Second Variable (Y) = #55 for "Seriousness of Unemployment"
- Options: #3-Select if Variable #55, "less than" (2) Value = 4 and (1) Variable #86 "less than" (2) Value = 4, 0 "None"
- Options: #1 Recode Variable #55 Recode statement (1 = 1)(2 – 3 = 2)
- Options: #1 Recode Variable #86 Recode statement (1 = 1)(2 = 2)(3 = 1)
- Select #6, "End task and write to disk"
- Execute now and start with Task 1

Note: Original value labels are not changed in the table and empty rows and columns result from the recodes and select. Also, the only measures of association provided are phi (or Cramer's V for larger than 2 × 2 tables) and the contingency coefficient. Lambda can be calculated from the data in the table.

Table 4.4 STATPAC
Crosstabulation Seriousness of Unemployment by Political Party

POLITICAL PARTY-(X Axis)
BY
SERIOUSNESS OF UNEMPLOYMENT-(Y Axis)

Number Row % Column % Total %		REPUB- LICAN 1	DEMO- CRAT 2	INDE- PENDENT 3	OTHER 4	DK 5	Row Totals
SERIOUS	1	118 42.9 44.2 21.8	157 57.1 57.3 29.0	0 0.0 0.0 0.0	0 0.0 0.0 0.0	0 0.0 0.0 0.0	275 50.8
SLIGHT	2	149 56.0 55.8 27.5	117 44.0 42.7 21.6	0 0.0 0.0 0.0	0 0.0 0.0 0.0	0 0.0 0.0 0.0	266 49.2
NO PROBLEM	3	0 0.0 0.0 0.0	0 0.0 0.0 0.0	0 0.0 0.0 0.0	0 0.0 0.0 0.0	0 0.0 0.0 0.0	0 0.0
DK	4	0 0.0 0.0 0.0	0 0.0 0.0 0.0	0 0.0 0.0 0.0	0 0.0 0.0 0.0	0 0.0 0.0 0.0	0 0.0
Column Totals		267 49.4	274 50.6	0 0.0	0 0.0	0 0.0	541 100.0

Corrected Chi square   = 8.770001   Valid cases   = 541
Degrees of freedom   = 1   Missing cases = 27
Probability of chance = 0.003   Response rate = 95.2%
Phi   = 0.127
Contingency coeff.   = 0.126

Note: 3 columns & 2 rows not included in Chi square calculations

A Review of Chi-Square Procedures and Nominal Measures of Association

Even though they are provided in the printed output, a review of the calculation of chi-square and nominal measures of association for the SPSS/PC+ and STATPAC outputs is provided below.

Formula   *Chi-Square*

$$\chi^2 = \Sigma \left[\frac{(O - E)^2}{E} \right]$$

Remember, expected frequencies for each cell are obtained by multiplying the cell's row total by the column total and dividing by the grand total.

$$\chi^2 = \frac{(118 - 135.72)^2}{135.72} + \frac{(157 - 139.28)^2}{139.28} + \frac{(149 - 131.28)^2}{131.28} + \frac{(117 - 134.72)^2}{134.72}$$

$$= 2.31 + 2.25 + 2.39 + 2.33 = 9.29$$

or

$$\chi^2 = \frac{N(ad - bc)^2}{(a + b)(c + d)(a + c)(b + d)} = \frac{541(118 \times 117 - 149 \times 157)^2}{275 \times 266 \times 267 \times 274} = 9.29$$

Formula   *Phi*

$$\Phi = \sqrt{\frac{\chi^2}{N}}$$

SPSS/PC+ uses uncorrected chi-square. STATPAC uses chi-square with Yates' correction:

$$\text{SPSS } \Phi = \sqrt{\frac{9.29151}{541}} = .13105 \qquad \text{STATPAC } \Phi = \sqrt{\frac{8.77459}{541}} = .127$$

Formula *Contingency Coefficient*

$$C = \sqrt{\frac{\chi^2}{\chi^2 + N}}$$

$$\text{SPSS/PC+ } C = \sqrt{\frac{9.29}{9.29 + 541}} = .1299$$

$$\text{STATPAC } C = \sqrt{\frac{8.77}{8.77 + 541}} = .126$$

Formula *Lambda, Asymmetric (with Unemp dependent)*

$$\lambda = \frac{E_1 - E_2}{E_1}$$

$$E_1 = 541 - 275 = 266$$

$$E_2 = (267 - 149) + (274 - 157) = 235$$

$$\lambda = \frac{266 - 235}{266} = \frac{31}{266} = .1165413$$

Interpretation of UNEMP BY POLPARTY Table

The output from either SPSS/PC+ or STATPAC should be used to construct a table, such as Table 4.5, that would appear in a paper or research report, and be discussed as follows:

Table 4.5 Perception of Seriousness of Unemployment by Political Party, CPS Respondents (%)*

Seriousness of Unemployment	Political Party		
	Republican/ Independent	Democrat	Total
Serious	44.2	57.3	50.8
Slight/No problem	55.8	42.7	49.2
Totals	100.0	100.0	100.0
(N)	(267)	(274)	(541)

*chi-square, corrected = 8.77, d.f. = 1, p < .01
lambda = .12, phi = .13, contingency coefficient = .13

Slightly over one-half of the CPS respondents (50.8 percent) think unemployment is a serious problem, and roughly one-half think it is only a slight problem or no problem (49.2 percent). However, the opinions of members of different political parties are quite different on this issue. Democrats are more likely than Republicans or Independents to view unemployment as serious. A majority of Democrats (57.3 percent) see unemployment as a serious problem, and the percentage of Democrats who view it as serious is 13 percentage points higher than the percentage of Republican/Independents who say it is a serious problem (44.2 percent). The chi-square test indicates that this is a statistically significant difference at the .01 level (chi-square = 9.29, Yates' correction = 8.77, 1 d.f., $p < .01$). The values of lambda (.12), phi (.13), and the contingency coefficient (.13) all indicate a weak association between these two variables.

Even though each nominal measure of association is calculated differently, all of them will indicate the same general degree of the strength of the association between the two variables. With lambda, a PRE measure, one can say that errors will be reduced by approximately 12 percent using the variable Political Party to predict views on the seriousness of unemployment over the alternative of making predictions without using it.

ORDINAL BIVARIATE DISTRIBUTIONS

Suppose you are interested in determining whether there is a relationship between age categories (ordinal) and perception of the seriousness of unemployment (ordinal). You hypothesize that as age increases, unemployment is likely to be perceived as a more serious problem. More specifically, your hypothesis is that older people (45 and over) are more likely to view unemployment as a serious problem than are younger people (under 45). An ordinal bivariate table is appropriate to examine this issue. In order to set up an ordinal table and use ordinal measures of association, both variables must be ordinal. However, it is possible to consider dichotomous nominal variables (those divided into two categories) as ordinal. Also, interval/ratio variables such as Age are ordinal when collapsed into fewer orderable, discrete categories, as was done in this case.

ORDINAL BIVARIATE TABLE CONSTRUCTION

The table-formatting procedures discussed earlier in the case of nominal bivariate table construction also apply here. In addition, it is important to adhere to the following procedures regarding the ordering of the categories of the independent and dependent variables:

1. Column category headings or values of the independent variable (X) should be arranged in ascending order (from low to high) as you move from the left to the right column in the table.
2. Row category headings or values of the dependent variable (Y) should be arranged in descending order (from high to low) as you move from the top to the bottom row of the table.

This arrangement will ensure that the sign (+ or −) of measures of association will be correct.

The Chi-Square Test for the Existence of a Relationship

The chi-square test is again used to answer the question of whether a relationship exists between two ordinal variables. See the previous portion of this section on nominal bivariate distributions for the computations of χ^2 for 2×2 and larger tables.

Ordinal Measures of the Strength of an Association

Ordinal measures of association indicate both the *strength* of the association between two variables on a proportional scale from 0 to ±1 and also the *direction* of the association: a positive value indicating a positive or direct association and a negative value indicating a negative or inverse association. Ordinal measures of association should only be used when both variables are ordinal. (Remember, dichotomous nominal variables can be treated as ordinal, for example, when religious affiliation is dichotomized into the two categories: Catholic and non-Catholic.)

The four most commonly used ordinal measures of association are: gamma, Somer's d, tau b, and tau c. All are PRE (Proportional Reduction of Error) measures. A brief description of each is provided here. Formulas and examples of the computation of each measure will be illustrated using SPSS/PC+ and STATPAC output in the next part of this section.

1. *Gamma* is perhaps the most widely used of the ordinal measures of association. It compares the number of times two variables are ordered or ranked the same with the number of times they are ordered differently (ignoring ties). It is symmetric in nature and does not specify which variable is independent. It can be used with any-sized table. In a 2 × 2 table gamma is also known as Yule's Q.

2. *Somer's d* is an asymmetric extension of gamma that differs from gamma in that ties* on the dependent variable are taken into account. It can be used in any sized table.

3. *Tau b* differs from gamma and Somer's d in that it considers ties on each variable. It should only be used on square tables with the same number of rows and columns (e.g., 2 × 2, 3 × 3).

4. *Tau c* is recommended instead of tau b for rectangular tables where the number of rows and columns are not the same (e.g., 2 × 3, 3 × 2, 3 × 4).

   Note that tau b, tau c, and Somer's d all yield smaller values than does gamma because they take ties into account.

The following are examples of the printed output of the crosstabulation of perception of the seriousness of unemployment by age from the CPS dataset. First, a 2 × 2 ordinal table (collapsing each variable into two categories) is produced. Then, a 3 × 4 ordinal table (using all three categories of UNEMP and the four AGE categories used in Section 2) is provided. Statistics used in the discussions of the chi-square test of significance and ordinal measures of association appropriate for each table are also provided.

A. *Crosstab of UNEMP BY AGE (2 × 2) Using SPSS/PC+*

Instructions:

```
SPSS/PC: SET PRINTER=ON. [Enter]
       : GET FILE='SPSSCPS'. [Enter]
```

---

*Ties occur when pairs formed within the same level of one variable have the same rank on the other variable.

```
: RECODE AGE (18 THRU 44=1)(45 THRU HI=2),
  [Enter]
: SELECT IF (UNEMP LT 4), [Enter]
: RECODE UNEMP (1=2)(2,3=1), [Enter]
: VALUE LABELS AGE 1 'Under 45' 2 '45 and over',
  [Enter]
: VALUE LABELS UNEMP 1 'Slight/No Prob'
  2 'Serious', [Enter]
: CROSSTABS TABLES=UNEMP BY AGE [Enter]
: /OPTIONS=4,8 [Enter]
: /STATISTICS=1,6,7,8,9, [Enter]
```

Note: OPTIONS = 4 displays column percentages.
OPTIONS = 8 orders rows by descending values.
STATISTICS: 1 = chi-square, 6 = tau b, 7 = tau c, 8 = gamma,
9 = Somer's d.

Table 4.6   SPSS/PC+

Crosstabulation: UNEMP   Seriousness of Unemployment
                   By AGE Age of Respondent

AGE→	Count Col Pct	Under 45 1	45 and over 2	Row Total
UNEMP Serious	2	160 46.8	125 56.6	285 50.6
Slight/No Prob	1	182 53.2	96 43.4	278 49.4
Column Total		342 60.7	221 39.3	563 100.0

Continued

Chi-Square	D.F.	Significance	Min E.F.	Cells with E.F.<5
4.75069	1	.0293	109.126	None
5.13440	1	.0235	(Before Yates Correction)	

Page 4   SPSS/PC+   8/7/8

Statistic	Symmetric	With UNEMP Dependent	With AGE Dependent
Somers' D	.09547	.09777	.09327

Statistic	Value	Significance
Kendall's Tau B	.09550	.0118
Kendall's Tau C	.09326	.0118
Gamma	.19391	

B. Crosstab of UNEMP BY AGE Using STATPAC

Instructions:
- Follow steps 1–10 in Appendix C
- Analysis type #4, "Crosstabs and Chi-Square Analysis"
- First Variable (X) = #75 for "Age"
- Second Variable (Y) = #55 for "Seriousness of Unemployment"
- Options: #3 Select if Variable #55, "less than" (2) Value = 4, 0 "None"
- Options: #1 Recode Variable #55 Recode statement (1 = 1)(2 − 3 = 2)
- Options: #1 Recode Variable #75 Recode (L0 − 44 = 01)(45 − HI = 02)
- Select #6, "End task and write to disk"
- Execute now and start with Task 1

Note: Only phi and contingency coefficient are provided by STATPAC. Other measures of association can be calculated from the data in the table. However, the rows will need to be rearranged in descending order.

Table 4.7   STATPAC

CROSSTAB UNEMP BY AGE

AGE-(X Axis)
BY
SERIOUSNESS OF UNEMPLOYMENT-(Y Axis)

Number Row % Column % Total %		1	2	Row Totals
SERIOUS	1	160 56.1 46.8 28.4	125 43.9 56.6 22.2	285 50.6
SLIGHT	2	182 65.5 53.2 32.3	96 34.5 43.4 17.1	278 49.4
NO PROBLEM	3	0 0.0 0.0 0.0	0 0.0 0.0 0.0	0 0.0
DK	4	0 0.0 0.0 0.0	0 0.0 0.0 0.0	0 0.0
Column Totals		342 60.7	221 39.3	563 100.0

Corrected Chi square = 4.75   Valid cases   = 563
Degrees of freedom   = 1   Missing cases = 9
Probability of chance = 0.029   Response rate = 98.4%
Phi   = 0.092
Contingency coeff.   = 0.091

Note: 2 rows not included in Chi square calculations

Formulas for and Calculations of Gamma, Somer's *d*, Tau *b*, and Tau *c*

Formulas for and calculation of ordinal measures of association are illustrated below using data from the preceding SPSS/PC+ and STATPAC output. Note that N_s and N_d are used in all formulas.

Formula   *Gamma*

$$G = \frac{N_s - N_d}{N_s + N_d}$$

where N_s = the number of times pairs are ranked the same

N_d = the number of times pairs are ranked differently

To calculate $N_s + N_d$ make sure the table is set up properly: column headings arranged in ascending order and row headings arranged in descending order.

Examples N_s: Start with the value in the *lower left* cell of the table. Multiply that value by the sum of all cell values above and to the right of it. (In tables larger than 2 × 2 continue to multiply every cell value that has cells above and to the right of it by the sum of the above-right cell values, and add all these products together.)

N_d: Start with the value in the *lower right* cell of the table. Multiply that value by the sum of all cell values above and to the left of it. Do the same for every cell value that has cells above and to the left of it. Then, add all the products together.

$$N_s = 182(125) = 22{,}750$$

$$N_d = 96(160) \;\; = 15{,}360$$

$$G \;\; = \frac{22{,}750 - 15{,}360}{22{,}750 + 15{,}360} = \frac{7{,}390}{38{,}110} = .19391$$

Remember that in a 2 × 2 table gamma is also known as Yule's Q. Therefore, Q = .19391.

Formula *Somer's d (Asymmetric)*

$$d = \frac{N_s - N_d}{N_s + N_d + T_y}$$

where T_y = the number of ties on the dependent variable

$N_s + N_d$ is calculated the same as in the case of gamma. T_y is calculated by multiplying all frequencies in each row by the sum of frequencies to the right of it and then adding all of them together.

$$T_y = 182(96) + 160(125) = 37,472$$

$$d = \frac{22,750 - 15,360}{22,750 + 15,360 + 37,472} = \frac{7,390}{75,582} = .09777$$

Formula *Tau b*

$$\text{tau } b = \frac{N_s - N_d}{\sqrt{N_s + N_d + T_y} \ \sqrt{N_s + N_d + T_x}}$$

where T_y = the number of ties on variable y

T_x = the number of ties on variable x

T_y is calculated the same as in the case of Somer's $d = 37,472$. T_x is calculated by multiplying all frequencies in each column by the sum of frequencies below it and then adding all of them together.

$$T_x = 160(182) + 125(96) = 41,120$$

$$\text{tau } b = \frac{22,750 - 15,360}{\sqrt{22,750 + 15,360 + 38,472} \ \sqrt{22,750 + 15,360 + 41,120}}$$

$$= \frac{7,390}{\sqrt{75,582} \ \sqrt{79,230}} = \frac{7,390}{274.92 \times 281.478} = \frac{7,390}{77,384.504} = .09550$$

Formula *Tau c*

$$\text{tau } c = \frac{2m(N_s - N_d)}{N^2(m - 1)}$$

where m = the smaller of the number of rows and columns

N = sample size

Therefore,

$$\text{tau } c = \frac{2(2)(22,750 - 15,360)}{(563)^2(2 - 1)} = \frac{4(7,390)}{316,969} = \frac{29,560}{316,969} = .09326$$

UNEMP BY AGE IN A 2 × 2 TABLE

Output from either SPSS/PC+ or STATPAC can be used to construct a table like Table 4.8. Such a table might appear in a research report and be discussed as follows:

Example   The results in Table 4.8 support the hypothesis that those over 45 years old are more likely to see a serious problem with unemployment than those under 45. Overall, about one-half of the respondents see unemployment as a serious problem and the other one-half see it as slight or no problem. Those respondents 45 and over are more likely to view unemployment as serious than are those under 45; roughly 10 percent more of those 45 and over see it as serious (56.6 percent versus 46.8 percent).

The relationship between age and perception of the seriousness of unemployment is statistically significant (chi-square, corrected = 4.75, 1 d.f., $p < .05$). Measures of association all indicate a somewhat weak association between these two variables (gamma = .194, asymmetric Somer's d = .098, tau b = .096). As age increases, the perception of unemployment as serious increases. If age is used to predict seriousness of unemployment, gamma indicates that 19 percent fewer errors would be made than if age is not used.

Table 4.8   Perception of Seriousness of Unemployment by Age of CPS Respondents(%)*

Seriousness of Unemployment	Age of Respondent		Total
	Under 45	45 and over	
Serious	46.8	56.6	50.6
Slight/No Problem	53.2	43.4	49.4
Totals	100.0	100.0	100.0
(N)	(342)	(221)	(563)

*chi-square, corrected = 4.75, d.f. = 1, $p < .05$
gamma = .194, asymmetric Somer's d = .098, tau b = .096

C. Crosstab of UNEMP BY AGE (3 × 4) Using SPSS/PC+

Instructions:

```
SPSS/PC:GET FILE='SPSSCPS', [Enter]
       :SET PRINTER=ON, [Enter]
       :RECODE AGE (18 THRU 24=1)(25 THRU 44=2)
       [Enter]
       :(45 THRU 64=3)(65 THRU HI=4), [Enter]
       :RECODE UNEMP (1=3)(2=2)(3=1), [Enter]
       :VALUE LABELS AGE 1'under 25' 2'25-44' [Enter]
       :3'45-64' 4'65 and over', [Enter]
       :VALUE LABELS UNEMP 1'NO PROBLEM' [Enter]
       :2'Slight' 3'Serious', [Enter]
       :SELECT IF (UNEMP LT 4), [Enter]
       :CROSSTABS TABLES=UNEMP BY AGE [Enter]
       :/OPTIONS=4,8 [Enter]
       :/STATISTICS=1,6,7,8,9,
```

Table 4.9 SPSS/PC+

Crosstabulation: UNEMP   Seriousness of Unemployment
                  By AGE   Age of Respondent

AGE→	Count Col Pct	Under 25 1	25-44 2	45-64 3	65 and over 4	Row Total
UNEMP Serious	3	34 46.6	126 46.8	83 58.0	42 53.8	285 50.6
Slight	2	35 47.9	134 49.8	52 36.4	30 38.5	251 44.6
No Problem	1	4 5.5	9 3.3	8 5.6	6 7.7	27 4.8
	Column Total	73 13.0	269 47.8	143 25.4	78 13.9	563 100.0

Continued

Chi-Square	D.F.	Significance	Min E.F.	Cells with E.F.<5
10.17566	6	.1174	3.501	2 OF 12 (16.7%)

Page 5   SPSS/PC+   8/7/88

Statistic	Symmetric	With UNEMP Dependent	With AGE Dependent
Somers' D	.06054	.05474	.06770

Statistic	Value	Significance
Kendall's Tau B	.06088	.0565
Kendall's Tau C	.05511	.0565
Gamma	.10000	

Number of Missing Observations = 1

D. Crosstab of UNEMP BY AGE (3 × 4) Using STATPAC

Instructions:

- Follow steps 1–10 in Appendix C

- Analysis type #4, "Crosstabs + Chi-Square Analysis"

- First Variable (X) = #75 for "Age"

- Second Variable (Y) = #55 for "Seriousness of Unemployment"

- Options: #3 Select if Variable #55, "less than" (2) Value = 4, 0 "None"

- Options: #1 Recode Variable #75 Recode statement (20 − 24 = 01) (25 − 44 = 02) (45 − 64 = 03) (65 − Hi = 04)

- Select #6, "End task and write to disk"

- Execute now and start with Task 1

Table 4.10   STATPAC

CROSSTAB UNEMP BY AGE

AGE-(X Axis)
BY
SERIOUSNESS OF UNEMPLOYMENT-(Y Axis)

Number Row % Column % Total %		1	2	3	4	Row Totals
SERIOUS	1	34 11.9 46.6 6.0	126 44.2 46.8 22.4	83 29.1 58.0 14.7	42 14.7 53.8 7.5	285 50.6
SLIGHT	2	35 13.9 47.9 6.2	134 53.4 49.8 23.8	52 20.7 36.4 9.2	30 12.0 38.5 5.3	251 44.6
NO PROBLEM	3	4 14.8 5.5 0.7	9 33.3 3.3 1.6	8 29.6 5.6 1.4	6 22.2 7.7 1.1	27 4.8
DK	4	0 0.0 0.0 0.0	0 0.0 0.0 0.0	0 0.0 0.0 0.0	0 0.0 0.0 0.0	0 0.0
Column Totals		73 13.0	269 47.8	143 25.4	78 13.9	563 100.0

Chi square   = 10.17   Valid cases   = 563
Degrees of freedom   = 6   Missing cases = 9
Probability of chance   = 0.117   Response rate = 98.4%
Cramer's V   = 0.095
Contingency coeff.   = 0.133

Caution: 2 cells contain an expected frequency less than 5
Note: 1 row not included in Chi square calculations

Calculations of chi-square and the various ordinal measures of association using data in the 3 × 4 tables are shown here.

Formulas *Chi-Square*

$$\chi^2 = \Sigma \left[\frac{O^2}{E} \right] - N_t \quad \text{or} \quad \Sigma \left[\frac{(O - E)^2}{E} \right]$$

The first formula above will be used here.

Expected Frequencies

	−25	25–44	45–64	65+
Serious	36.95	136.17	72.39	39.48
Slight	32.55	119.93	63.75	34.77
No Prob	3.50	12.90	6.86	3.74
	73.00	269.00	143.00	78.00

$$\chi^2 = \frac{(4)^2}{3.50} + \frac{(9)^2}{12.9} + \frac{(8)^2}{6.86} + \frac{(6)^2}{3.74} + \frac{(35)^2}{32.55} +$$

$$\frac{(134)^2}{119.93} + \frac{(52)^2}{63.75} + \frac{(30)^2}{34.77} + \frac{(34)^2}{36.95} + \frac{(126)^2}{136.17} +$$

$$\frac{(83)^2}{72.39} + \frac{(42)^2}{39.48} - 563$$

$$= 573.18 - 563$$

$$= 10.18$$

$$\text{d.f.} = (r - 1)(c - 1) = (3 - 1)(4 - 1) = (2)(3) = 6$$

$$\text{critical } \chi^2, p = .05 = 12.592 \text{ (See Table IV, Appendix D)}$$

$$p = .01 = 16.812$$

Formula *Gamma*

$$G = \frac{N_s - N_d}{N_s + N_d}$$

$$N_s$$

$$
\begin{aligned}
4(134+126+52+83+30+42) &= & 1{,}868 \\
+9(52+83+30+42) &= & 1{,}863 \\
+8(30+42) &= & 576 \\
+35(126+83+42) &= & 8{,}785 \\
+134(83+42) &= & 16{,}750 \\
+52(42) &= & \underline{2{,}184} \\
N_s &= & 32{,}026
\end{aligned}
$$

$$N_d$$

$$
\begin{aligned}
6(52+83+134+126+35+34) &= & 2{,}784 \\
+8(134+126+35+34) &= & 2{,}632 \\
+9(35+34) &= & 621 \\
+30(83+126+34) &= & 7{,}290 \\
+52(126+34) &= & 8{,}320 \\
+134(34) &= & \underline{4{,}556} \\
N_d &= & 26{,}203
\end{aligned}
$$

$$
G = \frac{32{,}026 - 26{,}203}{32{,}026 + 26{,}203} = .10000
$$

Formula   Somer's d, Asymmetric (with UNEMP dependent)

$$
d = \frac{N_s - N_d}{N_s + N_d + T_y}
$$

$$
\begin{aligned}
T_y = {} & 4(9+8+6) + 9(8+6) + 8(6) + 35(134 + \\
& 52 + 30) + 134(52 + 30) + 52(30) + 34(126 + 83 + \\
& 42) + 126(83 + 42) + 83(42) = 48{,}044
\end{aligned}
$$

$$
d = \frac{32{,}026 - 26{,}203}{32{,}026 + 26{,}203 + 48{,}044} = \frac{5823}{106{,}373} = .05474
$$

Formula   Tau b

$$
\text{tau } b = \frac{N_s - N_d}{\sqrt{N_s + N_d + T_y} \ \sqrt{N_s + N_d + T_x}}
$$

$$
\begin{aligned}
T_x = {} & 34(35 + 4) + 35(4) + 126(134 + 9) + 134(9) + \\
& 83(52 + 8) + 52(8) + 42(30 + 6) + 30(6) = 27{,}778
\end{aligned}
$$

$$
\text{tau } b = \frac{32{,}026 - 26{,}203}{\sqrt{32{,}026 + 26{,}203 + 48{,}044} \ \sqrt{32{,}026 + 26{,}203 + 27{,}778}}
$$

$$
= \frac{5{,}823}{95{,}649.474} = .06088
$$

Formula   *Tau* c

$$\text{tau } c = \frac{2m(N_s - N_d)}{N^2(m-1)}$$

$$\text{tau } c = \frac{2(3)(32,026 - 26,203)}{(563)^2(3-1)} = \frac{6(5,823)}{31,969(2)} = \frac{34,938}{633,938} = .05511$$

UNEMP BY AGE IN A 3 × 4 TABLE

Output from SPSS/PC+ or STATPAC can be used to construct a table like Table 4.11, which might appear in a report and be discussed as follows:

Example   The results in Table 4.11 show very little support for a consistent relationship between age, categorized in four groups, and view of the seriousness of unemployment. The group that sees unemployment as the most serious is the 45–64 age group (58 percent) followed by the 65-and-over group, 53.8 percent of whom see unemployment as serious. Less than a majority of both age groups under 45 see unemployment as a serious problem. The relationship between age and view on unemployment is not a linear one. A linear relationship is present when there is a steady increase or decrease in the column percentages as you move across a row of a table.

The chi-square test indicates that there is not a statistically significant relationship at the .05 level between age and perception of the seriousness of unemployment (chi-square = 10.18, d.f. = 6, n.s., $p > .05$).

Table 4.11   Perception of Seriousness of Unemployment by Age of CPS Respondents(%)*

Seriousness of Unemployment	Age of Respondent				Total
	Under 25	25–44	45–64	65 and over	
Serious	46.6	46.8	58.0	53.8	50.6
Slight	47.9	49.8	36.4	38.5	44.6
No Problem	5.5	3.3	5.6	7.7	4.8
Totals	100.0	99.9	100.0	100.0	100.0
(N)	(73)	(269)	(143)	(78)	(563)

*chi-square = 10.18, d.f. = 6, n.s. $p > .05$
gamma = .10, asymmetric Somer's d = .06, tau c = .055

Note that in the 2 × 2 table of UNEMP BY AGE there was a statistically significant relationship. This should alert you to be sensitive to the fact that the ways in which variables are categorized or catgories of variables are combined can have a considerable bearing on whether or not results will be significant. (The way in which results can change when a 3 × 3 table is constructed is discussed shortly.)

As you might expect, when there is not a statistically significant relationship, there will be virtually no association between the variables. Even when there is a significant relationship, measures of association may be somewhat weak if the relationship is not linear. In the 3 × 4 table here all the ordinal measures of association are weak: gamma = .10, Somer's d = .06, tau c = .055. These results indicate that age has very little influence on the opinions regarding the seriousness of unemployment.

UNEMP BY AGE IN A 3 × 3 TABLE

In the 3 × 4 table results were not statistically significant. However, if the two younger age categories are combined and the three age groups "Under 45," "45–64," and "65 and over" are compared concerning their views on the seriousness of unemployment, there are statistically significant differences among the age groups on this issue. In Table 4.12 chi-square = 9.58, d.f. = 4, $p < .05$.

Note in Table 4.12 that the middle age group (45–64) has the highest percentage considering unemployment as a serious problem (58 percent versus 46.8 percent for the younger age group and 53.8 percent for the older age group). As these percentages indicate, there is not a linear relationship between these two variables, and as a result the measures of association are weak (gamma = .12, Somer's d = .06, tau b = .06).

In summary, discussions of the findings that are presented in bivariate tables should include the following: (1) an examination of the relevant percentages that indicate if the relationship between the two variables exists as hypothesized; (2) an interpretation of the chi-square test to determine if the relationship is statistically significant; (3) mention of appropriate measures of association and what they indicate about the strength (and direction, if ordinal variables) of the relationship; and (4) a summary statement about what the findings in the table mean.

Table 4.12 SPSS/PC+

Crosstabulation: UNEMP   Seriousness of Unemployment
                    By AGE   Age of Respondent

AGE→	Count Col Pct	Under 45 1	45-64 2	65 and over 3	Row Total
UNEMP Serious	3	160 46.8	83 58.0	42 53.8	285 50.6
Slight	2	169	52 49.4	30 36.4	251 38.5	44.6
No problem	1	13 3.8	8 5.6	6 7.7	27 4.8
Column Total		342 60.7	143 25.4	78 13.9	563 100.0

Chi-Square	D.F.	Significance	Min E.F.	Cells with E.F.<5
9.58479	4	.0480	3.741	1 OF 9 (11.1%)

Page 5   SPSS/PC+   8/7/8

Statistic	Symmetric	With UNEMP Dependent	With AGE Dependent
Somers' D	.06426	.06399	.06453

Statistic	Value	Significance
Kendall's Tau B	.06426	.0527
Kendall's Tau C	.05253	.0527
Gamma	.11659	

Number of Missing Observations = 1

Exercise 4A:
Nominal Bivariate Tables

In the spaces below construct a nominal bivariate 2 × 2 table for Level of Education by Marital Status for the data in Table 2.13 of Section 2 exercises. For Education combine the "less than high school" and "high school" graduates into one category and combine "some college" and "college graduates" into the other. The two categories of Marital Status should be "married" as the first category and "never married, separated, widowed, and divorced" as the second category. Properly title, provide column and row headings for, and percentage the table (putting the percentages in the cells of the table) so that you can assess the effect of Marital Status on Level of Education. Then, calculate or answer the items below.

Table 4.13 _____ by _____ .

			Totals
Totals (%)			
(N)	( )	( )	( )

1. Chi-square =

2. Chi-square with Yates' correction =

3. Discuss whether there is a significant relationship between Marital Status and Level of Education at the .05 level. (Compare the obtained and critical χ^2 values.)

4. Phi =

5. Contingency coefficient =

6. Lambda =

7. Using the percentages, chi-square, and measures of association, discuss the results of this table.

Exercise 4B:
Ordinal Bivariate Tables

In the spaces below construct an ordinal bivariate 2 × 2 table for Income by Level of Education for the data in Table 2.13 of Section 2 exercises. For Income create two categories: "$20,000 or more" and "under $20,000." Use two categories for Education: "high school or less" and "some college and more." Properly title, provide column and row headings for, and percentage the table (putting the percentages in the cells of the table) so that you can assess the impact of Level of Education on Income. Then, calculate or discuss the items below.

Table 4.14 _____ by _____

_____

_____

_____ _____ _____ Totals

_____ _____ _____ _____

_____ _____ _____ _____

Totals (%) _____ _____ _____
(N)   (   )   (   )   (   )

1. Chi-square =

2. Chi-square with Yates' correction =

3. Discuss whether there is a significant relationship between education and income at the .05 level and at the 0.1 level. (Compare the obtained and critical χ^2 values.)

4. Gamma =

5. Somer's d =

6. Tau b =

7. Using the percentages, chi-square, and measures of association, discuss the results of this table.

Exercise 4C:
Computer Applications

Use SPSS/PC+ or STATPAC to obtain a 2 × 3 bivariate table of DIPLOMA by MARITAL for CPS respondents. For DIPLOMA use the categories 'high school or less' and 'some college and more.' For MARITAL use the categories 'married,' 'single,' and 'other' (combine divorced, widowed, separated, cohabiting). Obtain the chi-square and appropriate measures of association for this table. Attach your printed table to your report.

Using the percentages in the table, the chi-square, and measures of association, discuss the results of this table in the space below.

Exercise 4D:
Computer Applications

Use SPSS/PC+ or STATPAC to obtain a 2 × 4 bivariate table of INCOME by DIPLOMA for CPS respondents. For INCOME use the two categories "$30,000 and above" and "Under $30,000." For DIPLOMA use the four categories given. Obtain the chi-square and appropriate measures of association for this table. Attach your printed output to your report.

Using the percentages in the table, the chi-square, and measures of association, discuss the results of this table in the space below.

Exercise 4E:
Computer Applications

In this exercise you will use SPSS/PC+ or STATPAC to create two crosstabulations or bivariate tables that will enable you to examine two hypotheses concerning variables you select from the CPS. One table should be a *nominal* bivariate table and one should be an *ordinal* bivariate table. One table can be a 2 × 2 table, the other must be larger than 2 × 2.

Your typewritten analysis of each table should include:

1. Statement of the *hypothesis* (note the independent and dependent variables).
2. Specification of whether the variables are *nominal* or *ordinal*.
3. Examination and discussion of the relevant *percentages* that show if relationships between the variables exist as hypothesized.
4. Interpretation of the *chi-square* value and significance (Yates' correction, if appropriate) to determine whether or not the relationship is statistically significant.
5. Discussion of appropriate *measures of association* concerning the strength (and direction, if ordinal) of the association between the variables in your nominal or ordinal table.

The following shows the SPSS/PC+ and STATPAC commands needed to get a printout of a 3 × 2 crosstabulation of SEXDISC BY AGE. The RECODE statement creates two AGE categories. The SELECT IF statement drops the DK category from SEXDISC.

SPSS/PC+	STATPAC
`GET FILE='SPSSCPS',`	• Follow steps 1-10 in Appendix C
`SET PRINTER=ON,`	
`RECODE AGE`	• Analysis Type #4, "Crosstabs"
`  (LO THRU 39=01)`	
`  (40 THRU HI=02),`	• Variable X = #75
`SELECT IF (SEXDISC LT 4),`	• Variable Y = #49

```
CROSSTABS TABLES=
  SEXDISC BY AGE
/OPTIONS=4,8
/STATISTICS=1,6,7,8,9,
```

- Recode #75 (L0 − 39 = 01) (40 − HI = 02)
- Select if #49 "less than" (2) value = 4
- End task and write to disk

5
Forming and Testing Hypotheses

As hypotheses are formed and tested, researchers typically complete the steps in the research process discussed in Section 1: They (1) ask research questions, (2) form hypotheses, (3) construct research designs, (4) develop measures, (5) collect data, (6) analyze results, and (7) draw conclusions. Using hypotheses in research differs from the ways people often draw conclusions about the world.

USING HYPOTHESES RATHER THAN COMMONSENSE

Hypotheses are statements about how one or more variables are expected to be distributed or related; the seven research stages are completed to ascertain whether and to what extent evidence supports hypotheses. Researchers carefully follow the research process so that the information they gather and analyze (in the ways already discussed in Sections 2–4 and to be discussed further in subsequent sections) is representative and accurate enough to support valid conclusions (see Sections 6 and 7 on measurement and Section 8 on sampling).

In everyday life people often use very limited information—their personal experiences, something they read in newspapers or see on television, or things their friends tell them—to draw general conclusions about the world. Unfortunately, the information people receive from the media, their friends, or their personal experiences may not accurately picture either particular instances or the more general situation. For example, selective information about some welfare mothers (e.g., that they are not working) may be obtained and used to support the conclusion that most welfare mothers do not want to work. However, careful study of these particular welfare mothers, as well as representative samples of welfare mothers, may show that most *do* want to work, but circumstances such as child-care costs, domestic responsibilities, and lack of job skills hinder their chances for employment.

In contrast, researchers typically have well-informed perspectives about the world even before they undertake their research. How variables have been found to be distributed and interrelated in previous studies usually is known. Patterns of information that have accumulated as a result of prior research are called *empirical generalizations*. Empirical generalizations provide researchers with an awareness of patterns of relationships already known and, therefore, with guidelines for gathering additional appropriate information. For example, commonsense may lead many people to believe divorce results primarily from sexual incompatibility. Empirical generalizations about divorce, however, enable researchers studying marital dissolution to be aware that less obvious reasons for divorce, such as financial problems and the demands of early marriage and parenthood, are more important in the marital histories of divorced persons than are sexual problems. Using empirical generalizations means that researchers are guided by less obvious as well as more relevant information.

Researchers often form hypotheses on the basis of *theoretical statements*, which are logically interrelated and testable sets of hypotheses about the ways variables are expected to be distributed or interrelated. Such sets of hypotheses are often formed, combined, and expanded on the basis of a particular theoretical viewpoint or paradigm. A *theoretical paradigm* allows researchers to focus their research on several meaningfully interrelated hypotheses. While empirical generalizations have usually given support to some theoretical statements, the paradigm allows researchers to add new, related hypotheses that must be tested. For example, new theoretical statements about divorce may be based upon the paradigm that focuses on and interrelates untested aspects of early marriage and parenthood, such as income levels, employment of one versus both spouses, levels of parenting skills, parenting models spouses experienced as they grew up, and so on. Theoretical statements and the paradigms upon which they are based allow researchers to go beyond existent empirical generalizations.

Replication is the process by which theoretical statements that have been supported by research are retested (see Section 1). Replication is a continuous process because theoretical statements are retained by researchers only to the degree that, and for as long as, they are supported by empirical generalizations. As empirical generalizations change, the theoretical statements and the paradigms upon which they are based change as well. This dynamic interaction of theoretical statements and empirical generalization fuels continued research.

Unlike the process by which empirical generalizations and theoretical statements interact in the continuation of research, people often retain their beliefs about the world in spite of evidence and explanations that clearly contradict commonsense. Many people never make an attempt to understand less obvious but more correct explanations (i.e., theoretical statements and the paradigms upon which they are based). Many people do not make an effort to seek new and changing information about the world (i.e., current empirical generalizations). This is why commonsense often perpetuates continued misunderstanding of and ignorance about the world. In contrast, the research process better enables researchers to understand the complexities and dynamics of the world.

BIVARIATE HYPOTHESES

Hypotheses that involve an expected relationship between two variables are called *bivariate hypotheses*. Evidence presented in bivariate tables is used to test bivariate hypotheses (see Section 4).

A bivariate hypothesis is a clear statement of how change in one variable is expected to be related to change in another variable. "As people's education level increases, their level of earned income increases" is a hypothesis stating a positive (or direct) relationship: As educational level increases, earned income also increases. "As people's educational level increases, their level of racial prejudice decreases" is a hypothesis stating a negative (or inverse) relationship: The level of prejudice is expected to decrease as educational level increases. Hypotheses must make clear *how* two variables are related.

When nominal variables are involved in hypotheses, it is inappropriate to think of positive or negative relationships, because nominal variables do not increase or decrease. Instead, expected differences between the categories of the nominal variable must be clearly stated in hypotheses that involve nominal variables. "Men are more likely to earn higher incomes than women" and "Protestants are more likely to be Republicans than are Catholics and Jews" clearly state the expected differences in the categories of the nominal variables with regard to another variable.

Bivariate hypotheses usually relate an independent variable to a dependent variable. An *independent variable* is a variable that is expected to influence or cause a particular pattern of change in the dependent variable. The *dependent variable* (or effect) is the variable whose pattern of change results from changes in the independent variable. In social research independent variables such as gender, race, ethnicity, social class, level of education, and marital status may be used to explain dependent variables such as attitudes or behaviors that occur after or as a result of the independent variables. That independent variables precede dependent variables is one of the criteria for causal analysis (see Section 14).

In certain cases the independent variable in a relationship is obvious because one variable has occurred prior to the other variable. For example, if gender is related to income, gender obviously is the independent variable influencing one's earned income—income level could not be the independent variable determining whether one was a man or a woman. Or, level of education can be an independent variable influencing child rearing, but how children are raised usually does not determine how much education parents have. (There are, however, some instances where caring for children may affect parental pursuit or continuation of education, for example, adolescent pregnancy affecting completion of high school or college.) Cause and effect are not always clear-cut in social science research.

It is also important to realize that the same variable (e.g., children's self-esteem) can be either an independent or a dependent variable, depending on the research question. In the hypothesis "Children of divorced parents have lower self-esteem than children whose parents do not divorce," self-esteem is the dependent variable. Divorce is hypothesized to affect the level of self-esteem. In the hypothesis "Children with lower self-esteem are more likely to drop out of school than children with higher self-esteem," self-esteem is the independent variable because level of self-esteem is hypothesized to affect dropping out of school.

THEORETICAL VERSUS WORKING HYPOTHESES

A theoretical hypothesis must first be conceptualized and then be made specific in a working hypothesis before it can be tested with research results. *Theoretical hypotheses* are general and often abstract statements of an expected relationship. *Working hypotheses* provide specific indicators or measures of the concepts in a theoretical hypothesis. The process of choosing appropriate specific indicators of clear theoretical concepts for use in a working hypothesis is called *operationalization* (see Sections 6 and 7 on measurement).

In a theoretical hypothesis clear meanings are assigned to concepts, and statements about how these concepts are related are made. The process is often referred to as conceptualization. *Conceptualization* must be completed before operationalization can occur. The following discussions illustrate the steps in conceptualization and operationalization.

Example Suppose you think that the educational process exposes people to information about individual liberty and increases people's interest in preserving individual freedom. Suppose you also believe certain social programs violate human liberty. Notice that both these suppositions suggest consequences of the educational process and some social programs. With these ideas you are ready to further define these concepts and to develop a theoretical hypothesis. You could do so as follows:

Involvement in the educational process might be defined as being exposed to information that increases interest in preserving individual freedom. Social programs that deny liberty may be defined as those which do not allow people a choice whether or not to participate. These two examples illustrate how meaning must be assigned to concepts with definitions that clarify and delimit the meaning of the concepts (see Sections 6 and 7).

Once you have defined your theoretical ideas clearly, you can then state your theoretical hypothesis as follows:

"The more people have been exposed to information about individual freedom in the educational process, the less likely they are to support social programs that deny people a choice about participating."

You might justify your theoretical hypothesis with several untested assumptions, or *axioms*, such as:

"Better-educated people have been exposed to information that makes them more aware of supporting efforts to preserve individual liberty and opposing programs that deny freedom of choice."

Once a theoretical hypothesis is stated, you need to select a specific indicator of involvement in the educational process and an indicator of social programs that deny freedom of choice to participate. Many researchers select indicators for theoretical ideas from already existing datasets. Researchers who collect their own data must still choose or create indicators for theoretical ideas before they do their research. (Rules for selecting and evaluating indicators are discussed in Sections 6 and 7.)

Here we will use variables from the CPS as indicators. An indicator of involvement in the educational process is the variable DIPLOMA, with the categories "less than high school," "high school graduate or GED," and "some college or more." An indicator of a social program that denies freedom of choice to participate is DRUGEMP. This variable involves responses to the question "Are you in favor of, opposed to, or uncertain about mandatory drug testing for all employees?"

As you can see, clearly defining the concepts in a theoretical hypothesis is necessary and helpful in the selection of appropriate indicators. The above example illustrates the process of moving from conceptualization to operationalization.

Now, you are ready to state your working hypothesis:

"Those with higher educational degrees are less likely to support mandatory drug testing of employees than are those with lower educational degrees."

And for statistical testing in a bivariate table (see Sections 4 and 11), the working hypothesis would be translated into its null form:

"There is no difference between those with different educational degrees and their support for mandatory drug testing of all employees."

You are now ready to use SPSS/PC+ or STATPAC procedures to crosstabulate DRUGEMP by DIPLOMA in order to test your null hypothesis. Table 5.1 presents the SPSS/PC+ output you will generate.

A. *Crosstab at DRUGEMP BY DIPLOMA Using SPSS/PC+*

Instructions:

```
SPSS/PC:GET FILE='SPSSCPS', [ENTER]
       :SET PRINTER=ON, [ENTER]
       :RECODE DIPLOMA (3,4=3), [ENTER]
       :SELECT IF (DIPLOMA LT 5), [ENTER]
       :SELECT IF (DRUGEMP LT 3), [ENTER]
       :CROSSTABS TABLES=DRUGEMP BY DIPLOMA [ENTER]
       :/OPTIONS=4 [ENTER]
       :/STATISTICS=1, [ENTER]
```

Table 5.1 Mandatory Drug Testing by Diploma
Crosstabulation: DRUGEMP   Employee Drug Testing
                      By DIPLOMA   Highest Diploma of Respondent

DIPLOMA→ DRUGEMP	Count Col Pct	lt high school 1	hs grad or ged 2	some col 1/trade 3	Row Total
favor	1	72 71.3	72 58.1	114 46.5	258 54.9
oppose	2	29 28.7	52 41.9	131 53.5	212 45.1
	Column Total	101 21.5	124 26.4	245 52.1	470 100.0

Chi-Square	D.F.	Significance	Min E.F.	Cells with E.F.<5
18.38632	2	.0001	45.557	NONE

As can be seen in Table 5.1, two types of evidence enable you to reject your null hypothesis. First, the statistical results of the chi-square test indicate that the probability of such differences occurring by chance or sampling variability is less than .05 (in this case it is less than .001). Consequently, the decision can be made to reject the null hypothesis because the probability of rejecting a true null hypothesis is less than the commonly accepted "critical" probability value of .05 (see Section 11). There is a statistically significant negative relationship between level of education and support for mandatory employee drug testing. Those with lower levels of education are more likely to favor employee drug testing than those with higher levels of education.

Second, as can also be seen in Table 5.1, as level of education increases, there is a steady (or linear) decrease in the percentage of people who support mandatory drug testing for all employees. Over 71 percent of those with less than a high school degree support mandatory drug testing, but the percentages favoring it drop to 58.1 percent for high school/GED graduates and to 46.5 percent for those with college education.

Both the chi-square test and the percentage pattern enable you to reject the null hypothesis. The conclusion is that a statistically significant relationship does exist between level of education and support for mandatory drug testing of all employees. The percentage differences show that as educational level increases, the level of support for mandatory drug testing decreases. There is support for your working hypothesis that as educational level increases, support for mandatory drug testing of all employees decreases.

Results do not always so clearly sustain a working hypothesis, as the next example shows. In order to emphasize the steps in conceptualization and operationalization, we will proceed through them again before the results are considered.

Example   Suppose you believe that women are socialized in ways that make them both more aware of gender inequality in American society and more likely than men to experience the negative effects of gender inequality in areas such as hiring and promotion. You therefore hypothesize that women are more likely than men to feel that gender inequality exists in their community.

Using the CPS codebook you would obviously select the variable SEX for the indicator of gender. You could select the variable SEXDISC as an indicator of the belief that gender inequality exists in the United States. SEXDISC is the variable that orders responses to the question "Do you believe there is a problem with sex discrimination in this community?" into one of three categories: "serious," "slight," "no problem."

The working hypothesis is as follows:

"Women are more likely to view sex discrimination as a serious problem than are men."

And, for statistical testing (see Section 11), you would translate your working hypothesis into its null form:

"Women are no more likely to view sex discrimination as a community problem than are men."

The statistical evidence used to test your null hypothesis appears in Table 5.2, which presents the crosstabulation of SEXDISC by SEX.

B. Crosstab of SEXDISC BY SEX Using SPSS/PC+

Instructions:

```
SPSS/PC:GET FILE='SPSSCPS'. [ENTER]
        :SET PRINTER=ON. [ENTER]
        :SELECT IF (SEXDISC LT 4). [ENTER]
```

```
:CROSSTABS TABLES=SEXDISC BY SEX [ENTER]
:/OPTIONS=4 [ENTER]
:/STATISTICS=1, [ENTER]
```

Table 5.2 Seriousness of Sex Discrimination by Gender
Crosstabulation: SEXDISC   Seriousness of Sex Discrimination
                     By SEX   Sex of Respondent

SEX->	Count Col Pct	male 1	female 2	Row Total
SEXDISC				
serious	1	30 14.0	54 21.1	84 17.9
slight	2	135 63.1	147 57.4	282 60.0
no problem	3	49 22.9	55 21.5	104 22.1
	Column Total	214 45.5	256 54.5	470 100.0

Chi-Square	D.F.	Significance	Min E.F.	Cells with E.F.<5
3.99263	2	.1358	38.247	NONE

The results of the chi-square test that appear in Table 5.2 indicate
that the probability of the observed differences occurring by chance or
sampling variability is greater than the "critical" probability value of
.05. This means that the null hypothesis cannot be rejected; therefore,
the conclusion is that there is not a statistically significant relationship
between gender and viewing sex discrimination as a serious community
problem. Results do not enable you to accept the working hypothesis
that women are more likely than men to view sex discrimination as a
community problem. Results indicate that only 14.0 percent of the men
in the CPS sample and 21.1 percent of the women view sex discrimination as a serious community problem. In general, neither gender views
this problem as a serious one in the community. Even though the working hypothesis is not supported generally, there is evidence that women
are slightly more likely than men to view sex discrimination as a *serious*
community problem (21.1 percent versus 14.0 percent).

Although the results of research often do not fully support a working hypothesis, such outcomes should not be viewed as failures. Researchers learn as much when working hypotheses are not supported fully as when they are.

Forming and testing hypotheses are major parts of the research process (see Section 1). Tests of statistical significance that are used in the process of evaluating hypotheses fully combine methodological and statistical procedures. Social researchers carefully conceptualize and operationalize working hypotheses they use in research. Empirical generalizations and theoretical statements aid in the formulation of working hypotheses. Research findings are used to evaluate working hypotheses, and this process often results in new empirical generalizations and revision of theoretical statements. Research is a never-ending process because the use of hypotheses links predictions and evidence in a dynamic continuity.

Exercise 5A:
Empirical Generalizations

After each of the following hypothetical empirical generalizations, indicate—by checking yes or no—which of them could be used as theoretical statements consistent with the idea that people with lower status are more religious than are higher-status people.

	Yes	No
1. Poorer people donate more to television evangelists than do richer people.	_____	_____
2. Better-educated people attend fewer church services than do less-educated people.	_____	_____
3. Poorer families read the bible together more often than do richer families.	_____	_____
4. Richer people are more likely to belong to a church than are poorer people.	_____	_____
5. Unemployed people are less likely to believe in God than are employed people.	_____	_____
6. Less-educated people are more likely to believe in life after death than are better-educated people.	_____	_____

Exercise 5B:
Theoretical Statements

After each of the following theoretical statements, indicate—by checking the conflict or functionalist blank—which paradigm each could be derived from. (Note: The conflict paradigm focuses on how forms of conflict can improve social relationships, while the functionalist paradigm emphasizes how dividing tasks and cooperation make social relationships work better.)

	Conflict Paradigm	Functionalist Paradigm
1. Couples who openly express disagreements have happier marriages than those couples who do not argue.	_____	_____
2. Workers are more productive when they can challenge managerial roles than when they cannot.	_____	_____
3. Organizations work better when departments are highly specialized than when departments are not specialized.	_____	_____
4. Medical care is better when specialists refer patients to one another than when patients are treated by general practitioners.	_____	_____
5. Families are closer if members can express their household complaints than if they do not express dissatisfactions with family life.	_____	_____
6. Couples who share household duties are less likely to divorce than couples who do not share such duties.	_____	_____

Exercise 5C:
Independent and Dependent Variables

In the spaces next to each of the following hypotheses, identify the independent and the dependent variables.

	Independent Variable	Dependent Variable
1. Men are more likely to be aggressive than are women.	_____	_____
2. The lower married couples' combined incomes are, the more unhappy their marriage.	_____	_____
3. People who were abused as children are more likely to abuse their own children than are people who were not abused as children.	_____	_____
4. The earlier people marry, the more likely they are to divorce.	_____	_____
5. High school dropouts are more likely to have parents who have a low interest in education than are students who do not drop out.	_____	_____

Exercise 5D:
Hypotheses

In the spaces below provide the hypotheses indicated.

1. An hypothesis stating a negative relationship between parental supervision and delinquency:

2. An hypothesis stating a positive relationship between years of work experience and income:

3. An hypothesis relating gender and working part-time:

4. An hypothesis relating age and IQ level:

5. An hypothesis relating political party preference and social class:

Exercise 5E:
Null and Working Hypotheses

In the spaces below each of the following theoretical hypotheses, write an appropriate working hypothesis and an appropriate null hypothesis. Use the CPS Codebook to choose your indicators.

1. The greater people's entrenchment in a community (defined in terms of lack of geographical mobility), the higher their evaluation of community services (defined in terms of ratings given to various community services).
   a. working hypothesis:

   b. null hypothesis:

2. The higher people's social status (defined in terms of economic advantages), the less concern they have about less fortunate people in society (defined in terms of perceived seriousness of unemployment in the community).
   a. working hypothesis:

        b. null hypothesis:

3. The higher people's educational achievements (defined in terms of formal schooling), the greater their concern about educational problems in society (defined in terms of school problems in the community).
    a. working hypothesis:

        b. null hypothesis:

Exercise 5F:
Computer Applications

You are to test the following theoretical hypothesis with variables in the CPS dataset: "People who have a stable marital union are more likely to positively evaluate the quality of life in their community."

1. What variables in the CPS will you use as indicators of the following?
   a. stability of marital union:

   b. evaluation of quality of life in the community:

2. What is your working hypothesis?

3. What is your null hypothesis?

4. In the space below construct a bivariate table to test your null hypothesis; include in the table appropriate results that you obtained using SPSS/PC+ or STATPAC program commands. Follow the examples in Section 5. Be sure to obtain percentages and the chi-square.

5. Were you able to reject your null hypothesis at the .05 level of significance? Why or why not? Discuss the percentages and the chi-square.

6. Were you able to support your working hypothesis? Why or why not?

Exercise 5G:
Computer Applications

You are to test the following theoretical hypothesis with variables in the CPS dataset: "Those with higher educational attainment are more likely to feel that there are drug problems in the schools."

1. What variables will you use as indicators of the following?
   a. educational attainment:

   b. perception of drug problems in the schools:

2. What is your working hypothesis?

3. What is your null hypothesis?

4. In the space below construct a bivariate table to test your null hypothesis; include in the table appropriate results that you obtained using SPSS/PC+ or STATPAC program commands. Be sure to obtain percentages and the chi-square.

5. Were you able to reject your null hypothesis at the .01 level of significance? Why or why not? Discuss the percentages and the chi-square.

6. Were you able to support your working hypothesis? Why or why not?

Exercise 5H:
Computer Applications

The table below presents CPS findings that deal with the following working hypothesis: "The higher people's family income, the less likely they are to support a program providing services to the homeless." Answer the questions that follow the table.

Table 5.3 SPSS/PC+

Crosstabulation: HOMELESS   Need Services for Homeless
                    By INCOME   Total Family Income in 1986

INCOME-> HOMELESS	Count Col Pct	low 1	mod 2	hi 3	Row Total
yes	1	201	177	95	473
		92.2	90.8	88.0	90.8
no	2	17	18	13	48
		7.8	9.2	12.0	9.2
	Column Total	218	195	108	521
		41.8	37.4	20.7	100.0

Chi-Square	D.F.	Significance	Min E.F.	Cells with E.F.<5
1.55156	2	.4603	9.950	None

1. What is your null hypothesis?

2. Does the evidence allow you to reject your null hypothesis at the .01 level? Why or why not?

3. Does the evidence give any support for your working hypothesis? If so, what is it?

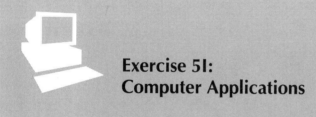

Exercise 5I:
Computer Applications

The table below presents CPS findings that deal with the following working hypothesis: "The higher people's family income, the more likely they will be registered to vote in elections." Answer the questions that appear below the table.

Table 5.4 SPSS/PC+

Crosstabulation: REGVOTER   Registered Voter?
               By INCOME   Total Family Income in 1986

INCOME-> REGVOTER	Count Col Pct	low 1	mod 2	hi 3	Row Total
yes	1	138 64.5	136 70.1	88 81.5	362 70.2
no	2	76 35.5	58 29.9	20 18.5	154 29.8
	Column Total	214 41.5	194 37.6	108 20.9	516 100.0

Chi-Square	D.F.	Significance	Min E.F.	Cells with E.F. <5
9.90233	2	.0071	32.233	None

1. What is your null hypothesis?

2. Does the evidence allow you to reject your null hypothesis? Why or why not?

3. Does the evidence give any support for your working hypothesis? If so, what is it?

6

Measurement

The general process of measurement involves an application and extension of conceptualization, operationalization, and hypothesis testing, all of which were discussed in the previous section (see Section 5). To measure anything, a researcher must do at least four things. First, a clear meaning must be assigned to the concept being measured (this is *conceptualization*). Second, a reasonable indicator of the meaning assigned to a concept must be selected (this is *operationalization*). Third, specific values or categories of the indicator must be considered (this is *structuring*). Fourth, whether or not the indicator is reliable and valid must be determined by testing specific hypotheses that relate the indicator to other variables (this is *reliability and validity testing*).

This section addresses the logic behind and procedures involved in conceptualization, operationalization, structuring of indicators, and assessment of reliability and validity in the relatively simple situation where a single item or indicator is used to measure something. For example, a researcher may contend that "social status" can be measured by income alone, or that "intelligence" can be measured by a score on a single test. Obviously, the world is more complicated than this—there are several types of status and several types of intelligence. Nevertheless, the researcher may wish to limit and simplify meaning in a certain study. The importance of assigning precise meaning to concepts, of carefully selecting an indicator of intended meaning, and of assessing both the reliability and validity of an indicator through hypothesis testing, discussed in this section in the context of a simple, single-aspect concept, also apply to more complex measures (discussed in Section 7).

CONCEPTUALIZING SINGLE-ASPECT CONCEPTS

For many research purposes assigning a single type of meaning to a concept makes good sense. If a researcher is studying differences in standards of living between single-parent and two-parent families, it may make sense to define "social status" in terms of "total family income." There may be no need to consider other dimensions of social status, such as parental educational levels and parents' occupational prestige. Although concepts can and do mean different things, often researchers deliberately restrict the meaning of a concept to the one meaning that is important for the purpose of their research. And single-meaning definitions frequently are the outcome of conceptualization. When researchers select and assign one specific meaning to a concept, the result is a *nominal definition*.

It is important to understand that the process of conceptualization (even when multiple-meaning concepts are involved) assigns a restrictive meaning to concepts. A nominal definition is never intended as a complete (or perfect or real) definition, which may be unattainable for any concept. Researchers seldom argue over the completeness or the exhaustiveness of definitions. But they *do* argue over the degree to which indicators reflect or index the meaning assigned by nominal definitions. For example, experienced researchers might question using grades in a statistics course as an indicator of "academic achievement" if the concept was defined to mean proficiency in *all* academic subjects.

OPERATIONALIZING SINGLE-ASPECT CONCEPTS

Once the meaning of a concept has been restricted to a single aspect or dimension, a relevant indicator of that particular meaning must be chosen. Two considerations need to be kept in mind when selecting "good" indicators. First, the indicator should provide an empirical referent to the meaning that has been assigned to the concept. The concept's theoretical meaning must match as closely as possible what is measured in the real, empirical world by its indicator; that is, it must have "face validity." Ultimately, this matching process is a matter of judgment.

Second, the indicator should provide as accurate a reflection of the meaning of the concept as possible, although accurate indicators are often difficult and expensive to obtain. For example, victimization rates during the previous year may be a more accurate way to measure the extent of such crimes as sexual abuse or rape than using rates of such offenses reported to the police. However, victimization rate indicators may be much more difficult to obtain. Often researchers may have to settle for an indicator that is not completely satisfactory and that has less face validity because of the expense of and difficulty in obtaining a more accurate form of the indicator.

STRUCTURING AN INDICATOR

After an indicator has been chosen, researchers must carefully consider what values or categories of the indicator will be used. For example, "total family income" might be chosen as an indicator of standard of living. If it is the standard of living of the poor or those with a marginal economic existence that is being studied, then more values in the lower range of total family income might be necessary than in the higher income range. Or, if the standard of living of high-income earners is being studied, then more high values or higher income divisions might have to be used. How many divisions or what range of values an indicator should have is an important issue when questions are structured for interviews or questionnaires (see Section 9).

All the critical values of an indicator that will be used to classify and render judgments about things or people must be included in an indicator's categorization scheme. If the critical value of "poverty" is earning $12,500, and if the critical value of "rich" is earning $100,000 or more a year, then these must be divisions of the total family income indicator.

JUDGING THE RELIABILITY AND VALIDITY OF AN INDICATOR

Whether or not an indicator that has been selected and structured by a researcher is a "good" indicator depends primarily on satisfactory answers to two questions: (1) Is the indicator reliable? and (2) Is the indicator valid?

An indicator is judged to be reliable if it provides consistent measurements—that is, if it produces the same results each time it is used. An indicator is valid if it actually and accurately measures the concept to which it has been assigned. Because an indicator may be reliable but not valid, the validity issue raises questions about the meaning of an indicator apart from how consistent outcomes are. Typically, therefore, reseachers first will attempt to demonstrate that the values obtained by using an indicator are reliable, and then will assess whether they are valid. To this end, researchers employ a number of methods.

Test-Retest Reliability Procedure

Researchers try to answer the question of reliability in several ways. One way is *test-retest reliability*, which involves using an indicator more than once. For example, a test measuring aggressiveness can be given to a group of children and then repeated with the same group four weeks later. If there is a high degree of similarity in the two measurements, the indicator is considered reliable. However, inflated estimates of reliability might result from the reactive nature of retesting, or the scores may not be similar but the indicator nonetheless be reliable. Change can occur over time—the longer the time between the first and the second measurement, the more likely change is to take place. Therefore, the length of time between measurements should be kept reasonably short.

Parallel or Alternate Forms Reliability Technique

Reliability can also be examined when measurement occurs at only one point in time. One method involves the *parallel* or *alternate forms* technique. Two alternate forms of an indicator, designed to be equivalent, are administered to the same group, and the correlation between the two forms is taken as an indication of the degree of reliability (see Section 13 for a discussion of correlation). For example, a very similar question related to a certain topic may be asked at two different points in an interview or on a questionnaire. If the items are reliable, respondents should answer the two items in a similar manner.

Split-Half Reliability Method

Another type of the parallel forms approach to reliability is the *split-half method*. This procedure requires the researcher to divide a scale or index containing several items into two sets or halves after the entire set of items has been administered to a group. Results in the two halves are compared; a high correlation between them is indicative of high reliability. Because the split-half procedure is best suited to complex indicators, it will be discussed in detail in Section 7.

Face Validity Procedures

Several approaches to answering the question of validity are used by social researchers. One, which was mentioned previously, is face validity. *Face validity* refers to the careful, but nevertheless subjective, judgment that an indicator does in fact measure the particular meaning assigned to a concept. The claim is made that the indicator appears, on the face of it, to measure the concept it is supposed to measure. All indicators *appear* to have this type of validity; otherwise, we would not have selected them to represent the concept. Assertions about face validity are often made in social research, but they may not always be compelling or satisfactory to those who raise questions about validity.

There are also several objective procedures that may be used to assess validity, including predictive and concurrent validity procedures. These methods are often referred to as empirically or criterion-based types of validity testing.

Predictive Validity Procedures

Predictive validity procedures are employed when an indicator is being used to help predict future outcomes. For example, college entrance tests were developed to help predict which high school graduates would succeed in post-secondary education. Vocational preference tests were developed to identify people who would be happier and more successful in certain types of occupations. The logic behind predictive validity is that scores on the indicator (e.g., the college entrance test) should be highly related to the future behavior (e.g., success in college) that the indicator is designed to predict. If this is generally the case for people who take the college entrance test, then the test is deemed valid.

Concurrent Validity Procedures

Concurrent validity procedures are logically equivalent to predictive validity, except that instead of a future event being compared to indicator results, another indicator of the same meaning is compared to the indicator being evaluated. For example, a person's score on the vocational preference test might be compared to another indicator of vocational interest or aptitude (e.g., hobbies or self-reported job interests). The concurrent validity of the vocational preference test is indicated by how well it corresponds with other known or presumed indicators of vocational interest.

Construct Validity Procedures

The most sophisticated way to determine an indicator's validity is *construct validity*. This procedure requires that prior (or current) research has tested (or will test) how several indicators of other concepts (called *constructs*) relate to an indicator similar to the one being evaluated. To understand this rather complex procedure, consider the following example: Suppose a researcher is evaluating whether income is a valid indicator of social status. First, the researcher must be able to find support for a series of hypotheses linking another indicator of status (e.g., educational attainment) to several constructs such as age, race, and gender. That is, suppose the researcher finds support in the data he or she has collected for the following theoretically justifiable hypotheses:

"Men have greater educational attainment than women."
"Whites have greater educational attainment than nonwhites."
"Older adults have greater educational attainment than younger adults."

To assess whether the income indicator of status is valid, the researcher would retest each of the hypotheses listed above by substituting income for educational attainment. If income is a valid indicator of status, then the researcher would find that whites had higher incomes than nonwhites, that men had higher incomes than women, and that older adults had higher incomes than younger adults. What is desirable, then, is finding that the same relationships exist between a similar indicator and certain constructs as exist between the indicator being evaluated and the same constructs. If similar relationships are found, support exists for concluding the indicator being evaluated is valid. If results are not the same, the indicator may not be valid, the constructs chosen may not be the proper ones, the hypotheses formulated may be incorrect, or some combination of these problems may exist. Deciphering why parallel outcomes do not occur when construct validity assessment is used is a difficult task.

An important point to mention about reliability and validity testing is that researchers often attempt to resolve or bypass these issues by using indicators that are considered to be valid and reliable because they were used in previous research. However, such an assumption may not be warranted, because evidence of validity or reliability may have been minimal or nonexistent in previous studies. Furthermore, indicators that were once valid and reliable may no longer be. Reliability and validity assessments thus are needed for both new and old indicators.

Exercise 6A:
Conceptualization, Operationalization, and Structuring

Identify each of the statements below as an example of one of the following:

Conceptualization (C)—what a concept means
Operationalization (O)—what indicator is used to represent or measure the concept
Structuring (S)—how the indicator is categorized

1. "Family income" is divided into four income brackets. __S__

2. "Religiosity" is defined as belonging to and attending church. __C__

3. "Achievement scores" of children in a classroom are grouped into three levels. __S__

4. "Believe in an afterlife" is measured by questions about belief in the existence of Heaven and Hell. __O__

5. "Marital discord" is defined in terms of arguments between spouses. _O C_

6. "Best product" is considered to be one that needs the fewest repairs. __C__

7. Dropout rates are used to study "student retention." __O__

In the spaces below indicate how you might conceptualize, operationalize, and structure the concepts of prejudice and child abuse.

	Prejudice	Child Abuse
Conceptualize:		
Operationalize:		
Structure:		

Exercise 6B:
Conceptualizing, Operationalizing, and Structuring

For each of the following items, complete the procedures of conceptualizing, operationalizing, or structuring in two different ways.

1. Conceptualize "being old."
   a. first way: *over a certain age*

   b. second way:
      – anyone who draws a pension

2. Operationalize "educational attainment."
   a. first way: *years completed in school*

   b. second way: *highest degree obtained*

3. Structure "social class."
   a. first way—to identify where in the class hierarchy most Americans are: *upper, middle, lower*

   b. second way—to enable a researcher to study upward social mobility:

4. Conceptualize "interpersonal conflict."
   a. first way: *an argument or disagreement characterized by conflict*

   b. second way: *physical violence and abuse*

5. Operationalize "political activism."
   a. first way: *[handwritten: voting]*

   b. second way: *[handwritten: participating actively in protest the]*

6. Structure "age."
   a. first way: *[handwritten: chronological]*

   b. second way: *[handwritten: child, teenage, adult, elderly etc]*

Exercise 6C:
Reliability and Validity

Complete each of the following aspects of reliability and validity analysis.

1. Discuss how you could use parallel forms to study the reliability of a work satisfaction question.
   a. first question:

   b. second question:

2. Identify how you would use predictive validity testing to evaluate a "leisure time preference measure."
   a. What would the future behavior be?

   b. What would the results of hypothesis testing be?

3. Assume you have an intelligence test for middle class whites (Test MCW) and an intelligence test for lower class whites (Test LCW). Use construct validity procedures to answer each of the following questions:
   a. What would the constructs be?

   b. What would be the relationships between Test MCW scores and the constructs?

   c. What would be the relationships between Test LCW scores and the constructs?

Exercise 6D:
Computer Applications

Evaluate the reliability of the variable YRSLIVED in the CPS data set by crosstabulating YRSLIVED by LIVEWC. (*Note:* Recode YRSLIVED into the following three categories: 0-11, 12-30, and 31-90.)

1. In the space below construct the appropriate table representing the crosstabulation of the recoded YRSLIVED by LIVEWC.

2. In the space below discuss the results of the table with respect to consistency between people's answers to the YRSLIVED and LIVEWC questions. Is there a relationship between the way people answered the two questions. If so, what is it?

Exercise 6E:
Computer Applications

Use construct validity procedures to evaluate the validity of the variable INCOME as a measure of "Status." The constructs you should use are SEX, RACE, and EMPLOYED. Use DIPLOMA as the other status variable to relate to the constructs.

Note: Recode INCOME as follows: $(1,2 = 1)(3,4 = 2)(5,6 = 3)$.
     Recode DIPLOMA as follows: $(1 = 1)(2 = 2)(3,4 = 3)$.
     Recode RACE as follows: $(1 = 1)(2,3 = 2)$.
     Relabel all recoded variables correctly.

1. In the space below construct and describe the results in the three bivariate tables that represent the crosstabulations of the recoded DIPLOMA variable by SEX, RACE, and EMPLOYED.

2. In the space below construct tables and describe results of the cross-tabulations of the recoded INCOME variable by SEX, RACE, and EMPLOYED.

3. Briefly explain the evidence that supports the conclusion that IN-COME is a valid measure of "Status."

7

Index Construction and Interpretation of Complex Concepts

Conceptualization of complex concepts involves clearly determining the meaning a concept will have (and by implication the meanings it will not have). The range of possible meanings a concept will have is called the concept's *universe of meaning*. Note that many concepts have a universe of meaning that includes more than one aspect or dimension. How large a concept's universe of meaning is must be made clear by a researcher in a nominal definition (see Section 6). For example, in a study of religiosity, a narrow universe of meaning might restrict its meaning to regularity of church attendance. However, a researcher studying religiosity may need a broader universe of meaning, which might include church attendance, religious beliefs, and rituals that take place in the home. Many concepts used by researchers have several elements or dimensions in their universe of meaning.

Once the components of a complex concept's universe of meaning have been identified by a researcher, he or she may select several indicators of each dimension of meaning. There are several reasons for selecting more than one indicator for each component of a concept's universe of meaning. First, a particular element of meaning may be inadequately represented if only one indicator is used. Second, if one indicator does not actually measure the aspect of meaning very well, then the others used may. Third, using several indicators of each aspect of meaning allows a researcher to conduct the parallel forms type of reliability testing.

INDEX CONSTRUCTION

Some variables may be easily measured by one indicator. For example, Marital Status is adequately determined simply by establishing a respondent's marital status: married, single, divorced, widowed, separated, cohabiting. However, other variables may require several indicators because they are complex and consist of several components. Socioeconomic status might be determined by indexing the three indicators of occupation, education, and income—that is, by combining them into one measure.

An *index* is a summary measure of a complex concept that is obtained by adding up the values of the indicators used to measure the concept's universe of meaning. Indexes often have five or more items, and some have many more items. A typical number of index components in social research is probably from four to nine items, given that the concepts indexes usually measure may have two or three dimensions, each being measured by two or three indicators.

Summated Index

There are several ways to combine the values of the indicators that comprise an index. One way is by what is called a *summated index*. This type of index is made up of indicators that have two values: either 1 or 0. The value of 1 corresponds to a "yes" or "agree" response, while the 0 represents a "no" or a "disagree" response. When a summated index is used, the total score for a particular person or thing is obtained by adding up all the 1's. On a five-item summated index, for example, the maximum total score possible is 5, while the minimum total score possible is 0.

Example Suppose we wished to construct a summated index measuring the extent to which people favored mandatory or coercive measures to correct community problems. From the CPS we select the following five items, which we think reflect that complex concept: #16 Mandatory Employee Drug Testing, #17 Drug Testing for H.S. Athletes, #18 Mandatory Seat Belt Use, #19 No Smoking Areas in Work Places, and #20 Ban on New

Shopping Centers. Responses of "favor" on each item are scored 1, and responses of "oppose" are scored 0 ("uncertain" responses are disregarded or combined with "oppose" to form the other category). Scores could range from a high of 5, indicating a high degree of support for mandatory measures, to a low of 0, indicating no support for mandatory measures (or at least no support for these particular mandatory measures). Whether this index is a valid measure of this complex concept needs to be assessed, as does the question of whether or not items on the index are reliable.

Likert Scaling

A second procedure for combining the values of the indicators that comprise an index is called *Likert scaling*, although the Likert procedure for complex variables is really an index construction technique (see the discussion on scaling that concludes this section). The Likert procedure is the most popular way of constructing indexes, especially those which measure attitudes. Every indicator (usually a question) on a Likert scale can be scored with any one of five possible values, either from 1 to 5 or from 0 to 4. Thus, the Likert technique increases the variation in possible scores over that obtained with the summated index technique. The possible responses to which the values are assigned usually are: "strongly agree," "agree," "don't know" (or "uncertain"), "disagree," and "strongly disagree." What numerical value a particular response in this *foil* (sequence) receives depends on the syntax of the question asked—that is, on whether the Likert items are phrased positively (e.g., "This product is good") or phrased negatively (e.g., "This product is inadequate"). The answer sequence is constant for all items. This is one of the defining characteristics of a "matrix" question format. (Question formats are discussed more fully in Section 9 on questionnaire construction.)

The assignment of values to responses on Likert index items is as follows: Usually, the "strongly agree" response on the positive items receives a value 5, the "agree" response a value of 4, and so on. Or, if the 0–4 value scale were used, the two responses just mentioned would receive values of 4 and 3, respectively. To ensure that each person's opinions are coded in a logically consistent manner, the numerical values assigned to responses to negative items are reversed. The "strongly disagree" response to negative items receives a value of 5, while the "strongly agree" option receives a value 1. The person who favors the issue should strongly agree with the positive statements about it and also strongly disagree with the negative statements about it. On a five-item Likert scale the range of possible total scores would be either from 5 through 25 or from 0 through 20, depending on which typical range of numerical values, either 1–5 or 0–4, a researcher decided to use.

Example
A Likert index on satisfaction with community services could be constructed out of the following five items from the CPS: #26 Quality of City Government, #28 Police Protection, #29 Fire Protection, #33 Medical Facilities, and #34 Shopping Facilities. Here, instead of using a five-point "strongly agree" to "strongly disagree" scale, a five-point grading scale of A to F is used, with A given a value of 5 and F a value of 1. Scores could range from a low of 5 (F's on all items, indicating very low satisfaction with community services) to a high of 25 (A's on all items, indicating great satisfaction with community services).

Whether a researcher uses a summated index or a Likert index depends upon the type of structuring he or she needs in order to adequately measure conceptual meaning. A Likert index may be appropriate for measuring certain attitudes or orientations where a fuller range of values, including the uncertain response posssibility, given by the "SA, A, DK, D, SD" or "A, B, C, D, F" foils is needed. Although Likert scales usually have five categories, they can have more or fewer than five. Summated indexes, on the other hand, may be useful for measuring clusters of events, behaviors, or attitudes where the forced choices of "yes" or "no," "agree" or "disagree," "present" or "absent" are adequate.

Factor Scaling

There are also other ways to structure the assignment of numerical values to index items. A frequently encountered, though complex, way is called *factor scaling*. This procedure is based on a computerized analysis routine called *factor analysis*, which examines how subsets of index items are interrelated to one another but not to other subsets of items. In fact, factor analysis is often used to help define the different aspects or dimensions of meaning in a complex concept's universe of meaning. This topic is beyond the scope of this text and will only be discussed here in general terms. The results of factor analysis show the degree to which subsets of index items are related to separable dimensions, or factors, of meaning. The degree to which subsets of items are differentially related to a separate factor of meaning is measured in a way analogous to a correlation between each item in the subset and the factor of meaning. For those items in a subset that relate to a particular factor, the values of this "correlation" usually range from .4 to .7, or higher (see Section 13).

Researchers who use indexes successfully do so because they are quite familiar with the previous body of research in that area. They know how previous researchers have conceptualized and operationalized the universe of meaning concepts have. They are also aware that some particular indicators of meaning have worked better or more consistently than others. Finally, they are aware that every indicator used must be re-evaluated in the context of their own research, so they ask the same questions that would be asked if that indicator were the only one being used to measure meaning:

1. Does the indicator have face validity?
2. Is the indicator reliable in the sense that its outcomes are similar to those achieved in like attempts at measurement?
3. Is the item valid in the sense that its outcomes are related to indicators of other concepts to which it may be expected to be related?

To be somewhat facetious, researchers who use indexes must not only be well informed, they must also be somewhat compulsive and suspicious (paranoid?). Because items have worked previously for other researchers does not mean they do in the present researcher's context. We now turn to the ways in which suspicious and compulsive researchers decide to keep or eliminate index items.

RETAINING OR ELIMINATING INDEX ITEMS

Once the results in a research project are obtained, some items may turn out not to be adequate as index items. Whether or not an item should be retained or eliminated from an index depends on the answers to the questions always asked to determine adequacy of measurement: (1) Are index items reliable? and (2) Is the index a valid measure of the concept's universe of meaning? Even though the questions asked to determine and measure adequacy for indexes are similar to those asked in determining whether single-item measures are "good," the answers are sought differently.

Although a high degree of reliability (or outcome similarity) is desirable for single-item measures, only a moderate degree of consistency is desirable as far as the outcomes of various index indicators are concerned. The reason for the difference between the two types of measurement is that indexes are intended to measure several aspects of a concept's meaning, not just one. If an index does measure different aspects of a concept's meaning in a valid way, then the outcomes based on the index items should not be too highly related. If the measurement outcomes are highly related, then the items are measuring the same aspect of meaning, which defeats the purpose of having the items in the index. Too much consistency in measurement outcome between index items is called *autocorrelation*. Such a pejorative label signifies that having duplicate indicators is not desirable for items on an index.*

When index items are evaluated for reliability and validity, the following interrelationships are expected: First, there should be meaningful but rather moderate relationships among all the index items. Second, there should be meaningful and moderate relationships between each of the index items and variation in total index scores. The most popular methods used to assess these types of relationships will now be discussed.

Inter-Item Analysis

There are two common ways to answer the first issue concerning inter-item relationships between index items. Both approaches illustrate what is called *inter-item analysis*. One approach is to crosstabulate the outcomes of all possible pairs of index items when ordinal levels of measurement have been used. The other approach is to calculate correlation coefficients (r's) for the outcomes of all possible pairs of index items when interval/ratio levels of measurement have been used (see Section 13 for discussion of correlation coefficients). Because crosstabulation is more cumbersome when the number of items is large and there are several categories for each item, the correlational approach is more often used. Today, researchers increasingly treat ordinal measures as if they were interval/ratio measures. In both approaches the researcher hopes to find meaningful but moderate relationships between the outcomes of all possible pairs of index items, using measures such as gamma (see Section 4) in crosstabulation and Pearson's correlation coefficient (see Section 13) in the correlational approach.

Each of these two approaches to inter-item analysis is illustrated next with three slightly revised items from the CPS.

---

*Note: This discussion does not refer to the need for including parallel forms of items for purposes of split-half reliability testing.

Example   Suppose a researcher is interested in evaluating the following three
items for use in an Index of Opinion on the Seriousness of Youth Drug
Problems. The items are numbered as follows:

1. DRINKING—Is underaged drinking a serious community problem?
    Yes = 1, No = 0
2. SMOKING—Is underaged smoking a serious community problem?
    Yes = 1, No = 0
3. DRUGHS—Is drug use among high school students a serious commu-
    nity problem? Yes = 1, No = 0

Below appear the summary results of a crosstabulation of item outcomes and a summary of correlations between item outcomes:

	Crosstabulations (Gamma's)				Inter-Item Correlations (r's)		
	Item				*Item*		
	1	2	3		1	2	3
1	____	____	____	1	____	____	____
Item 2	.72*	____	____	Item 2	.40*	____	____
3	.71*	.55*	____	3	.36*	.25*	____

*Significant at the .01 level.

Both approaches show that there are statistically significant and
moderate relationships between all possible pairs of index items. Consequently, a researcher would be justified in including all three items in an
Index of Opinion on the Seriousness of Youth Drug Problems.

Whether a researcher uses crosstabulations of outcomes or inter-
item correlational analysis for ordinal (and sometimes nominal) data
depends upon how comfortable he or she is in assuming that ordinal/
nominal items can be measured at an interval/ratio level.

Item Total Score Correlation

The procedure for examining the relationship between each index item
and the total index score is an *item total score correlation*. Here researchers must and do assume items measure at the interval/ratio level.

The statistic used in this procedure is the *alpha statistic*, which measures the average correlation between split-half total scores of items that make up an index. Remember, first, that split-half total scores should be similar if support for parallel forms reliability exists (see Section 6). For example, in a Likert index, the total score on one-half of the items should be similar to that on the other half of the items. A *split-half total score correlation* is a summary statistic that measures the overall correlation between split-half total scores for all the things or persons studied. That alpha is an *average* of several split-half correlations results from the fact that there are several ways of dividing the items on an index into separate halves. Each different division into halves has its own split-half correlation. Alpha is the arithmetic mean of all such split-half correlations. It is desirable to have an alpha value of .7 or greater for an index to be considered reliable.

Computerized routines exist to calculate alpha. After the value of alpha is determined, the computerized routine proceeds to recalculate alpha as each index item in turn is eliminated from the index. As each index item is removed, alpha is recalculated to show the overall average split-half reliability if the outcomes of that particular item are eliminated. What the researcher hopes to find for each such recalculated alpha value is that it is less than the alpha obtained when all items were included. In other words, if the overall split-half reliability is less when an item is deleted, then the variation in outcomes of that item helps contribute to the overall consistency in index outcomes. Conversely, if the alpha value obtained when an item is dropped is greater than the alpha with all items included, the item should be removed from the index because the overall outcome of measurement is more consistent without than with the item.

Remember that good research is based upon conducting careful inter-item correlation *and* item total score correlation analyses *every time* a group of index items is used in research. Good index items are not necessarily ones that have worked in past research or that the present researcher thought would work. Good index items are those which actually do work in the present research context. Evaluating index items requires that statistical and methodological techniques be combined.

Even when all index items interrelate properly with one another and with total index score variation, researchers must ask additional questions about the validity of the index. First, do all of the items on the index have face validity? Presumably, this issue was addressed before items were used, but face validity is an issue that must continually be reconsidered as research proceeds. Second, total index score variation must be related to indicators of other concepts in theoretically expected ways. If the index is being used to predict a future event (e.g., hospitalization or promotion readiness), then total index scores should in fact be related to future outcomes. Or, total index score variation should be related in theoretically expected ways to various constructs. For example, if an index is in fact a valid measure of marital stability, then variation in index scores should be interrelated in expected ways with constructs known to predict marital continuity: age at marriage, similarity of backgrounds of the spouses, and other factors (see Section 6).

Keep in mind that evaluating indexes is based upon techniques that are extensions of, but logically the same as, the ways in which single-item measures are evaluated. One need not be or become an expert in actually using complex index evaluation procedures to understand (1) why such techniques are used and (2) what the basic principles and logic involved in such techniques are.

STRUCTURING INDEXES AS VARIABLES

Once the items that will be used on an index are determined to be reliable and valid indicators of meaning, the researcher must decide how the index will be dealt with as a variable in analysis procedures. There are two basic choices. First, the researcher may choose to use the index as an interval/ratio variable that will be correlated with other variables in analyses involving correlations, as well as multiple correlation analysis and multiple regression analysis (see Sections 13 and 15). In such analyses the index variable may be used as a dependent variable to be explained or as an independent variable used to explain something else.

Second, the researcher may choose to structure the index into an ordinal variable composed of several (usually three) categories. As was pointed out, social researchers may be able to accomplish their research objectives by rank-ordering groups of things or people. A more detailed gradient of difference may not be necessary. Given that an ordinal structure of an index is often used, the steps in using SPSS/PC+ and STATPAC commands to trichotomize the three-item Index of Opinion on Youth Drug Problems, previously discussed in this section, is now provided.

The range of values on the index is not structured into a trichotomy until and unless all the index items have undergone reliability and validity testing to ensure that they are all "good" index items. The three CPS variables that compose the index in this example—DRINKING, SMOKING, and DRUGHS—are recoded as "forced-choice" attitude questions. This is done by combining the responses "no" and "a slight problem" into "no" and retaining the response "a serious problem" as "yes." As usual, "yes" = 1 and "no" = 0. Their new values will be combined into a summated Index of Opinion on Youth Problems, ranging in value from 0 to 3.

The following SPSS/PC+ and STATPAC commands recode the variables and produce a frequency distribution of the values of the new distribution that enable the researcher to trichotomize the distribution in an appropriate way.

A. Three-Variable Index Using SPSS/PC+

Instructions:

```
SPSS/PC:GET FILE = 'SPSSCPS', [Enter]
        :SET PRINTER = ON, [Enter]
        :SELECT IF (DRINKING LT 4), [Enter]
        :SELECT IF (SMOKING LT 4), [Enter]
        :SELECT IF (DRUGHS LT 4), [Enter]
        :RECODE DRINKING (1=1) (2,3=0) [Enter]
        :/SMOKING (1=1) (2,3=0) [Enter]
        :/DRUGHS (1=1) (2,3=0), [Enter]
        :VALUE LABELS DRINKING 0'No' 1'Yes' [Enter]
        :/SMOKING 0'No' 1'Yes' [Enter]
        :/DRUGHS 0'No' 1'Yes', [Enter]
        :COMPUTE DRUGHS = DRINKING + [Enter]
        :SMOKING + DRUGHS, [Enter]
        :FREQUENCIES VARIABLES = DRUGS, [Enter]
```

Table 7.1 SPSS/PC+

DRUGS

Value Label		Value	Frequency	Percent	Valid Percent	Cum Percent
		0.0	47	9.6	9.6	9.6
		1.00	66	13.5	13.5	23.2
		2.00	129	26.4	26.4	49.6
		3.00	246	50.4	50.4	100.0
		TOTAL	488	100.0	100.0	
Valid Cases	488	Missing Cases	0			

B. Three-Variable Index Using STATPAC

Instructions:

- First add the variable Drugs—variable #89—to the CPS codebook (CPSCODE)
- Follow steps 1–10 in Appendix C
- Run Frequency Analysis for variable #89
- Select if variables #42, #43, and #45 are less than 4
- Recode #42 (1 = 1)(2 = 0)(3 = 0)
  #43 (1 = 1)(2 = 0)(3 = 0)
  #45 (1 = 1)(2 = 0)(3 = 0)
- Compute statement: V89 = V42 + V43 + V45
- Save to disk and execute starting with Task 1

Table 7.2 STATPAC

drugs	Number	Percent	Cumulative
0 =	47	9.6%	9.6%
1 =	66	13.5%	23.2%
2 =	129	26.4%	49.6%
3 =	246	50.4%	100.0%
Total	488	100.0%	100.0%

Missing cases = 0
Response percent = 100.0%

With the above information, a researcher might proceed to trichotomize the Index of Opinion on Youth Drug Problems as follows: Values 0 and 1 might be combined as "low" (N = 113, 23.1 percent), 2 might be considered "moderate" (N = 129, 26.4 percent), and 3 might be regarded as "high" (N = 246, 50.4 percent) concern.

A BRIEF DISCUSSION OF SCALES

Technically speaking, there is an important difference between an "index" and a "scale": While an index can yield a particular total score in more than one way, a scale yields a certain total score in only one way.

This is because there is an intensity structure linking the items that compose a scale. Stated another way, there is a primary pattern by which responses to the scale items are ordered. Items are arranged in order of intensity so that the first item will be agreed with most often and the last item least, with decreasing likelihood of agreement as one moves from the first to the last item. A "no" to an earlier item should be followed by "no" to all subsequent items.

Consider the following four items, which could form a marital violence scale. Notice that the four items can be arranged in order from least to most violent:

least violent:	spouses have disagreements*
somewhat more violent:	spouses verbally abuse each other during disagreements*
even more violent:	spouses strike each other during disagreements*
most violent:	spouses seriously injure one another during disagreements*

What remains to be determined after responses to the items have been obtained is whether or not the vast majority of people answer the marital violence questions in one of the following ways:

	Answer Patterns				
Intensity Order	(1)	(2)	(3)	(4)	(5)
least violent	no	yes	yes	yes	yes
somewhat more violent	no	no	yes	yes	yes
even more violent	no	no	no	yes	yes
most violent	no	no	no	no	yes

If the vast majority of people do answer the items in patterns that reflect a single-intensity structure, then the items are said to form a scale. The technique for determining whether or not most answer patterns do conform to a single-intensity structure is called *Guttman scaling analysis*. Essentially, this technique consists of finding that answer patterns do in fact reflect a single-intensity structure approximately 90

*Codes: "yes" = 1, "no" = 0.

or 95 percent of the time in a particular dataset. The statistic yielding the percentage of answer patterns that reflect a single-intensity structure is called the *coefficient of reproducibility*, or CR. The value of the CR should be .9 or larger. Items that form such a scale are said to compose a Guttman scale.

Although Guttman scales and other types of multiple-item measures such as Thurstone scales have single-intensity structures and are used periodically in social research, most multiple-item measures used by social researchers are indexes, not scales. One reason for this is that the world is not structured enough that broad-ranging scales occur frequently. It is much easier to scale aspects of meaning in the world when only a limited number of yes/no items are considered. Another reason why researchers do not attempt to form scales is that a single-intensity structure is often unnecessary. Knowing, for example, that couples who score 7 or more on a 10-item summated index of marital violence are more violent than other couples is usually sufficient. This degree of severity is usually enough to suggest counseling or to identify potential problems such as spouse abuse. For these reasons indexes, rather than scales, have been emphasized in this section.

One final point on indexes and scales: Whether or not items form an index or scale, they must be reassessed every time they are used in research. The fact that items have formed an index or a scale in previous research does not mean they do in the current research context.

Exercise 7A:
Indexing for Complex Concepts

Do the following with regard to developing an index for the complex concept of either (1) "political interest" or (2) "perception of community problems."

1. Briefly, define three different aspects or dimensions of meaning for the concept you have selected.
   Concept:
   a. first aspect:

   b. second aspect:

   c. third aspect:

2. Based on the aspects of meaning you have chosen for your concept, in the following space provide a nominal definition of the concept that reflects its universe of meaning.

3. In the spaces below list two indicators of each aspect of meaning you
gave to the concept.
a. first aspect's indicators:

b. second aspect's indicators:

c. third aspect's indicators:

These six indicators now constitute an index.

Exercise 7B:
Split-Half Reliability Procedures

Using split-half reliability procedures, evaluate items in the index of "political interest" or "perception of community problems" that you developed for Exercise 7A.

1. Split the index items into halves.
   a. items in the first half:

   b. items in the second half:

2. Briefly explain why you divided the items as you did.

3. Assuming your index was a summated index where "yes" = 1 and "no" = 0, answer the following questions about it:

a. What is the range of possible index values?

b. What is the range of values in a split-half?

c. What would be three different answer patterns that would result in a total index score of 4?

   i.

   ii.

   iii.

4. Briefly describe how people's split-half scores should be related if the index is reliable.

Exercise 7C:
Construct Validity Procedures

Use construct validity procedures to assess the validity of the index constructed in Exercises 7A and 7B.

1. If you had to select one single-item indicator of "political interest" or "perception of community problems" from the CPS variables, what would it be?

2. If you had to select three constructs that would be related to the indicator of "political interest" or "perception of community problems," what would the three constructs be?
   a. first construct:

   b. second construct:

   c. third construct:

3. State an hypothesis that clearly relates each of the above constructs to the indicator of "political interest" or "perception of community problems."
   a. first hypothesis:

   b. second hypothesis:

   c. third hypothesis:

4. State hypotheses that make clear how you would expect your index to be related to each of the three constructs:
   a. first hypothesis:

   b. second hypothesis:

   c. third hypothesis:

Exercise 7D:
Computer Applications

Develop a three-item summated index where "yes" = 1 and "no" = 0 to measure "Opinion on Employment Problems," using variables in the CPS dataset.

1. What are your three indicators?
   a. first:

   b. second:

   c. third:

2. Based upon your indicators, how would you define the universe of meaning of "Opinion on Employment Problems"?

3. Use SPSS/PC+ or STATPAC to obtain crosstabulations between indicators. Do the inter-item relationships indicate that all indicators should be kept in the index? Attach the tables and include a discussion of results in the space below. (*Note:* Remember to recode each indicator appropriately.)

4. Use SPSS/PC+ or STATPAC to obtain the frequency distribution of your index. Decide and indicate in the space below what categories of the index will result. Attach table results.

Exercise 7E:
Computer Applications

Use construct validity procedures to assess the validity of your index of "Opinion on Employment Problems" from Exercise 7D. Answer the following questions.

1. Select a comparison indicator.

2. What are three constructs that could be related to a comparison indicator?

   a. first construct:

   b. second construct:

   c. third construct:

3. After recoding all constructs into trichotomies, use SPSS/PC+ or STATPAC to crosstabulate the comparison indicator by each construct. Attach the tables and include a brief discussion of results in the space below.

4. Use SPSS/PC+ or STATPAC to crosstabulate your index results (trichotomize your index variable) by each of the constructs. Attach the tables and include a brief discussion of results in the space below.

5. What evidence is there that your Index of "Opinion on Employment Problems" is valid?

8
Sampling Procedures

The aim of social research is to draw conclusions and make generalizations about an entire population, such as all voters in the United States or all graduates of a university. However, it is impractical and usually impossible to study an entire population. Social researchers, therefore, collect and analyze data from a smaller, and hopefully representative, sample of the population. In this section types of nonprobability and probability sampling techniques are discussed. Because the latter sampling methods give more representative pictures of populations, they are emphasized in this section.

NONPROBABILITY SAMPLING

Nonprobability sampling techniques are ones in which the things or people being sampled do not have a known probability of being selected. Some researchers are tempted to use nonprobability samples because they are more convenient, less expensive, and easier to collect than probability samples. However, all forms of nonprobability sampling suffer from a distinct and damaging disadvantage: The likelihood or probability of error in such samples cannot be estimated, which means the accuracy or inaccuracy of the results obtained can never be determined.

There are several types of nonprobability sampling—judgmental sampling, convenience sampling, quota sampling, theoretical sampling—each of which may have specific (though limited) use in social research.

Judgmental Sampling

In *judgmental sampling* a researcher makes sample selections based on informed guesses about the most representative cases. For example, some exit polling in elections is done by sampling voters in so-called key precincts, chosen because past experience or present political wisdom judges them representative of all voters. The problem is that prior judgments about the representativeness of key cases simply may be wrong.

Convenience Sampling

In *convenience sampling* the researcher takes samples from large groups of accessible but unrepresentative cases, such as students in a large lecture class or people in a shopping center. This method of sampling can be and often is used to pretest preliminary versions of questionnaires. However, convenient groups of cases are seldom representative of general populations.

Quota Sampling

In *quota sampling* researchers make selections from all important groupings or categories of a population. The important groupings compose a *quota matrix*, which is a chart that includes up-to-date estimates of cases in all important categories. Researchers then make some selections in every "cell" of the matrix; results are often multiplied by that value which will increase selected cases' aggregate value up to the estimate of the size of the grouping in the matrix. For example, a certain, and often equal, number or quota of cases may be selected from combinations of categories, such as men and women, blacks and whites, young and old people, and married and unmarried people. Results from all quotas are then multiplied by numbers that reflect the relative size of each category in the population. Thus, if the category "married" is three times as large as the category "unmarried," the results of the former quota are multiplied by 3.

There are several problems with quota sampling. First, not all groupings or types of cases can be included in the matrix; some are always excluded. Second, the size of the category or grouping in a population often cannot be determined until after the results of sampling are in. Third, selections within a category or grouping in the quota matrix may not be representative of that type or group. Quota sampling often leaves the decision as to which particular cases will be sampled up to interviewers or others trying to collect data. When selection procedures are so subjective, quota sampling amounts to nothing more than another form of convenience sampling.

Theoretical Sampling

In *theoretical sampling* (or availability or purposive sampling)—another form of judgmental sampling—the researcher purposely picks cases that are extremes or that illustrate contrasting types or various categories of theoretical interest. For example, a researcher could pick some school districts that experienced racial desegregation smoothly and some that experienced it with great rancor to draw distinctions between the social environment of the two types of school districts. Or, researchers could purposely pick the inner-city schools that have the lowest dropout rates in order to characterize key features of the "best" inner-city schools. Although useful in helping to draw and crystallize hypothetical distinctions, theoretical sampling is best viewed as exploratory research, because claims that the sample is representative of a larger population cannot be made. Results using theoretical samples should be tested more systematically by using probability sampling techniques.

PROBABILITY SAMPLING

If things or people did not vary, there would be no need to worry about sampling—any given case would do as well as any other for purposes of research. Obviously, things and people in the social world vary considerably; this is why sampling carefully to represent such variation in a population is extremely important. As mentioned earlier in this section, a *population* is that large and heterogeneous group of things or people that the research is about. Many populations studied by social researchers are social categories like "senior citizens" or "college graduates" or "middle-class families." Because populations are too large and dispersed and diverse to study as wholes, however, researchers take samples from populations. A *sample* is that proportion of the population actually selected for study. Samples should be *representative*; that is, samples should be realistic, though smaller, versions of the actual diversity and dispersion of a population. Careful sample selection using one of the methods of probability sampling enhances the likelihood that samples will be representative.

Probability sampling is used by social researchers for another even more important reason. The results of any one probability sampling procedure can be placed in a larger known pattern of variation. From the central limit theorem (discussed in Section 10) the known pattern of variation in sample statistics, such as averages or proportions, if many fairly large probability samples are drawn from a population, can be determined; this known variation is called a *sampling distribution*. A sampling distribution refers to variation in the values of sample summary statistics (such as average income of the sample, or the proportion of the sample composed of retired persons), not to variation between the individual elements within a sample. By taking the known variation of sample statistics into account, social researchers use the results of one sample to estimate actual (but unknowable) population values, called *parameters*. Knowing the sampling distributions of sample statistics enables a social researcher to give a range or interval that is likely to include the parameter a known percentage of the time. These are called *confidence intervals* (see Section 10).

The value of a sample statistic based on probability sampling should not be construed as the real population value. However, the sample statistic does suggest that a certain range of estimation will include the real population value, say, 95 times out of 100 (a 95 percent confidence interval), or 99 times out of 100 (a 99 percent confidence interval). Therefore, a researcher's faith or confidence is not in the sample result, but in the method of probability sampling that allows the laws of probability to be applied in using sample statistics in intervals of estimation to estimate population values. In this way researchers combine statistical and sampling procedures in the research process (see Sections 1 and 10).

We now turn to the major ways to draw probability samples.

SIMPLE RANDOM SAMPLING

In a *simple random sample* everyone or everything in the population has an equal and known probability of being selected for or included in the sample. Often, social researchers make an assumption of simple random sampling in most statistical tests of hypotheses (see Section 11). However, researchers seldom actually use this particular form of probability sampling because it is difficult and sometimes impractical or impossible to conduct. In order to take a simple random sample, one must first have a complete listing of all the elements in the population, with the elements numbered consecutively from 1 to N. Then, a table of random numbers or a computerized routine for randomly selecting numbers is used to draw the desired sample size. (A table of random numbers and an explanation of how to use them is provided in Table V of Appendix D.)

The main problem with taking a random sample is that actual and complete listings of the population may not be available or accessible. For example, listings of all the people who live in a community or all the employees of a large corporation may not exist or may not be obtainable. Even when such listings (or an approximate listing in the case of a directory of phone numbers) are available, the time needed to number the list, especially if it is a lengthy one, and then match randomly selected numbers to it may be prohibitive. Because simple random samples are often difficult to obtain, other probability sampling techniques, discussed below, are usually used.

SYSTEMATIC SAMPLING

Some researchers view systematic samples as acceptable alternatives to or approximations of simple random samples because they are much more economical and expeditious to conduct. *Systematic sampling* consists of selecting every Kth case from a listing after the first case has been selected at random from the first K cases. The interval (K) from which the selection is made is calculated by dividing the population size by the sample size.

Example   Suppose a researcher wanted a systematic sample of 500 from a listing of 10,000. The interval of selection (K) would be calculated as follows:

$$K = \frac{\text{population size}}{\text{sample size}} = \frac{10,000}{500} = 20$$

To systematically sample 500 from a population listing of 10,000, make a random selection from the first 20 on the list, and then proceed to select every twentieth case after that until the end of the list is reached and 500 have been selected. Suppose the random start was 03. In a systematic sample keep adding the interval of selection, 20, to the random start, 03, until the number of things or people on the list (N = 10,000) is exhausted. The first five selection numbers would be 03, 23, 43, 63, and 83; the final number would be 9,983.

Systematic sampling is much easier to do than simple random sampling because only one random number needs to be generated. After that, it is a simple matter of adding a constant (K) to the randomly selected initial number until the number of elements listed is exhausted. Such a sample is still random because a constant added to a random beginning means that all selections are still random.

If there is any reason to suspect that the listing of things or people is arranged in a way that might introduce a bias, then systematic sampling should not be used until the list is rearranged. If, for example, every homeroom class roster begins with the "best" student listed first, and if most homerooms have 30 children, a systematic sample of the children might be seriously biased. If the interval of selection were any multiple or fraction of 30, then it is possible that the sample would overselect or underselect "best" students. Thus, the homeroom lists should be rearranged (e.g., alphabetized) so that the "best" student is not always listed first.

STRATIFIED SAMPLING

For some research projects it may be necessary to stratify a population before conducting a random or systematic sample. *Stratified sampling* entails dividing or separating a population into separate subpopulations, or strata, and then sampling within each stratum. Stratification guarantees that important population subgroupings are represented. Without stratifying there is a chance that the natural variation in sampling results will, in any given instance of sampling, overrepresent some subpopulations and underrepresent or perhaps not even include others.

Although it is impractical to stratify on a large number of criteria at once, it is often convenient to stratify on the basis of two or three. For example, university students could be stratified by class level (freshman, sophomore, and so on), by gender, by local residence (on- or off-campus housing), or by a combination of class, gender, and residence. Similarly, drawing on census data, nationwide interview sampling designs often stratify on the basis of race, social class, and size of community. The stratification criteria are usually chosen because the subpopulations created by them are viewed as crucial groupings in the research.

There are two major types of stratified samples: proportionate stratified samples and disproportionate stratified samples.

Proportionate Stratified Sampling

In a *proportionate stratified sample* the proportions of sample selections in each stratum are similar to the proportions of the various strata found in the population. That is, the same proportions exist between stratum sample sizes as exist between stratum subpopulation sizes. If, for example, among three population strata the largest one is three times as big as the smallest, and the middle-sized one is twice as large as the smallest, then these same ratios, 3:2:1, should exist after samples are drawn from each stratum. The way such ratios are preserved is to use the same interval of selection (K) if systematic sampling procedures are used to sample from all the strata.

Example Suppose that a high school is composed of 1,500 sophomores, 1,000 juniors, and 500 seniors, and a sample of 300 students is desired. In a proportionate stratified systematic sampling the same interval of selection for all strata ($K = 3,000/300 = 10$) would be used and would result in a selection of 150 sophomores, 100 juniors, and 50 seniors.

Some researchers might question whether enough seniors have been sampled, however. Fifty (50) would be enough to apply the laws of probability in estimating parameters that apply to all seniors. However, 50 would not be enough to allow further breakdowns or analyses of seniors by gender, local residence, or grade point average.

For most research purposes a minimum of 100 cases is recommended for each sample stratum. If 100 seniors were to be included in the example above, then the overall sample size would have to be increased, or a different form of sampling design would need to be used.

Disproportionate Stratified Sampling

One way of increasing sample size for certain strata is through disproportionate stratified sampling. In a *disproportionate stratified sample* proportions of each stratum in the sample are not the same as the proportions in the population. Random selections within or different intervals of selection for each stratum are used to select a sufficiently large ($N = at$ $least$ 100), and often equal, number of cases from each stratum. The major reason for sampling disproportionately is that some very important strata in the real world are much smaller than others. To study a small stratum adequately, a larger number must be included in the sample than would ordinarily appear through simple, systematic, or proportionate stratified sampling procedures.

Example Suppose that a researcher was using disproportionate stratematic sampling to obtain samples of 150 students in each of the following strata: sophomores ($N = 1{,}350$), juniors ($N = 900$), and seniors ($N = 450$). The intervals of selection would be as follows:

$$\text{interval for sophomores } K = \frac{1{,}350}{150} = 9$$

$$\text{interval for juniors } K = \frac{900}{150} = 6$$

$$\text{interval for seniors } K = \frac{450}{150} = 3$$

This procedure would provide the researcher with sufficient numbers of cases in all strata so that analyses of the differences within and between strata could be conducted. As long as these intra- or interstrata comparisons are the focus of the research, disproportionate sampling provides no distortion of results. However, if estimates of overall parameters of the entire student population are needed, the distortions caused by disproportionate sampling must first be corrected. The problem is that samples have been selected with intervals that do not preserve the population size proportions among the strata. In order to estimate population parameters the results in each stratum must be weighted to make the sample reflect the actual proportions in the population.

Weighting Procedures

Weights restore unequal population size relationships between strata that have been obscured by obtaining samples of the same number of cases from each stratum. Results in a stratum are multiplied by the number, or weight, that restores the original population size relationships between the strata. (See Table 8.1.) In the above example the junior population and its selection interval (K) are twice as large as the senior population and its interval; and the sophomore population and its selection interval are three times as large as the senior population and its interval. Therefore, the results for and the sample size of juniors need to be multiplied by two, and the results for and the sample of sophomores by three, in order to weight the results properly. These weights would be used only when results are pooled in order to estimate an overall population value.

Table 8.1   Illustration of Weighting Necessary to Estimate
Overall Proportion of Students Who Are Receiving Financial Aid

| Strata | Pop Size | Samp Size | # Rec Aid | Weights | Weighted Results | |
					Sample	# Rec Aid
Sophomores	1,350	150	109	3	450	327
Juniors	900	150	86	2	300	172
Seniors	450	150	77	1	150	77
Totals	2,700	450	272		900	576

Example   Suppose a researcher wants to estimate the overall proportion of students who are receiving financial assistance. As the information in Table 8.1 shows, without weighting one might erroneously estimate that 60.4 percent (272 of 450) are receiving financial aid. However, after results have been properly weighted, the correct estimate is that 64.0 percent (576 of 900) are receiving such aid.

Notice in the above example that the smallest stratum (seniors) has a weight of 1, which is equivalent to saying that cases in the smallest stratum are not weighted. When weighting is necessary to estimate population parameters, results in the smallest stratum are not adjusted.

Weighting is not necessary when strata are being analyzed separately or when the results for each stratum are being compared to one another. Weighting is only used to estimate overall population parameters. Disproportionate stratified systematic sampling is a technique (1) that ensures that enough cases are selected from all strata, including small ones, and (2) that enables a weighted estimation of overall population parameters. This sampling technique is therefore both very powerful and very adaptable to the needs of social researchers when sampling diverse population strata.

CLUSTER SAMPLING

Cluster samples are multistage samples where a population is first divided into primary areas and subsequently divided into smaller segments or clusters. Then, samples of clusters are chosen from the population, using either random or systematic sampling selection procedures. Cluster sampling is often used when complete listings of the things or people in various parts or areas of a population are not available or are impractical to assemble.

For example, suppose researchers wanted to sample residents of a large city or the members of a large religious denomination in the United States (e.g., Roman Catholics). Cluster sampling does not require actual listings of the current populations in the areas of the city or in the churches that comprise the American Catholic Church. Reliable and current estimates of population sizes, however, are necessary. The residents of the city might first be divided or grouped into geographical areas consisting of city blocks or census tracts. Catholics might be grouped by the churches they attend. A sample of blocks or a sample of churches can be selected; and then, within each grouping, a sample of households or members could be selected. Usually, the number of elements chosen for each block or church, called the *cluster size*, is relatively small. It is not desirable to have the cluster size too large because of similarity among people who live in the same city block or who attend the same church. As a consequence of keeping cluster size small (usually around five), a relatively large number of blocks or churches must be selected to obtain the desired sample size. For example, if cluster size is five, then 200 city blocks or churches are needed for a sample of 1,000. Limiting cluster size and increasing the areas or divisions of the population studied is the preferred way to make cluster samples as representative as possible.*

Once blocks have been selected, then the samples of households may be randomly or systematically selected from a listing of the addresses on the selected blocks. Sometimes, researchers leave the actual selection of households in the clusters to interviewers or other data collectors. As was pointed out in the discussion of convenience and quota sampling, however, such a selection process can be risky, yielding unrepresentative segments of the general population.

It is desirable that project directors also randomly select the actual persons in a selected household who are to be interviewed or studied. This is necessary in order to represent the diversity of respondents in the selected households and to prevent certain types of individuals from being selected more often than they should be.

---

*This is a simplified example of two-stage cluster sampling. More complex cluster sampling is used to take nationwide area samples; however, such procedures are beyond the scope of this book.

RANDOM DIGIT DIALING TELEPHONE SAMPLING

Today, the vast majority of American households have at least one telephone. It is true that some specific types of households—very poor, homeless, rural, nonwhite, students, and divorced or separated persons, for example—are underrepresented in telephone interviewing. Nevertheless, more and more social researchers, both commercial and academic, now believe that telephone interviewing utilizing random digit dialing techniques is a feasible and efficient way to sample general populations. In fact, telephone interviews that employ random digit dialing are becoming the most popular way to interview sample households.

Random digit dialing refers to the various ways of sampling a population by generating a list of random-digit phone numbers and, with the aid of computer-aided telephone interviewing systems (sometimes referred to as CATI systems), randomly dialing a sample of telephone numbers among those in the telephone exchanges that define the geographical boundaries of the population to be sampled. Random digit dialing techniques can be modified and customized for specific geographical areas. In addition, with Wide Area Telephone Service (WATS) lines, regions of the country, or the whole nation, may be less expensively sampled and interviewed by phone.

Random digit dialing has several advantages over selecting telephone numbers from directories. First, directories, which may be outdated, are not needed. Second, unlisted and new residential numbers are automatically included among the potential sample numbers. There is also a practical drawback to using randomly selected telephone numbers: More numbers must be dialed than the desired sample size requires given that some randomly selected phone numbers will be nonresidential (e.g., businesses, governmental agency offices, schools, hospitals) and others will be nonworking numbers (e.g., disconnected, never connected, moved, temporarily not in service).

Assuming that proportionate sampling is used, the desired number of telephone numbers in each exchange must be increased as a function of two major factors: (1) the proportion of exchange numbers that are nonresidential and nonworking and (2) the proportion of residential numbers that will not yield an interview, for reasons that include no one being at home and refusals. The first proportion can be roughly established from information obtained from the telephone companies or from directories. The second proportion can be adequately approximated with evidence from prior research or with current estimates of nonresponse available from recent surveys. A realistic range of proportions to use as an adjustment for nonresponse would be from 33 to 40 percent.

Random Digit Dialing and the CPS

The sample design used in the CPS was a combination of a proportionate stratified probability sample using a random digit dialing procedure for the four major telephone exchanges serving the county and a systematic sample of the three smaller exchanges in the county.

The sample selection procedure was designed to yield approximately 600 completed interviews, with each of the county telephone exchanges represented in the sample in approximately the same proportion as it exists in the telephone subscriber population. The steps in the sampling process were as follows:

1. Information on the number of residential telephone numbers in each exchange in the county was obtained from the telephone company.

2. The proportion of all residential numbers in the county in each exchange was calculated; and the number of completed interviews desired from each exchange was determined by distributing the 600 total interviews needed according to the percentage of residential phone numbers in each exchange. For example, the 781 exchange had 26.95 percent of the residential numbers in the county, and 26.95 percent of the 600 desired interviews as well (N = 162).

3. The desired total of telephone numbers in each exchange was adjusted upward based on the empirical probability of obtaining a residential number in that exchange. In the 781 exchange, for example, 6,428 of the 10,000 possible phone numbers were residential. So, the number of desired interviews (N = 162) was divided by .6428, the probability of obtaining a residential number in the 781 exchange. This yielded approximately 250 numbers needed for that exchange. Probabilities of obtaining residential numbers in the four major exchanges were determined from information on the number of residential listings in each exchange provided by the phone company. Telephone numbers in the three smaller exchanges were drawn from residential directory listings. Systematic sampling was used, and the intervals of selection were determined by dividing the total number of residential numbers in an exchange by the desired sample size after adjustments.

4. Desired sample sizes in each exchange were further adjusted upward by 40 percent to take into account no-answers and refusals. This last adjustment resulted in a total sample size of 350 in each of the major exchanges, and 35, 35, and 14, respectively, in the three smaller exchanges. The required number of random four-digit numbers for the

four major exchanges was selected using a basic four-digit random-number-generating computer program. Listings of 350 randomly generated numbers in each exchange were printed, and duplicate numbers were eliminated. Altogether, nearly 1,500 telephone numbers were needed to yield slightly over 600 interviews.

Note that certain modifications in the random digit dialing method can and should be made depending upon the particular circumstances and needs of a research project.

Although random digit dialing sampling techniques are the "state of the art" in telephone surveying, other survey options are available, as we shall see in Section 9.

Exercise 8A:
Nonprobability Sampling

Identify each of the following specific types of nonprobability sampling as either C (convenience sampling), J (judgmental sampling), Q (quota sampling), or T (theoretical sampling).

1. A selection of the 10 best and the 10 worst kindergarteners in a school to study family attitudes toward education   _____

2. A study of voting behavior by sampling people who mail back responses to an ad in the newspaper   _____

3. A researcher who selects 30 "average" ex-spouses to study the effects of divorce   _____

4. A selection of 10 cases from each of the major types of clients in a public service agency   _____

5. A study of campers conducted by passing out questionnaires to campers who use a particular state park during early summer   _____

6. A professor who uses students in a large "intro" class to study relationships between social class and health   _____

7. A national TV network gauging public opinion on an issue by asking viewers to call a 1-900 telephone number   _____

8. A market researcher who selects 20 each of six different types of consumers and asks about preferences for a product   _____

9. A study comparing differences in adjustment of 30 "reporting" and 26 "nonreporting" victims of rape who volunteer to be interviewed   _____

Exercise 8B:
Simple Random Sampling

Discuss below the procedures you would use to take a simple random sample of 30 registered voters from a list of 2,100 registered voters. Using random numbers from Table V in Appendix D, record the numbers of your sample of 30 below. Then, perform the operations indicated.

1. Procedure:

2. Numbers of sample from Table V:

1. _____	11. _____	21. _____
2. _____	12. _____	22. _____
3. _____	13. _____	23. _____
4. _____	14. _____	24. _____
5. _____	15. _____	25. _____
6. _____	16. _____	26. _____
7. _____	17. _____	27. _____
8. _____	18. _____	28. _____
9. _____	19. _____	29. _____
10. _____	20. _____	30. _____

3. Using the *left-most* random digits from the following five-digit random numbers, place a check mark next to each of the random numbers that would be included in the sample.

a. 84855 _____

b. 02008 _____

c. 15475 _____

d. 48413 _____

e. 49513 _____

Exercise 8C:
Systematic Sampling

Discuss the procedures you would use to take a systematic sample of 20 university students from a list of 2,600. Be sure to indicate what your interval of selection (K) is, and show how you arrived at it. Also, indicate what your random start is, and list your 20 selection numbers for sampling the students.

Exercise 8D:
Stratified Sampling

You plan to sample students from each of the following strata: sophomores, $N = 1,000$; juniors, $N = 500$; seniors, $N = 300$. Answer the questions below, and complete the table, as indicated.

1. If you take a proportionate stratified systematic sample of 300 students, indicate what the selection interval is and how many sophomores, juniors, and seniors will be in the sample.

   a. Selection interval:

   b. Sample sizes
      Sophomores:
      Juniors:
      Seniors:

2. If you take a disproportionate stratified systematic sample of 100 students in each of the stratum, what will the interval of selection (K) be for each stratum?

   a. Interval for sophomores:

   b. Interval for juniors:

   c. Interval for seniors:

3. What weights would be used when pooling results to estimate a population parameter? Show your math.

   a. Weight for sophomores:

b. Weight for juniors:

c. Weight for seniors:

4. Complete the following table, applying appropriate weights to estimate the overall percentage of students who are members of Greek organizations.

Strata	Pop Size	Samp Size	# of Greeks	Weighted Results		
				Weights	Sample	# Greeks
Sophomore	___	___	10	___	___	___
Junior	___	___	30	___	___	___
Senior	___	___	50	___	___	___
Totals						

5. Estimate the overall percentage of students in Greek organizations.

Exercise 8E:
Cluster Sampling

Discuss how you might develop a two-stage cluster sample design to select a sample of 200 elementary school children in a metropolitan area. There are 40 elementary schools in the metro area, each with approximately 300 students. Also, explain what you could do to ensure that students in all grades are represented.

Exercise 8F:
Random Digit Dialing

Assume you are using random digit dialing to conduct a telephone survey of a community that is served by three telephone exchanges, with prefixes 781, 842, and 843. You find out from the telephone company that the numbers of residential phones in each exchange out of 10,000 are as follows: 781 = 6,000; 842 = 4,000; and 843 = 2,000. You wish to draw a proportionate stratified sample of 600 numbers. Fill out the following worksheet to determine:

1. What is the proportion of residential numbers in each exchange?

2. What is the desired number of interviews from each exchange based on a proportional distribution?

3. What is the empirical probability of obtaining a residential number using random digit dialing in each exchange?

4. What are the desired numbers of interviews needed, adjusting for the probability of obtaining a residential number?

5. What number of interviews are needed in each exchange if the estimates in step d are adjusted upward by 40 percent for no-answers and refusals?

6. What is the total number of random-digit numbers needed to obtain a sample of 600 completed interviews?

	Exchanges			
	781	842	843	*Total*
1. Proportion residential				
2. Desired interviews				
3. Residential empirical probability				
4. Adjusted desired number				
5. Number adjusted for no-answer and refusal				

6. Total number needed =

9
Survey Research

Survey research involves asking a sample of a population a number of questions and recording answers for subsequent analysis. Just as there are several ways to sample populations (see Section 8), there are several ways to collect survey data. Depending on the research questions, the nature of the unit of analysis of the population, and factors such as time and cost, surveys may be conducted in mass audience situations, by mailed questionnaires, by telephone, or by face-to-face interviews. Survey researchers carefully construct questions to ensure that answers are reliable and valid and that ethical guidelines are followed.

UNITS OF ANALYSIS

The *unit of analysis* is the social entity that is analyzed in a particular research project. Not all survey research deals with the same kind of unit. Some survey projects analyze individuals, others investigate organizations, still others involve geographical units such as cities, and some are concerned with very large units such as societies or nation-states. Researchers select a unit of analysis appropriate for answering their research question. For example, the question "Why do some people vote and others not vote in elections?" is addressed by selecting individuals as the units of analysis. "How do social clubs elect leaders?" is answered through selecting particular types of organizations as the unit of analysis. "How open are national elections in developing countries?" is addressed by selecting particular types of societies as the units of analysis.

Once the appropriate unit of analysis is determined, the survey researcher must define the population of such units eligible for study. Recall that the population of units of analysis is the entire range of appropriate units that could be studied to answer the research question. Depending on the scope of the research project, level of funding, and availability of adequate data, the population of units may be defined to include all such units that exist, or some smaller portion of them. All the units that exist comprise the *universe* of units, while the smaller portion actually studied in a research project is referred to as the *study population*. For example, to answer the first research question posed above, the universe of units might be all citizens of the United States who are eligible to vote. The study population, on the other hand, might be all registered voters in a particular locality, state, or region who voted or did not vote in general elections. Because many researchers cannot afford or manage the study of a universe of units, study populations or samples within such study populations are more often employed.

Some narrowing of scope is nearly always a part of the process by which study populations are defined. Often, researchers judge that sufficiently reliable and relevant data will be obtained by limiting the study population to adults, as was done when the CPS study population was limited to all residents of a county 18 years of age or older. Obviously, the broader the scope of the study population, the more generalizable the results. Most researchers attempt to obtain as broad a study population as is practicable.

It is often too costly and impractical, however, to collect data from the entire study population. Consequently, researchers are likely to analyze data obtained from a sample of the study population. Recall that a sample is a smaller, though representative, version of the study population, and is usually selected by using one of the probability sampling techniques discussed in Section 8. Probability sampling techniques generally result in greater representativeness, and the range of error in making population estimates can be determined when such techniques are employed. It is important to remember that very accurate estimates of population parameters can be obtained from carefully drawn samples of 1,200 no matter how large the study population (see Section 10).

Once appropriate units of analysis have been sampled for study, a broad range of data can be collected from the sampled units. If individuals have been sampled, a number of attitudinal and/or behavioral data can be gathered, along with many social and demographic traits, such as the individual's age, race, educational level, and income. If organizations have been sampled, then data on a wide variety of organizational attributes can be obtained, such as size, turnover rate, and supervisor-staff ratios, along with many contextual measures, such as location, range of operations, and typical consumer or service outlets. If whole societies have been sampled, data on a wide variety of societal traits, such as age-sex structures, death rates, and life expectancies, can be included, along with many socioeconomic measures, such as occupational activity, educational level, and literacy rates.

FALLACIOUS INFERENCES

Data collected on the units of analysis in a particular survey research project are appropriate only for those units and the particular research question for which selection of the units made sense. Researchers must be very careful to avoid making inferences about units of analysis that were not studied from those units that were studied. Fallacious inferences about units not studied usually involve either the individualistic fallacy or the ecological fallacy.

Individualistic Fallacies

The *individualistic fallacy* involves making unwarranted inferences about larger social units from data about individuals. For example, CPS respondents gave a higher percentage of "A" and "B" grades to the quality of shopping facilities in the community than they did to the quality of the schools or the cultural facilities in the community. It would be inappropriate, and perhaps incorrect, to infer that the educational system and cultural atmosphere of the community are deficient. Assessments of the educational and cultural systems must be based on specific measures of them, not on the opinions of individuals. Individuals' opinions about education or culture are independent of, and may be quite different from, the structure of the educational and cultural environments in which they live.

Ecological Fallacies

The *ecological fallacy* involves unwarranted, and possibly erroneous, inferences about individuals when groups have been the units of analysis. For example, suppose an analysis of CPS data had revealed that neighborhoods with the highest percentage of older people also had the highest percentage of respondents who thought crime was a serious problem. To naively and incorrectly infer that older people are more likely than young people to see crime as a serious problem would be an example of an ecological fallacy—the finding concerning neighborhoods cannot be transferred to the individual. Differences between young and old people on this issue would have to be investigated using the individual as the unit of analysis. It is not appropriate to draw conclusions about individual opinions from data collected on groups, because individuals' attitudes and behaviors can and often do vary independently of group-level characteristics. Individuals must be studied using data collected about them, not data collectd on the groups to which they belong.

CONTEXTUAL EFFECTS

It is possible to study both individuals and groups in the same survey research project to see how individuals' attitudes and/or behaviors are influenced by the types of groups to which they belong. Such research may or may not yield evidence of a contextual effect. A *contextual effect* exists when different types of individuals have similar attitudes or display the same behaviors in particular group situations. For example, both younger and older workers may be more productive in companies that have profit sharing. Or, both working-class and middle-class students may have higher achievement scores in high schools that emphasize academics.

Data collected in the CPS enable contextual analyses using both individuals and groups. For example, CPS respondents were asked several questions about the households in which they lived, including whether any members of the household were under the age of 18. Respondents were also asked their opinion on the seriousness of underage drinking as a community problem. Whether or not there are persons under 18 in the household is a group-level attribute, while opinion on underage drinking as a community problem is an individual-level opinion variable. Results of the CPS study revealed a difference between married women and married men concerning whether there was a problem with underage drinking (a higher percentage of women thought it was a serious problem—75 percent versus 62 percent). However, in households where there were children under 18, the problem was seen as less serious by married women, and the difference between married women and married men narrowed considerably—68 percent versus 62 percent, respectively, a difference that was not significant (chi-square = .49, d.f. = 1, $p > .05$).

TYPES OF SURVEY RESEARCH DESIGNS

Different research questions call for different survey research designs. There are two main types of survey research designs: cross-sectional surveys and longitudinal surveys.

Cross-Sectional Versus Longitudinal Surveys

A *cross-sectional* survey collects data from a cross section, or a presumably representative segment, of the population at one point in time. Cross-sectional surveys are the most prevalent and most frequently encountered type of survey. They yield data that are pertinent to many research questions, such as providing estimates of population characteristics and revealing whether differences or relationships exist between variables. The CPS is an example of a cross-sectional survey. In the CPS a representative sample of adult residents of a county was interviewed by telephone and data were obtained on a wide variety of issues and respondent characteristics. On one question—"What percentage of adults in the community have college degrees?"—findings from the CPS indicated that 25.6 percent of the respondents had college degrees.

In contrast, a *longitudinal* survey collects data at more than one point in time. Though both more time consuming and more difficult to conduct, longitudinal surveys are the best means of answering questions about how communities, societies, and people have changed over time. There are three basic types of longitudinal surveys: trend studies, cohort studies, and panel studies.

Trend Studies

Trend studies involve an examination of changes observed by comparing data collected in cross-sectional surveys taken at different points in time. "Is the percentage of college graduates increasing in the community?" is a question that must be answered by longitudinal survey research; data from the CPS cannot answer this type of question. However, if the CPS were repeated at a future date, the percentage of college graduates obtained in that study could be compared to the 25.6 percent figure obtained in the original CPS, and both figures could be used to determine whether or not the percentage of college graduates has increased.

Change over time in the percentage of adults in a community who are college graduates—or who are married, who are homeowners, and so on—illustrates the concept of a trend, a *trend* being the pattern of change in a general population observed over time. Trends must be studied with longitudinal rather than cross-sectional survey research.

Cohort Studies

Cohort studies examine the same cohort of people (usually a certain age group) with data obtained from a series of cross-sectional surveys. Surveys of general populations can be repeated periodically (e.g., every 10 years), and data obtained can be used to do a cohort analysis. Enough people in various age groups must be sampled for conclusions about changes in specific cohorts to be reliably judged (see Section 8). For example, there were 151 respondents age 30–39 in the CPS. These people were born between 1948 and 1957 and could be considered a cohort. If the CPS were to be repeated 10 years after it first was conducted, the people in this cohort would be 40–49 years old. Given that enough of such people (at least 100) were included in the CPS follow-up, then changes in, say, the proportion of the cohort who were married or divorced could be studied. Researchers would have to make sure, however, that the members of the cohort studied subsequently were people who had lived in the community since the first survey. This would ensure that observed changes did not occur because different types of people comprised the cohort in the two surveys.

Panel Studies

Panel studies examine changes in the same set of people who are interviewed at several points in time. If the same set of respondents who were interviewed in the CPS were to be reinterviewed in a subsequent survey or surveys, then those types of surveys would constitute a longitudinal panel design. Panel designs are best for describing changes and persistence over time and for unraveling cause and effect, (e.g., determining whether unemployment problems precede or follow a divorce). The biggest drawbacks to panel studies are the heavy investments of both money and time that are required to locate the same people over an extended period of time.

Some survey researchers are tempted to draw inferences about changes in people's lives by looking at the differences between age groups discovered in a cross-sectional survey. For example, among CPS respondents, the older respondents are, the more likely they are to view drug use among adults as a serious problem in the community. Because the relationship between opinion on seriousness of drug use among adults and age of respondents is statistically significant (chi-square = 8.06, d.f. = 1, $p < .05$), one might be tempted to conclude from these results that people become more concerned about adult drug use as they grow older. However, such a conclusion is unwarranted because the data do not reflect changes in opinion of individuals on this issue as they age. Instead, differences between age groups may reflect societal changes; that is, people who were born more recently may have different attitudes about drug use than those born during an earlier period. People born more recently may always be less fearful of and less concerned about drug use among adults. Differences may reflect societal changes rather than maturational changes. The latter changes must be analyzed using cohort studies.

DATA COLLECTION TECHNIQUES

Survey research is one of the most widely used methods of obtaining data in the social sciences (see Section 1). There are two basic ways in which survey researchers can collect data from respondents: questionnaires—mass-administered or mailed—and interviews—face-to-face or telephone.

Mass-Administered and Mailed Questionnaires

Mass-administered questionnaires are distributed to groups of respondents such as classrooms of students or assembled members of organizations. *Mailed questionnaires* are mailed out to respondents' homes and are mailed back to researchers upon completion.

In both mass-administered and mailed surveys questionnaires are used. *Questionnaires* are booklets of structured, standardized, precoded, and sometimes open-ended questions that are read by respondents, who record their own answers. Whenever questionnaires are used, survey researchers must be confident that the respondents have sufficient reading skills to comprehend the questions. The issue of question clarity is crucial, and great care must be taken to make questions short and clearly worded. (See the rules for question writing later in this section.)

Face-to-Face and Phone Interviews

In both *face-to-face interviews*, which usually take place in respondents' homes, and *telephone interviews*, an interview schedule is used. *Interview schedules*, like questionnaires, are booklets of structured, standardized, precoded, and sometimes open-ended questions. In this case, however, questions are read to respondents by an interviewer, who records respondents' answers and probes or follows up for clear and complete answers should respondents not provide them. Interviewers must be able to interact easily and professionally with others and should not be easily offended by respondent refusals or by the content of the interview.

Question Structure

In all these data collection techniques questions are usually structured—that is, they have predetermined answer alternatives—and they are standardized—that is, the same questions are asked in the same order for all respondents. A typical question asked of respondents might be the following:

4. *What is your marital status? (circle one)*

    1 *Never married*   4 *Married*
    2 *Divorced*   5 *Separated*
    3 *Widowed*

As in the example above, questions are usually precoded, meaning that the answer alternatives are numbered so that the number of the answer(s) selected by a respondent can be transferred to a data record directly from the interview form or questionnaire. Note that respondent choices are usually clearer to interpret on questionnaires if answer alternatives are circled. Filling in boxes or checking blanks is a more cumbersome and confusing way to format questions.

An unstructured, or open-ended, option is often included as the last item in a listing, or inventory, of alternative answers. The use of completely unstructured questions is not recommended because answers to such questions are very difficult to codify and require much effort to manage. An *inventory* is a listing of answer options that researchers either construct or borrow from those used by previous researchers.

Factors Affecting the Choice of Data Collection Technique

Survey researchers choose one of the survey data collection techniques on the basis of the following criteria:

1. The complexity of the information sought
2. The sensitivity of the information sought
3. The reading level of the study population
4. The time and money available for data collection
5. The geographical dispersion of the study population

Complex information should be collected through interviews rather than by questionnaires. Interviewers can explain the meaning of questions and can probe to ensure that respondents have not forgotten aspects of information sought. Such topics as employment or fertility histories and other retrospective series of questions are best dealt with by interviews. Even lengthy interviews are possible because respondents usually enjoy providing answers to a sincere, polite and non-theatening interviewer.

Sensitive topics, such as mental or physical health matters or deviant behavior, are best dealt with by using data collection techniques that ensure anonymity, and not simply confidentiality. *Anonymity* is when the identity of a respondent is not and can not be known. *Confidentiality* is when the identity of a respondent is known by the researcher but will not be made known to others, including those who work on the research project. Usually, respondents feel freer to openly and honestly respond to sensitive questions if they feel their identity is not known. Techniques that guarantee anonymity include using random digit dialing (which selects respondents by phone number rather than by name) to conduct telephone interviewing and using questionnaires without names or ID numbers. Use of questionnaires with ID numbers or names and home interviewing are methods that guarantee only confidentiality.

Interviewing is preferred to the use of questionnaires when the ability of respondents to read, to understand, and to answer questions is in doubt. Even when questionnaires are judged appropriate, researchers must be careful that the reading level of instructions and questions does not exceed that of the typical respondent. Through pretesting, expert judgment, and computer analysis of wording level (based on number and frequency of polysyllabic words per sentence), researchers attempt to match the wording level of the material on the questionnaire to that of the respondents (e.g., school children, lesser-educated adults, and so on).

Mass-administered questionnaires are the least expensive and quickest form of data collection in survey research. Not only can large groups of assembled respondents complete a lengthy questionnaire in one-half hour or less, but the cost of distributing and collecting mass-administered questionnaires, as opposed to face-to-face or long-distance telephone interviewing, is minimal. Mailing costs are fixed regardless of where questionnaires are mailed in the United States, and short questionnaires—four sides or less—and their accompanying material usually weigh less than one ounce.

Short questionnaires save considerable mailing costs, and business-reply envelopes are less costly than first-class, stamped envelopes. However, people may be more likely to reply if first-class stamps are used on both mailed and return envelopes (see the discussion on response rates in this section). Short-distance telephone interviewing costs less than telephoning over a more widely dispersed geographical area, although Wide Area Telephone Service (WATS) lines may make long-distance telephone interviewing cost effective.

A geographically dispersed study population is more efficiently dealt with by either telephone interviewing or mailed questionnaires. The managerial aspects of distributing mass-administered questionnaires and completing face-to-face interviews nationwide are both complex and more costly, because travel expenses and salary costs are increased. The least expensive way to contact a dispersed study population is by mailed questionnaires; much academic and nonacademic survey research involving nationwide samples is done this way. Telephone interviewing has become more popular than face-to-face interviewing in nationwide studies because it is much less expensive to undertake than sending interviewers out to respondents' homes. In addition, people today are more concerned about personal safety and thus may prefer to be interviewed on the telephone rather than face-to-face in their homes (see the discussion of random digit dialing in Section 8).

GUIDELINES FOR CONSTRUCTING GOOD QUESTIONS AND QUESTIONNAIRES

Great care and attention needs to be devoted to the construction and revision of a questionnaire or interview schedule for a survey research project. Development of appropriate instruments is influenced as much by creativity and experience as it is by science. In a sense each survey research project is unique. Questionnaires have to be customized and tailored to the specific research questions at hand.

Improperly or carelessly worded questions receive improper, useless, or biased answers. Such questions also frustrate potential respondents and increase the chance they will refuse to complete the interview or questionnaire or will answer it carelessly. Badly worded questions taint respondents' feelings toward the whole survey experience. In contrast, well-worded questions not only obtain the information sought but also enable the respondent to complete the survey experience in a straightforward and satisfying manner. Good questions increase rates of response to surveys. The following guidelines should help you write good questions:

1. *Questions should be as short as possible.* Early drafts of the questions to be asked on a questionnaire or interview should be edited until they are as short as possible. Saving a few words on every question can make the questionnaire easier to read and complete. Shortening questions will also reduce the costs of printing and mailing. It is nearly always possible to shorten the early drafts of all questions. For example, the question

   "What is the size of the community in which you reside?" (circle one)
   1 rural or farm area
   2 small city or town (under 25,000)
   3 larger city or town (25,000–49,999)
   4 smaller metro area (50,000–249,999)
   5 larger metro area (250,000 and above)

   can be shortened to

   "How big is your community?" (circle one)
   1 rural or farm area
   2 town or small city (under 50,000)
   3 medium city/metro area (50,000–249,999)
   4 large city/metro area (250,000 and above)

2. *Questions should be clear.* Questions can almost always be edited to make them clearer. This will make questions more understandable and ensure that respondents interpret the question's meaning similarly. After all, the goal of the questionnaire is to ask standardized

questions. This is why unstructured questions should be avoided and structured questions be made as clear as possible. Consider the following unclear questions:

"What was your income in 1988?"

"What do you think about the quality of the fire department?

Each can be more clearly stated as follows:

"In 1988 what was your total income from all sources?"

"What grade (A, B, C, D, F) would you give to the quality of fire protection where you live?"

3. *Questions should avoid jargon or slang.* The level of wording may alienate, offend, or frustrate respondents. Scientific jargon or argot involves using words that are too complex, and slang involves using words whose meaning may be unknown or offensive to respondents. Each of the following questions are inappropriately worded for respondents who are employed mothers:

"Do you experience role conflict between family roles and work roles?"

"Do you and your husband reach equalitarian decisions about child-raising responsibilities?"

Each question could be reworded as follows:

"Have you had problems handling both work and family responsibilities?"

"Do you and your husband share equally in the raising of your children?"

4. *Double-barreled questions should be avoided.* Questions should inquire about a single thing. One of the most common mistakes in asking survey questions is to ask two questions in one. This is the so-called double-barreled question. Such questions are useless because the meaning of a respondent's answer to them is unclear. If two issues are included in the same question, a "yes" may mean "yes" to one

issue, "yes" to the other issue, or "yes" to both issues. Each of the following questions is double-barreled:

"Do you listen to a commercial or public radio station at least once a day?"

"Do you talk to friends or neighbors at least once a week?"

In each case the question must be broken down into two separate questions.

5. *Questions should be placed in logical, consistent order.* All the questions that deal with the same types of issues or topics should be grouped together and asked in similar fashion. For example, the CPS questionnaire (see Appendix E) grouped together all questions about aspects of the community—such as city government, shopping facilities, and so on—that were to be graded by respondents, and all questions had the same answer possibilities: "A" through "F." Likewise, all the questions about opinions on community problems were grouped together and asked with the same answer options: "serious," "slight," "no problem," or "don't know." The questions that belong together and have the same answer options comprise a *matrix*.

6. *Simple and less threatening questions should precede complex and more threatening questions.* The CPS questionnaire began with simple questions about how respondents viewed the community as a place to live, where in the community they lived, and how long they had lived in the county. Such simple questions are easier to answer and "warm up" the respondent for more complex questions that require judgments and evaluations. Simple questions also heighten respondents' interest in and orient their thinking on the subject matter of subsequent questions. This is the reason for asking questions 3, 8, and 9 early in the CPS questionnaire. More sensitive personal questions—such as on race, occupation, family income, political party affiliation, and voter registration status—are among the very last to be asked on the CPS questionnaire (questions 82–87). These questions are purposely asked last, after the respondent has completed the majority of the interview and is thoroughly immersed in the interview process. Questions that are personal or that may threaten a respondent should never be asked early in a questionnaire or interview.

7. *Question wording should not bias or lead the respondent's answer.* Leading questions are self-fulfilling prophecies—they obtain sought-for answers by providing clues as to the more desirable response.

References to authority figures such as "doctors" or to majority opinion with the phrase "most people" will lead the respondent to give the "usual" answer for fear of appearing odd or deviant or unusual. Absence of a "face-saving" phrase will also result in a bandwagon effect, as will negatively phrased questions. Consider the following biased or leading questions:

"Most people want to send their children to college. Do you?"

"Patriotic Americans exercise their right to vote. Did you vote in the last general election?"

"You don't use cocaine, do you?"

These questions could be rephrased as follows to avoid appearing biased or leading:

"Some people want their children to attend college and others do not. Do you want your children to attend college?"

"Some people find time to vote and others do not. Did you vote in the last general election?"

"Some people use cocaine and others do not. Do you?"

8. *Questions should be asked only of those to whom they apply.* It is unnecessary for the researcher to ask, and bothersome for the respondents to answer, questions that do not apply. The way to avoid asking inapplicable questions is to first ask a filter question and then follow up with contingency questions. A *filter question* is a question that determines to whom a topic or issue applies. *Contingency questions* are asked only of those persons to whom an issue applies. For example, question 83 on the CPS questionnaire was a filter question on employment, and question 84 was a contingency question on occupation.

9. *Sensitive questions should be asked in a relatively nonthreatening way.* There are several ways to ask sensitive questions in a non-threatening way. A face-saving phrase may be used. The "rightness" or "wrongness" of a reply can be diffused through question wording. Questions about sensitive issues such as illnesses and deviant behavior can be asked in an inventory or checklist format. Each of

the following illustrates a less threatening way to ask sensitive questions:

"Children often hurt playmates at one time or another. Has your child hurt a playmate in the last six months?"

"Have you used any of the following drugs in the last three months?" (circle either "1" or "2" for each)

No	Yes	
1	2	*coffee*
1	2	*cocaine*
1	2	*tobacco*
1	2	*aspirin*
1	2	*barbiturates*
1	2	*amphetamines*
1	2	*heroin*

10. *Questionnaires should be constructed using computerized formats.* Questionnaires should look uncluttered and should be printed with different-sized type (or in different fonts), with major sections highlighted and emphasized through use of larger, bolder type, and answer alternatives and items in checklists condensed and downplayed through use of smaller type. Using a word processing routine and a laser-jet printer allows much more material to be condensed and clearly printed and presented on a single page than is possible with a typewriter. In addition, respondents are more likely to complete and return a questionnaire that looks professionally printed than one that looks as if it has been run off on a ditto machine.

OVERALL RESPONSE RATES

Type of Data Collection Technique

The various survey data collection techniques tend to have somewhat different rates of response. Face-to-face and telephone interviews have relatively high response rates, customarily around 80 percent or higher. Personal contact and the impressions created by sincere and professional interviewers enhance response rates. Survey researchers may also send letters to respondents' homes before the interview occurs, to legitimate the interview process. Researchers who use telephone interviewing often advertise the forthcoming interview to enhance the credibility of the interview process and to increase response rates.

Mass-administered questionnaire surveys usually have quite high response rates (as high as 95 percent), because only those absent from the group on the day of questionnaire administration are nonrespondents (e.g., school children absent from school).

Mailed questionnaire surveys usually have the lowest overall response rate (30–60 percent). Lower response rates result because respondents are very likely to throw questionnaires away or forget to complete and return them. Researchers use several techniques to entice respondents to complete and return mailed questionnaires, including keeping the questionnaires short and making the wording and format easy to follow. In addition, they may write appealing cover letters that explain the purpose of the research and the reasons why each respondent's reply is important. Techniques that guarantee anonymity, such as not using names or ID numbers on questionnaires, are used. Follow-up reminders and requests for participation are sent. Sometimes, a postcard reminder is sent two weeks after the questionnaire was mailed, and two weeks after that another questionnaire is sent to nonrespondents. To avoid repeating a mailing to a respondent, when ID numbers or names are not on questionnaires, researchers may use separate return postcards so the name of respondents will be known. And, where first-class stamped envelopes are used, the increased costs are often offset by resulting higher response rates.

Representativeness

Representativeness is the goal of all sampling procedures (see Section 8). Consequently, even though an overall response rate will probably be less than 100 percent, researchers are primarily concerned with whether or not the sample actually obtained is still representative. Provided the final sample size is large enough to enable reasonably close estimates of population traits (see Section 10), a smaller than expected sample size can still be both large enough and representative enough. Whether a sample is representative usually is assessed by comparing characteristics of the sample with known values of population traits. For example, the CPS sample was judged to be representative by comparing characteristics of the sample (e.g., distribution by residence and race) with census data.

Item Nonresponse

Another problem frequently encountered is that not all items or questions in an interview or questionnaire may be answered. *Item nonresponse* refers to how frequently a particular item is not answered by respondents. Researchers take care to avoid this by properly wording and formatting questions and by identifying problematic questions in a pretest of the questionnaire or interview schedule on a group of people similar to the respondents. Though more sensitive questions usually have higher refusal rates, careful researchers usually ask such questions in ways that prevent refusal rates from becoming too high for reliable and valid conclusions. For example, the more sensitive background questions in the CPS questionnaire on total family income and political party preference did have refusal rates higher than other background questions (9.3 percent and 4.4 percent, respectively), but these rates were still low enough for the CPS results to be considered reliable and valid.

In the case of items that comprise an index (see Section 7), researchers have two options when respondents have answered some but not all of the items. Such respondents may be removed from the analysis, or some means of estimating missing answers may be devised. One way to estimate missing answers is to assign the modal or median response obtained from all those who did respond to the item (see Section 3 on measures of central tendency). Another way is to assign the modal or median response the respondent has given to the other items that comprise the index. There is no best way to assign missing values. The method chosen (if any) will depend upon the particular research situation and the nature of the particular index being constructed. The best solution to this potential problem in index construction is to use wording and other questionnaire formats that motivate respondents and make it easy for them to answer all the items. In the case of sensitive questions very careful wording and formatting is especially important. Similar care needs to be taken on items that will be used in multivariate analyses (see Sections 14 and 15), because nonresponses to certain items may have to be excluded from the analyses.

ETHICAL GUIDELINES IN SURVEY RESEARCH

Survey researchers follow ethical as well as statistical and methodological guidelines when they conduct research. Ethical guidelines are as important as the guidelines by which survey research designs are selected, sampling strategies chosen, measures developed, and various statistical analyses conducted. *Ethical guidelines* refer to those proper standards of conduct agreed upon by researchers. Various disciplines and professional associations have written codes of ethics outlining the behavioral standards that practitioners should follow as they conduct and report the results of their research. These written ethical codes typically relate to five basic principles: (1) informed consent to participate, (2) right to privacy, (3) avoiding harm to participants, (4) objectivity, integrity, and honesty in reporting procedures, and (5) honesty in reporting results.

1. Informed Consent to Participate

People who are studied (e.g., survey research respondents) can be encouraged to participate but must be informed that their participation is voluntary. People should not be coerced or required to participate, and they should be informed about what the purpose of the research is. This principle is referred to as *informed consent to participate*.

2. Right to Privacy

The individual identities of those who participate in research (e.g., respondents) and other personal information (e.g., individuals' answers or behaviors they report) should never be disclosed in research reports or in any other way be made public. Techniques ensuring anonymity or confidentiality are crucial ways by which this principle of the *right to privacy* is maintained. And, research reports are summarized (e.g., through aggregated data or use of pseudonyms) so as to guarantee that information is not linked to individuals and that no reference is made to particular people.

3. Avoiding Harm to Participants

Care must be exercised so that research is conducted in ways that are least likely to harm or offend respondents. The principle of *avoiding harm to participants* is sometimes subtle. Obviously, torturing participants or humiliating them is unacceptable. But dealing with sensitive topics—such as drug use, mental illness, and employment histories—

can be potentially damaging to people's self-images. Researchers should avoid wording that labels people as good or bad, normal or deviant. Moreover, they should make it clear that information is being collected to help understand people rather than judge them. Such reassurances are necessary so that survey participants do not feel degraded or stigmatized.

4. Objectivity, Integrity, and Honesty in Reporting Procedures

Researchers should exercise the utmost care in accurately describing the research procedures they have used. These are the principles of *objectivity, integrity, and honesty in reporting procedures*. It is unethical, for example, to report that certain sampling procedures or statistical tests have been conducted if they have not actually been used. Untruthful discussions of inadequate research procedures—including failure to acknowledge shortcomings and inability to generate a large and representative sample—are not only misleading but also unethical.

5. Honesty in Reporting Results

Researchers must carefully and honestly report research results. This is the principle of *honesty in reporting results*. Negative findings and the failure to establish statistically meaningful relationships must be reported as scrupulously as positive and significant outcomes. The dynamic nature of the relationship between empirical generalizations and theoretical statements (see Sections 1 and 5) in the research process means that negative results are just as informative and valuable as positive results. Nevertheless, ethical guidelines motivate researchers to avoid falsifying results to enhance the fit between results and predictions.

Ethical guidelines are applied in various ways. Federal agencies use them before granting funds for specific research projects and while such projects are under way. Many universities have committees that monitor the ethical aspects of campus research projects. Many research firms follow ethical guidelines similar to those to which academic groups adhere. Most importantly, most researchers are personally aware of and guided by the ethical guidelines for research that are established in their academic disciplines and professional associations. This internalization of appropriate behavioral standards explains why most research is ethically as well as methodologically sound.

Exercise 9A:
Units of Analysis

For each of the following questions on the CPS interview schedule (see Appendix E), indicate whether the unit of analysis is I (individuals) or G (groups).

1. #3   (opinion on the county as a place to live)   _____

2. #10 (opinion on merging city and county government)   _____

3. #53 (opinion on pornography as a problem)   _____

4. #40 (rating parks and recreational facilities)   _____

5. #64 (opinion on building new public swimming pool)   _____

6. #77 (number of people in household)   _____

7. #74 (sex)   _____

8. #85 (total family income)   _____

9. #75 (age)   _____

10. #81 (renting the place of residence or owning)   _____

Exercise 9B:
Units of Analysis

For each of the research questions below, indicate whether the unit of analysis is I (individuals), G (groups), or IG (both individuals and groups.

1. Are couples without children happier than couples with children? _____

2. Do sociology departments have more majors than psychology departments? _____

3. Do families with three or more children eat out more frequently than families with fewer children? _____

4. How do the grade point averages of Greek-affiliated college men and women compare to the grade point averages of non-Greek-affiliated college men and women? _____

5. Do college men vote more regularly than college women? _____

6. Are divorced people less happy than married people? _____

7. Do families with VCRs spend more leisure time together than families without VCRs? _____

8. Do small colleges attract a higher proportion of merit scholars than larger universities? _____

9. Are both boys and girls less adjusted when both parents work as compared to when only fathers work? _____

10. Who cleans the house in American families? _____

NAME _____   DATE _____

Exercise 9C:
Populations and Samples

Identify each of the following as U (a universe), SP (a study population), or S (a sample).

1. All college graduates in the United States   _____

2. The alumni of a researcher's home university   _____

3. All registered voters in the county a researcher is
   studying to find opinions on local government   _____

4. The 611 households in the CPS   _____

5. The people who were interviewed in the latest
   nationwide Gallup Poll   _____

6. All college and university basketball players in a
   researcher's home state   _____

7. All day-care centers in a researcher's hometown   _____

8. The Decennial Census of the United States   _____

9. The 1 in 8 households in the United States that
   complete the longer Decennial Census forms   _____

10. The approximately 40,000 households that comprise
    the monthly Current Population Survey conducted by
    the Census Bureau   _____

Exercise 9D:
Fallacious Inferences

Identify each of the following as involving either IF (the individualistic fallacy), EF (the ecological fallacy), or FF (fallacy-free research).

1. Using data on suicide rates in Protestant and Catholic countries to determine whether Protestants or Catholics are more likely to commit suicide _____

2. Using people's opinions on candidates to study their voting preferences _____

3. Using data showing that Catholics are just as likely to use birth control as Protestants as evidence that the position of the Church has changed on this issue _____

4. Using dropout data from a number of high schools for the last 10 years to study the trends in retention in the schools _____

5. Using neighborhood crime rates to study who commits crimes _____

6. Using precinct voting rates to study why people vote _____

7. Using data showing that regions of the country with a higher percentage of foreign-born individuals have higher literacy rates as evidence that foreign-born individuals are likely to be more literate than the native born _____

8. Using CPS respondents' ratings of parks and recreational facilities to evaluate the quality of such facilities in the community _____

9. Using CPS respondents' opinions on the seriousness of crime to study how serious a problem crime is considered to be in the community   ———

10. Using data on CPS respondents' diplomas to study levels of education attained in the community   ———

Exercise 9E:
Survey Research Designs

Identify each of the following as either CSS (a cross-sectional survey), TS (a trend study), COS (a cohort study), or PS (a panel study).

1. Repeated CPS surveys to study changes in people's opinions of the community _____

2. Repeated CPS surveys to see how people's incomes change as they age from their twenties to their thirties _____

3. Repeated surveys of the same sample of university alumni every five years _____

4. A survey like the CPS done in your home county _____

5. A survey of all alumni of a state university _____

6. A study of differences in family income by age in the CPS _____

7. The Current Population Survey (CPS) conducted by the U.S. Census Bureau _____

8. Repeated surveys of a class of students as they progress through high school _____

9. The results of a particular Gallup Poll _____

10. Repeated study of the same customers of a car dealership _____

Exercise 9F:
Survey Research Designs

For each question below select the most appropriate research design: CSS (cross-sectional survey), TS (trend study), COS (cohort study), or PS (panel study).

1. Are married couples with children more satisfied with life than childless adults? _____

2. How much has the average age at marriage increased in the United States since 1980? _____

3. Does marijuana smoking among high school students lead to later cocaine use? _____

4. Do more men than women in the United States exercise at least once a week? _____

5. Do people vote more as they mature? _____

6. How does retirement influence men? _____

7. How is the proportion of childless couples changing in the United States? _____

8. Do more older than younger people attend church regularly in the United States? _____

9. Is the proportion of people over the age of 65 increasing in the United States? _____

10. In the United States do wives do more housework than husbands? _____

Exercise 9G:
Survey Research and the CPS

Refer to the CPS interview schedule (Appendix E) to answer the following questions.

1. List the number of every unstructured question in the CPS interview.

2. Briefly discuss how the precoding of answers to CPS questions 10–24 might be changed. Why might a change be necessary?

3. Is the precoding for the answers to question 76 (marital status), question 80 (highest diploma), and question 86 (political party preference) appropriate? Why or why not?

4. Identify a CPS question that still seems unclear. Why is it not clear? Rewrite it to make it clearer.

Exercise 9H:
Data Collection Techniques

Select the most appropriate survey data collection technique to address each of the following research projects. In each case state why you chose the data collection technique you did. Remember: Information from questionnaires can be obtained in either anonymous or confidential ways.

1. The opinions of elementary school children about drugs in a community

2. A study that must be completed quickly of political preferences among a national sample of Americans

3. A detailed study of how families in a community budget family resources

4. With a fairly large budget, a nationwide study of opinions on alcohol abuse

Exercise 91:
Interviews and the CPS

Refer to the CPS interview schedule (Appendix E) to answer the following questions.

1. Identify and briefly describe the major features of a matrix you find in the CPS interview.

2. Identify and briefly describe the major features of filter and contingency questions in the CPS interview, other than questions 83 and 84.

3. For better order, might any of the CPS interview questions 74–88 be reordered? Which one (or ones) and why?

4. Select a CPS interview question that contains jargon or slang. Reword it to make the wording more appropriate.

5. Select a CPS interview question that seems too long. Provide a shortened version.

Exercise 9J:
Guidelines for Good Questions

In the blank after each question indicate the number(s) of the guide-line(s) for good questions that are violated, where

1 = short questions
2 = clear questions
3 = no jargon or slang
4 = no double-barreled questions
5 = logical ordering
6 = simple, less threatening questions first
7 = unbiased wording
8 = asked only of those to whom they apply
9 = nonthreatening, sensitive questions
10 = computerized formats
11 = clear answer formats
12 = structured questions preferred

1. The first question asked: How old are you? ____   _____

2. All respondents are asked: How many children
   do you have? ____   _____

3. How many of your relatives are drug addicts or
   drunks? ____   _____

4. Most people go to church. Do you? (circle one)
   1 yes   2 no   _____

5. Do you often go to the movies or rent movies at
   a video outlet? (circle one)
   1 yes   2 no   _____

6. Do you agree with the INF treaty provisions, especially on intermediate ground-based missiles? (circle one)
   1 agree   2 disagree   _____

7. What influenced you to attend college? ___   _____

8. Doctors say you should not smoke. You don't smoke, do you? (circle one)
   1 yes   2 no   _____

9. How many times a year do you overdraw your checking account? (check one)
   ___ once ___ twice
   ___ three times ___ four times
   ___ five times ___ six times
   ___ seven times ___ eight times
   ___ nine times ___ ten times or more   _____

10. All respondents are asked: Do you and your spouse have "knock-down, drag-out" fights? (circle one)
    1 yes   2 no   _____

11. How often do you get drunk? _____   _____

12. Who did you vote for in the last election? ___   _____

Exercise 9K:
Guidelines for Ethical Research

In the blank after each brief description of a research project, indicate which of the ethical guidelines for research is violated, where:

1 = informed consent to participate
2 = right to privacy
3 = avoidance of harm to participants
4 = objectivity and honesty in reporting procedures
5 = honesty in reporting results

1. Students in a class are required to fill out a drug-use questionnaire. _____

2. Without parental permission, children's school records are used in research on deficient school progress. _____

3. A research report discusses results without mentioning that convenience sampling was used. _____

4. Prisoners are promised prison privileges if they will volunteer for research on criminal behavior. _____

5. Researchers discuss results by deciding to interpret relationships as significant at the .10 level of probability because more positive results are found using that scheme. _____

10
The Bases of Inferential Statistics

In inferential or sampling statistics, data from samples are used to make inferences or generalizations about the populations from which they are drawn. The normal distribution is very important from both a theoretical and practical point of view. Because much data either approximate or are assumed to approximate a normal distribution, we can describe empirical and sample distributions based on properties of the theoretical normal curve.

THE NORMAL CURVE

Knowledge of the normal curve is essential to understanding the notions of probability involved in inferential statistics and hypothesis testing.

The normal curve is perhaps one of the most widely recognized mathematical shapes (see curve A in Figure 10.1). Sometimes called the bell-shaped curve, the *normal curve* actually consists of numerous bell-shaped curves portraying the distribution of scores or values in a population or sample. Some normal curves are wider and flatter than the standard shape; others are narrower with a more pronounced peak. The

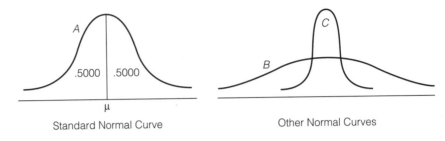

Figure 10.1 Shapes of the normal curve

shape reflects the variance of values around the mean of the distribution. For example, when values are widely dispersed around the mean, the shape of the distribution is similar to the one depicted by curve B in Figure 10.1; and when values in a distribution are tightly clustered around the mean, the shape of the distribution is similar to the one depicted by curve C in Figure 10.1.

Despite variations in shape, all normal distributions and curves share these characteristics:

1. The total area under the curve = 1.00; that is, 100 percent of all values and scores lie under the curve.

2. The mean of the distribution lies at the middle of the curve. It is located on the horizontal axis at the point at which a vertical line drawn from the highest point in the curve meets the horizontal axis.

3. One-half of the area of the curve—.50 or 50 percent of the values or scores—lies on each side of the middle line. Or, 50 percent of the values are below the mean and 50 percent are above. Both sides of the curve are symmetrical. If the curve were folded along the middle line, one side would be the mirror image of the other (see curve A in Figure 10.1).

4. There is a fixed proportion of values or scores between a vertical line erected at one point on the horizontal axis and a vertical line at any other point. For example, in all normal curves the proportion of values that lie
   a. between the mean (μ) and ± 1 standard deviations (σ) = .3413 or 34.13 percent of all values

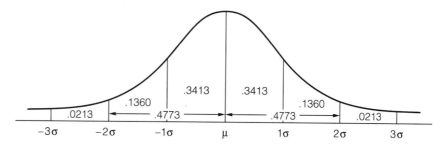

Figure 10.2 Areas of proportions under the normal curve

   b. between 1σ and 2σ (or -1σ and -2σ) = .1360 or 13.6 percent
   (therefore, between the mean and $+2\sigma$ or between the mean and
   -2σ = .4773 or 47.73 percent)
   c. between 2σ and 3σ (or -2σ and -3σ) = .0213

Over 95 percent of the values or cases in a distribution lie with $\pm 2\sigma$ of
the mean (.4773 + .4773 = .9546 or 95.46 percent). Virtually all of
the values in a distribution (99.72 percent) fall between $\pm 3\sigma$ (see Figure 10.2).

Z-SCORES

A useful and common way of summarizing the position of a particular
value in a distribution relative to the mean in a normal distribution is
through Z-scores. *Z-scores* are standardized scores that express the distance of a value or score from the mean in units of the standard deviation. They tell us how many standard deviations higher (if positive) or
lower (if negative) from the mean a particular value is.

Formula   *Z-Score for Populations*

$$Z = \frac{x - \mu}{\sigma}$$

     where x = a value or score in a distribution
          μ = the mean in a population distribution
          σ = the standard deviation of the population
             distribution

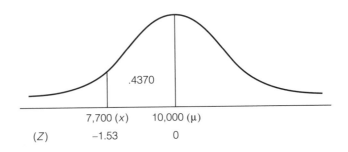

Figure 10.3 Normal distribution with $\mu = 10,000$, $\sigma = 1,500$, $x = 7,700$

Example Suppose the income distribution of a population has the following characteristics: $\mu = \$10,000$ and $\sigma = \$1,500$. You are interested in the position of a value of $7,700.

To find the proportion of values that fall or lie between the value of
7,700 and the mean of 10,000 in this population distribution, first calculate the Z-score for the value 7,700 and then consult Table I, 'Z-Scores
and Areas Under the Normal Curve,' in Appendix D. (Note that a Z-score
of 0 is in the exact center of the curve where the mean is.)

$$Z = \frac{x - \mu}{\sigma} = \frac{7,700 - 10,000}{1,500} = \frac{-2,300}{1,500} = -1.53$$

Therefore, the value of 7,700 is -1.53 standard deviations lower than
the mean. The area or proportion of values corresponding to a Z-score of
$-1.53 = .4370$. (This is also the area corresponding to a Z-score value of
1.53. See Table I, Appendix D.) This means that between $7,700 and the
mean of $10,000 lie .4370, or 43.70 percent, of all the values in the
distribution.

A graphic display of the above information is provided in Figure 10.3.
When working with the normal curve and Z-scores, remember to
proceed as follows:

x ---------> Z ----------> *proportion or percentage of total area*

1. Start with an actual value (x), convert to a Z-score using the Z-score
   formula, and then obtain the proportion or percentage of total area of
   the curve corresponding to the Z-score.

$$\text{proportion} \text{ ----------} \rangle Z \text{ ----------} \rangle x$$

2. Or, if you start with a percentage or proportion, obtain the Z-score that corresponds to it from the body of Table I in Appendix D and then solve for x using the Z-score formula.

Z-Scores and Proportions in a Normal Distribution

Below are procedures to follow for determining proportions of values or scores in a normal distribution. These examples will give you experience in working with Z-scores and Table I in Appendix D. A drawing of the normal curve helps you to visualize what procedures are required; and you are strongly advised to sketch a crude drawing of a normal curve to help you whenever you are working with Z-scores and the normal curve. The procedures described below in examples *a* to *h* are visually displayed in Figure 10.4.

Location of Values	*Procedure*
a. Between a Z-score of 0 and a positive or negative Z-score (or between the mean and a particular value of x):	Find the proportion corresponding to the Z-score in Table I, Appendix D.

e.g.,
between $Z = 0$ and $Z = 1.53$ = prop. = .4370
between $Z = 0$ and $Z = -1.53$ = prop. = .4370

b. Between a positive and a negative Z-score:	*Add* the proportions corresponding to both Z-scores, because they are on opposite sides of the mean and the entire area between the two scores is desired.

e.g.,
between $Z = 2.14$ and $Z = -1.33$: prop. for $Z = 2.14$ = .4838
prop. for $Z = -1.33$ = .4083
prop. = .4839 + .4083 = .8921

c. Between two positive or two negative Z-scores:	*Subtract* the smaller proportion from the larger proportion, because both are on the same side of the mean and the area between the two scores is desired.

e.g.,
between $Z = 2.14$ and $Z = 1.33$ = .4838 − .4083 = .0755
between $Z = -2.14$ and $Z = -1.33$ = .4838 − .4083 = .0755

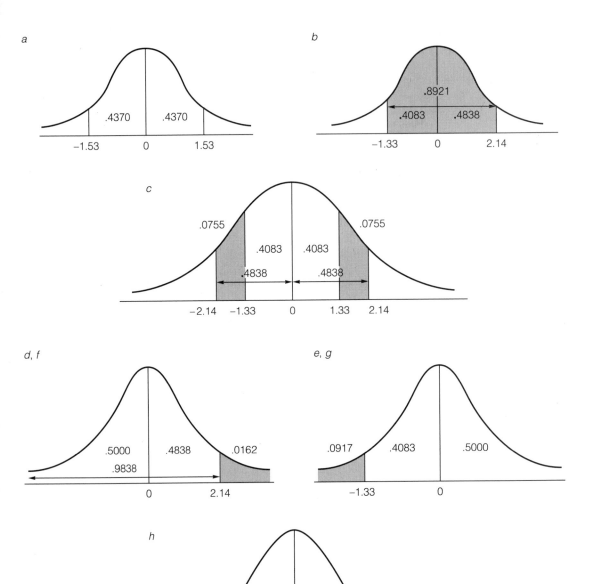

Figure 10.4 Finding proportions between, above, and below Z-scores

d. To the right of (or are greater than) a positive Z-score:

Subtract the proportion from .5000, because only the area in the right tail is desired.

e.g.,
prop. $> Z = 2.14 = .5000 - .4838 = .0162$

e. To the right of (or are greater than) a negative Z-score:

Add .5000 to the proportion, because this area and the other one-half or side of the curve are desired.

e.g.,
prop $> Z = -1.33 = .5000 + .4083 = .9083$

f. To the left of (or are smaller than) a positive Z-score:

Add .5000 to the proportion, because this area and the other one-half or side of the curve are desired.

e.g.,
prop. $< Z = 2.14 = .5000 + .4838 = .9838$

g. To the left of (or are smaller than) a negative Z-score:

Subtract the proportion from .5000, because only the area in the left tail is desired.

e.g.,
prop. $< Z = -1.33 = .5000 - .4083 = .0917$

h. To the right and left of (or are higher and lower than) a positive and negative Z-score:

Subtract each proportion from .5000 and add together, because the sum of both tails is desired.

e.g.,

$$
\begin{aligned}
\text{prop.} > \text{and} < Z = \pm 1.33 = \quad & .5000 - .4083 = .0917 \\
+ & .5000 - .4083 = .0917 \\
\hline
& \text{prop.} = .1834
\end{aligned}
$$

Illustrative Uses of Z-Scores and the Normal Curve

In a population income distribution with a mean = $10,000 and a standard deviation = $1,500, what proportion of values or incomes are lower than $9,000?
Here is the procedure:

$$x \dashrightarrow Z \dashrightarrow \textit{proportion below 9,000}$$

$$Z = \frac{9,000 - 10,000}{1,500} = \frac{-1,000}{1,500} = -.67$$

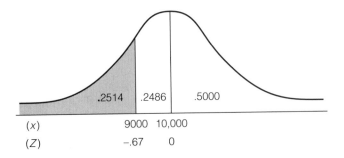

.2514	.2486	.5000

(x) 9000   10,000

(Z) −.67   0

Figure 10.5   Proportion of values lower than 9000

The proportion corresponding to $Z = -.67$ is .2486 (see Figure 10.5). The proportion of incomes lower than \$9,000 $= .5000 - .2486 = .2514$; or, 25.14 percent of incomes or values in the income distribution are lower than \$9,000. Because the normal curve is a theoretical probability distribution, we can also say that the probability of randomly selecting or finding a value lower than \$9,000 is .2514; and the probability of finding a value higher than \$9,000 is .7486 (.2486 + .5000).

In an income distribution with a mean = \$10,000 and a standard deviation = \$1,500, what value or income is needed to be in the top 10 percent of the distribution?

Here is the procedure:

proportion in top 10% ----------〉 Z ----------〉 x

The top 10 percent, or .10, is in the extreme right tail of the curve (see Figure 10.6). That leaves .4000 in the area between μ and x. From Table I in Appendix D, the Z-score most closely corresponding to a proportion of .4000 is $Z = 1.28$ (prop. = .3997). Plug these values into the Z-score formula and solve for x:

$$1.28 = \frac{x - 10,000}{1,500}$$

$$1,920 = x - 10,000$$

$$x = 11,920$$

An income or value of \$11,920 is needed to be in the top 10 percent of the distribution.

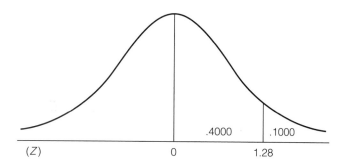

Figure 10.6 The value in the top 10 percent of the distribution

THE CENTRAL LIMIT THEOREM

Populations in the real world often do not have normal distributions. However, repeated random samples taken from them have sample means ($\bar{x}$) that form a normal distribution. This fact is the foundation of statistical inference and probability sampling (see Section 8). The Central Limit Theorem states:

If repeated random samples of equal-sized N (at least size 100) are se-lected from a population with a mean = μ and standard deviation = σ that is or is not normally distributed, then the means of the samples will form a distribution (the sampling distribution of the sample means) that will be approximately normally distributed with a mean of the sample means $\mu_{\bar{x}} = \mu$ (the population mean) and a standard deviation of the distribution of sample means (or standard error) $\sigma_{\bar{x}} = \sigma/\sqrt{N}$.

In reality, when we do a study, we take only one sample and not repeated samples. However, the Central Limit Theorem guarantees that a given sample mean will come close in value to the population mean and will become a closer estimate of the population mean as the sample size increases. The standard error decreases as N becomes larger.

The Z-score for sample means ($\bar{x}$), when the population standard deviation (σ) is known, is calculated as follows:

Formula *Z-Score for Sample Means*

$$Z = \frac{\bar{x} - \mu}{\dfrac{\sigma}{\sqrt{N}}}$$

Example Suppose in a population the mean number of years of school attained was 11.5 years, with a standard deviation = 3.4 years. If you randomly selected a sample of N = 125: (a) What proportion of sample means would be expected to be above 12 years? (b) Between what two values will 95 percent of the sample means lie? (c) What proportion of sample means will be above 12 if the sample size is increased to 400?

a.
$$Z = \frac{\bar{X} - \mu}{\frac{\sigma}{\sqrt{N}}} = \frac{12 - 11.5}{\frac{3.4}{\sqrt{125}}} = \frac{.5}{.304} = 1.64$$

From Table I in Appendix D, the proportion corresponding to Z = 1.64 is .4495. Thus, the proportion above 12 years = .5000 − .4495 = .0505.

b. A Z-score of ±1.96 contains 95 percent of all values in a normal distribution. (Verify this by drawing a normal curve and checking with Table I in Appendix D.) Again, use the Z-score formula, this time solving for $\bar{x}$:

$$Z = \frac{\bar{X} - \mu}{\frac{\sigma}{\sqrt{N}}} \quad \text{or} \quad \pm 1.96 = \frac{\bar{X} - 11.50}{.304}$$

$$\pm .59584 = \bar{X} - 11.50$$

$$\bar{X} = 10.904 \text{ and } 12.10$$

Therefore, 95 percent of the sample means lie between 10.904 and 12.10, which is expressed in statistical notation as follows:

$$10.90 < \mu < 12.10$$

c. If sample size is increased to 400, the standard error decreases.

When N = 125	When N = 400
$\sigma_{\bar{x}} = \dfrac{3.4}{\sqrt{125}} = .304$	$\sigma_{\bar{x}} = \dfrac{3.4}{\sqrt{400}} = .17$

Therefore, the proportion of sample means greater than 12 will also decrease.

$$Z = \frac{12 - 11.5}{.17} = 2.94$$

The proportion corresponding to 2.94 = .4984. Therefore, the proportion above 12 years = .0016.

The above formulas are seldom used, however, because σ is rarely known. All that is usually provided when data are collected for a study are sample statistics. For sample means when only the sample standard deviation (s) is known, it is necessary to use the following formula:

Formula *Standard Error of Sample Means*

$$\sigma_{\bar{x}} = \frac{s}{\sqrt{N-1}*}$$

where s = the sample standard deviation

N = the sample size

When you use the SPSS/PC+ Frequency procedure or the STAT-PAC Descriptive Statistics procedure, the standard error ($\sigma_{\bar{x}}$) is calculated and displayed along with the mean and standard deviation (see output in Tables 3.3 and 3.4).

Remember:

μ = the mean for a population

σ = the population standard deviation

x̄ = the mean for a sample

s = the sample standard deviation

$\sigma_{\bar{x}}$ = the standard error of the sample mean

For samples when σ is unknown and s is used, the Z-score formula is:

Formula Z-Score

$$Z = \frac{\bar{x} - \mu}{\frac{s}{\sqrt{N-1}}}$$

*Instead of N, here N − 1 is used as an adjustment for the bias of s. Some texts use N. However, when N is sufficiently large—usually over 100—the value of s/√N − 1 will be virtually the same as s/√N.

ESTIMATION—CONFIDENCE INTERVALS FOR MEANS

When we collect sample data, we assume that our sample statistic is a good estimate of the population value (i.e., that $\bar{x}$ is a good estimate of μ). However, we know that the estimate is subject to error due to sampling variability. *Confidence intervals* tell us within what range the true population value is likely to lie and what the probability is that the population value will be within that range.

By rearranging the Z-score formula we can obtain the general formula for a confidence interval for sample means:

Formula *Confidence Interval for Sample Means*

$$\text{C.I.} = \bar{x} \pm Z\left[\frac{s}{\sqrt{N-1}}\right]$$

where Z = the Z-score corresponding to the desired level of confidence

From the normal curve and Table I in Appendix D it can be seen that:

1. 90 percent of the values in a normal distribution lie between Z-scores of ± 1.65.
2. 95 percent of the values in a normal distribution lie between Z-scores of ± 1.96.
3. 99 percent of the values in a normal distribution lie between Z-scores of ± 2.58.

Therefore:

1. A 90 percent C.I. uses a Z-score of ± 1.65.
2. A 95 percent C.I. uses a Z-score of ± 1.96.
3. A 99 percent C.I. uses a Z-score of ± 2.58.

In hypothesis testing reference is made to an alpha (α) or Type I error. An α or Type I error refers to the probability of rejecting a null hypothesis of no difference when it is true.

1. An $\alpha = .10$ is equivalent to a C.I. of 90 percent.
2. An $\alpha = .05$ is equivalent to a C.I. of 95 percent.
3. An $\alpha = .01$ is equivalent to a C.I. of 99 percent.

A confidence interval of 95 percent means that 95 out of 100 times the true population mean will lie between the two values indicated, and that we only commit an α error 5 percent of the time or are likely to be wrong only 5 in 100 times in assuming the true population value lies within the confidence interval. The alpha error of .05 is the one most commonly used by social researchers when they establish confidence intervals.

Confidence Intervals	α	Z-Score
90%	.10	± 1.65
95%	.05	$\pm .1.96$
99%	.01	± 2.58

Example   A survey reveals the following information concerning hours of TV watched daily. Construct confidence intervals for $\bar{x} = 5.2, s = .75, N = 157$:

$$90\% \text{ C.I.} = 5.2 \pm 1.65 \left[\frac{.75}{\sqrt{157 - 1}} \right] = 5.2 \pm 1.65(.06) = 5.2 \pm .099$$

$$90\% \text{ C.I.} = 5.10 < \mu < 5.30$$

This means that 90 percent of the time the actual mean number of hours of TV watched will lie between 5.10 and 5.30 hours.

$$95\% \text{ C.I.} = 5.2 \pm 1.96 \left[\frac{.75}{\sqrt{157 - 1}} \right] = 5.2 \pm .12$$

$$95\% \text{ C.I.} = 5.08 < \mu < 5.32$$

$$99\% \text{ C.I.} = 5.2 \pm 2.58 \left[\frac{.75}{\sqrt{157 - 1}} \right] = 5.2 \pm .15$$

$$99\% \text{ C.I.} = 5.05 < \mu < 5.35$$

Note: As the confidence increases, the interval surrounding the mean increases.

The 95 percent and 99 percent confidence intervals are provided in STATPAC's Descriptive Statistics output. For example, STATPAC output for the CPS data on Age (see Table 3.4) gives a 95 percent confidence interval of 42.43–45.17 and a 99 percent confidence interval of 42.00–45.60. The same confidence intervals can easily be constructed with output from the Frequency or Descriptive Statistics procedures in SPSS/PC+ (see Table 3.3). For example:

$$95\% \text{ C.I.} = 43.8 \pm 1.96(.699) = 43.8 \pm 1.37$$
$$\text{(mean)} \quad Z(\text{std. err.})$$

$$95\% \text{ C.I.} = 42.43 > \mu > 45.17$$

$$99\% \text{ C.I.} = 43.8 \pm 2.58(.699) = 43.8 \pm 1.80$$

$$99\% \text{ C.I.} = 42.00 > \mu > 45.60$$

ESTIMATION—CONFIDENCE INTERVALS FOR PROPORTIONS

The estimation procedure for sample proportions (or percentages) is very similar to that for sample means. A modification of the Central Limit Theorem holds that repeated large random samples will yield a distribution of sample proportions that will be approximately normal with the mean of the sample proportions $P_s = P_\mu$ (the population proportion) and the standard deviation or standard error of the sample proportions $\sigma_p = \sqrt{P_\mu(1 - P_\mu)/N}$.

The Z-score for sample proportions and the confidence interval for proportions are calculated as follows:

Formulas *Z-Score for Sample Proportions*

$$Z = \frac{P_s - P_\mu}{\sqrt{P_\mu(1 - P_\mu)/N}}$$

Confidence Interval for Proportions

$$\text{C.I.} = P_s \pm Z \sqrt{\frac{P_\mu(1 - P_\mu)}{N}}$$

where P_s = the proportion in the sample (in decimal form)

Z = the appropriate Z-score for the C.I. chosen

N = sample size

P_μ = the proportion in the population
(It is customary to set P_μ at .5 $(1 - P_\mu = .5)$ to maximize the standard error of the proportions.)

Example   If 44 percent answered "yes" to a particular question in a survey where the sample size was 100, the 99 percent and 95 percent confidence intervals would be:

$$99\% \text{ C.I.} = .44 \pm 2.58 \sqrt{\frac{(.5)(.5)}{100}} = .44 \pm 2.58(.05)$$

$$= .44 \pm .13 \text{ (here the error is } \pm.13 \text{ or } \pm13 \text{ percent)}$$

$$99\% \text{ C.I.} = .31 < P_\mu < .57$$

The actual population proportion will lie between .31 and .57 99 percent of the time.

$$95\% \text{ C.I.} = .44 \pm 1.96(.05) = .44 \pm .10 \text{ (error of } \pm10 \text{ percent)}$$
$$95\% \text{ C.I.} = .34 < P_\mu < .54$$

The actual population proportion will lie between .34 and .54 95 percent of the time.

As sample size increases, the standard error is reduced and the confidence interval becomes narrower. For example, if sample size in the above example is increased from 100 to 600, at the 99 percent C.I. error is reduced from .13 to .05, or from ±13 to ±5 percent $[2.58(\sqrt{(.5)(.5)/600} = .053 = .05]$; and at the 95 percent C.I. error is reduced from .10 to .04, or from ±10 to ±4 percent $[1.96(\sqrt{(.5)(.5)/600} = .04]$.

DETERMINING SAMPLE SIZE

If a researcher wanted to limit his or her error to ±3 percent at the 95 percent confidence level, how large a sample would be needed? This question can be answered by using the following formula:

Formula   *Sample Size*

$$N = \frac{Z^2(P_\mu)(1 - P_\mu)}{E^2}$$

where N = the sample size needed

Z^2 = the appropriate Z-score squared for the confidence level selected (1.96^2 for 95 percent C.I.; 2.58^2 for 99 percent C.I.)

P_{μ} = the population proportion (use .50 to maximize the value of the numerator)

E^2 = the amount of sampling error expressed in decimal form and squared (3 percent is .03²)

Based on the formula above:

$$N = \frac{1.96^2(.5)(.5)}{.03^2} = \frac{.9604}{.0009} = 1{,}067.11$$

Thus, a sample size of 1,067 is needed to assure accuracy within ±3 percent at the 95 percent confidence interval.

Using this formula, sample sizes needed for various sampling errors at the 95 percent and 99 percent confidence levels are indicated below:

Sampling Error (%)	Approximate Sample Size (N) Needed at 95%*	at 99%
± 10	100	166
± 7	200	340
± 5	400	666
± 4	600	1,040
± 3	1,000	1,849
± 2.5	1,500	2,663
± 2	2,400	4,160
± 1	9,600	16,641

*Figures here are not exact, but rounded.

It is important to emphasize here something that seems contrary to common sense or intuition. When random samples are taken, it is the size of the sample, not the proportion of the population in the sample, that is the prime determinant of sampling error. The CPS that is referred to in this text had a sample of approximately 600 respondents from a county of about 100,000 population. The sampling error is ±4 percent at the 95 percent confidence level. Likewise, national surveys of 600 respondents in a country of about 250,000,000 people also have a sampling error of ±4 percent at the 95 percent confidence level.

The complete formula for sampling error is:

Formula   *Sampling Error for Means*   *Sampling Error for Proportions*

$$\sigma_{\bar{x}} = \frac{\sigma}{\sqrt{N}}(\sqrt{1 - f}/1) \qquad\qquad \sigma_p = \sqrt{\frac{P(1 - P)}{N}} \; (\sqrt{1 - f}/1)$$

where f = the sampling fraction

The part of the formula to the right in parentheses is not normally included in the calculation of sampling or standard error because if only a small proportion of a population is included in the sample, f is very close to zero, making the overall value of the entity within the parentheses essentially 1; hence, it does not affect the rest of the formula. The sampling fraction only has an effect when samples are taken from small populations, and it should be included in those cases.

Recognition of the fact that an appropriately selected random probability sample of $N = 600$ will provide accurate results to within ± 4 percent and one of $N = 1,000$ will be accurate to within ± 3 percent should give you a good idea of why polling, survey, and market research projects are so widespread and influential today. All reputable professional pollsters, media (TV and newspaper) surveys, market research firms, and social science research studies routinely report sampling error and sample size. And, although it may not be explicitly mentioned, the 95 percent confidence level is usually used. Always look for this information, and be suspicious of, and generally disregard, any study results that omit it. When you see it, you should know how researchers determined the error and what the error means.

Exercise 10A:
Proportions of the Normal Curve

In the normal curve determine the proportion of values or cases for the following:

1. Between $Z = 0$ and $Z = +1.44$
2. Between $Z = 0$ and $Z = -.53$
3. Between $Z = -.53$ and $Z = +1.44$
4. Between $Z = -.53$ and $Z = -1.44$
5. Between $Z = +.53$ and $Z = +1.46$
6. Higher than $Z = +1.88$
7. Higher than $Z = -1.88$
8. Lower than $Z = +1.88$
9. Lower than $Z = -1.88$
10. Higher than $Z = +2.33$ and lower than $Z = -2.33$

Exercise 10B:
Proportions of the Normal Curve

For a normally distributed population with a mean = 50 and a standard deviation = 10, answer or calculate the following.

1. What proportion of values or scores:
   a. fall between the mean and a score of 47?

   b. are higher than 47?

   c. are lower than 53?

   d. are between 35 and 65?

   e. are between 40 and 47?

   f. are above 72?

   g. are below 31 and 69?

   h. are between 55 and 62?

2. What score would you need to be in the top 15 percent of the distribution?

3. What score do you need to be in the bottom 5 percent of the distribution?

4. A score of 55 exceeds what percentage of scores in the distribution?

Exercise 10C:
Confidence Intervals for Means

A survey of 75 faculty members reveals the following information about the age at which they would take early retirement: sample mean = 60.0, sample standard deviation = 6.3. Answer or calculate the following.

1. What proportion of sample means would be expected to be greater than 62?

2. Construct 90 percent, 95 percent, and 99 percent confidence intervals around the mean:
   a. 90 percent C.I. =

   b. 95 percent C.I. =

    c. 99 percent C.I. =

3. What happens to the intervals as the confidence increases?

4. What would happen to the confidence intervals if N increased to 500? Illustrate by comparing the 95 percent C.I., $N = 75$, with the 95 percent C.I., $N = 500$.

Exercise 10D:
Confidence Intervals for Proportions

In a survey of 400 respondents you find 57.0 percent favor more child-care services. Answer or calculate the following.

1. Construct 90 percent, 95 percent, and 99 percent confidence intervals around the proportion:
   a. 90 percent C.I. =

   b. 95 percent C.I. =

   c. 99 percent C.I. =

2. What happens to the interval as the confidence increases?

3. If sample size decreases to 200, what happens to the confidence intervals? Illustrate by comparing the 95 percent C.I., N = 400, with the 95 percent C.I., N = 200.

4. How large a sample would you need to limit error to ±3 percent at 99 percent C.I.? (Show your work.)

(500)

Exercise 10E:
Computer Applications

Run the Frequency procedure (including STATISTICS = ALL) in SPSS/PC+ or the Descriptive Statistics procedure in STATPAC for variable #79, GRADE. Then answer or calculate the following.

1. Record the values for:
   a. sample mean $\bar{x} =$
   b. sample standard deviation $s =$
   c. standard error $\sigma_{\bar{x}} =$
   d. sample size (valid cases) $N =$

2. Verify that the standard error can be obtained with the formula $\sigma_{\bar{x}} = s/\sqrt{N}$.

3. Using the formulas for Z-scores and estimation of means for sample data, determine the following:
   a. 95 percent confidence interval for the mean number of years of school completed

   b. 99 percent confidence interval for the mean number of years of school completed

4. What sample mean would be needed to be in the top 10 percent of the distribution of sample means?

Exercise 10F:
Computer Applications

Run the Frequency procedure in SPSS/PC+ or the Frequency Distribution procedure in STATPAC for variable #58, CHILABUS. Then answer or calculate the following. (Note: Disregard output concerning mean, standard deviation, and standard error. They are computed based on the codes of 1 = Yes, 2 = No, and 3 = DK, and are inappropriate and meaningless here.)

1. a. Proportion saying "Yes" to needing more child-abuse services:
   P_s =

   b. Sample size (valid cases):
   N =

2. Calculate the standard error with the formula $\sigma_p = \sqrt{P(1 - P)/N}$.

3. a. What is the sampling error at the 95 percent C.I. $[Z(\sigma_p)]$?

   b. What is the sampling error at the 99 percent C.I.?

4. Construct:
   a. 95 percent confidence interval for the proportion favoring more child-abuse services

   b. 99 percent confidence interval for the proportion favoring more child-abuse services

5. How large a sample would you need to have in order to limit sampling error to ±3 percent at the 99 percent confidence level? (Show your work.)

11

Inferential Statistics: Hypothesis Tests

In this section several of the most common types of hypothesis tests or tests of significance for sample means, proportions, and variances are discussed. In each case use of inferential statistical techniques permits a decision to be made, with a known probability of error, about whether a sample characteristic is different from a population characteristic (the single sample cases), or whether differences between samples are large enough to allow the conclusion that the populations represented by the samples are different on a certain characteristic (the cases with two or more samples).

The tests covered in this section are:

1. Z-test for a single sample proportion
2. t-test for a single sample mean
3. Z-test for two sample proportions
4. t-test for two sample means
5. t-test for before/after or paired samples
6. F-test for variances
7. ANOVA one-way test for three or more sample means

THE BASICS OF HYPOTHESIS TESTING

Hypothesis tests are used to make inferences and draw conclusions about population parameters based on results from probability samples (ideally simple random samples; see Section 8). Before using any inferential statistical test of an hypothesis, the assumptions concerning the data and sample requirements of the test should be checked. For the tests considered in this section the following assumptions are necessary:

1. Variables should be measured at the interval/ratio level for tests involving means or variances. Categories of nominal variables are used in tests involving proportions.
2. The samples are randomly and independently selected.
3. The sample distributions are normally distributed.
4. The variances are equal (for two sample means and ANOVA).

The hypothesis-testing procedure is similar for all the statistical tests considered here and consists of the following four steps, which address the statistical components of the logic and procedure of hypothesis testing discussed in Section 5.

1. State the Null and Alternative Hypotheses

The null hypothesis (H_0) states that there is no difference, or that means, variances, or proportions are equal. The alternative hypothesis (H_1) states that there is a difference and may specify the direction of the difference (see discussion of working hypotheses in Section 5).

In all of science and in all tests of hypotheses in social research, it is always and only the null hypothesis that is tested. Tests of hypotheses provide information on the probability of rejecting a true null hypothesis. The error of rejecting a true null hypothesis is called an alpha (α) or Type I error (see Section 10).

The error of failing to reject a false null hypothesis is called a beta (β), or Type II, error. As the likelihood of committing an alpha error is reduced, the probability of committing a beta error increases. However, the magnitude of the beta error depends on what exact value of the alternative hypothesis is specified. Because beta, or Type II, errors are infrequently discussed, only alpha, or Type I, errors will be considered here.

The decision to reject a null hypothesis occurs only if the probability of committing an alpha error is at an acceptably low level, customarily $\alpha = .05$ or $\alpha = .01$.

Social research is inherently conservative. Rejections of null hypotheses of no difference are purposely made difficult so that the alternative hypotheses that there are differences (or new findings) are not easily accepted. The decision of what alpha level is to be used in hypothesis testing is an arbitrary one; however, the .05 level is probably the most widely used, as well as the minimum level accepted, by researchers for rejecting a null hypothesis. Most researchers feel confident in rejecting a null hypothesis as long as there is a less than 5 in 100 (α = .05) or a less than 1 in 100 (α = .01) chance of being wrong.

An alternative hypothesis (H_1) may be one of two types:

1. *Two-tailed H_1*: where the hypothesis states merely that sample statistics and population characteristics are different, or not equal, without specifying a direction of difference. For example, the hypothesis that a sample proportion is different from a population proportion is a two-tailed test because the sample proportion could be higher or lower—the direction is not specified.

2. *One-tailed H_1*: where the hypothesis states that the sample mean or proportion is greater than or less than the population value, or that one population value is greater than or less than another. Direction of difference is specified in a one-tailed alternative hypothesis.

Examples of and symbolic notations for null and alternative hypotheses for single sample proportions and means are presented below:

Single Sample Proportion Hypotheses

$$H_0: P_s = P_\mu \text{ (sample proportion is equal to population proportion)}$$

two-tailed $H_1: P_s \neq P_\mu$ (sample and population proportions are not equal)

one-tailed $H_1: P_s > P_\mu$ (sample proportion is greater than population proportion)

or

$$P_s < P_\mu \text{ (sample proportion is less than population proportion)}$$

Single Sample Mean Hypotheses

$$H_0: \overline{x} = \mu \text{ (sample mean is equal to population mean)}$$

two-tailed $H_1: \overline{x} \neq \mu$ (sample and population means are not equal)

Table 11.1   Critical Z-Values

Alpha Level	H_1		
	One-Tailed >	One-Tailed <	Two-Tailed
.05	1.65	−1.65	±1.96
.01	2.33	−2.33	±2.58

one-tailed H_1: $\overline{x} > \mu$ (sample mean is greater than population mean)

or

H_1: $\overline{x} < \mu$ (sample mean is less than population mean)

2. Select the Appropriate Test and Critical Value of the Test Statistic

The critical value of the test statistic for any test depends on the form of the alternative hypothesis (H_1) (i.e., whether it is one- or two-tailed and what alpha is selected). Critical values for the Z-test are listed in Table 11.1.

In a distribution of Z-scores in a normal curve (see Section 10), 95 percent of the values lie between a Z-score of −1.96 and a Z-score of +1.96, and 99 percent of the values lie between a Z-score of −2.58 and a Z-score of +2.58. Therefore, the critical values of Z for a two-tailed H_1 are:

$$\pm 1.96 \text{ for } \alpha = .05 \text{ and } \pm 2.58 \text{ for } \alpha = .01$$

Because the direction of the difference is not specified in a two-tailed alternative hypothesis, the probability of rejecting a true H_0 is represented by the sum of the proportions in the tails at both ends of the curve.

In a distribution of Z-scores 95 percent and 99 percent of the values will lie below a Z-score of 1.65 and 2.33, respectively; and 95 percent and 99 percent of the values will lie above a Z-score of −1.65 and −2.33, respectively. Therefore, the critical values of Z for a one-tailed H_1 are:

1.65 for $\alpha = .05$ (H_1: >)	2.33 for $\alpha = .01$ (H_1: >)
−1.65 for $\alpha = .05$ (H_1: <)	−2.33 for $\alpha = .01$ (H_1: <)

Because the direction of the difference is specified in a one-tailed alternative hypothesis, the probability of rejecting a true H_0 lies in the area at only one end of the curve.

It is important to remember that the critical value of the test statistic depends on both the form of the alternative hypothesis and the alpha level chosen by the researcher.

3. Compute the Obtained Value of the Test Statistic

The Z-score, t-value, or F-value that is calculated becomes the obtained value of the test statistic.

4. Make a Decision

Making a decision is a very straightforward process involving a choice between one of the following two options: (1) Reject H_0, or (2) Fail to Reject H_0. Whether you reject H_0 or fail to reject H_0 depends on the result of the following comparisons:

1. If the obtained value of the test statistic is greater than (>) the critical value of the test statistic: Reject H_0.
2. If the obtained value of the test statistic is less than (<) the critical value of the test statistic: Fail to reject H_0.

Consider the following alternative hypotheses for sample proportions, the obtained and critical values of Z, and the appropriate decisions:

H_1	Obtained Z	Critical Z	α	Decision
$P_s = P_\mu$	-2.02	± 1.96	.05	reject H_0
$P_s > P_\mu$	1.88	± 2.33	.01	fail to reject H_0
$P_s < P_\mu$	-3.11	-1.65	.05	reject H_0
$P_s = P_\mu$	2.57	± 2.58	.01	fail to reject H_0

Note that in computer output for some of the tests of hypotheses in SPSS/PC+ and STATPAC, the probability of the obtained test statistic is always provided. In such cases, reject H_0 if the probability indicated is less than the alpha level chosen.

If H_0 is rejected, then H_1, the alternative, is tentatively accepted. If the decision is to fail to reject H_0, then the hypothesis of no difference still holds.

When researchers claim that results are "statistically significant at the .05 level," this means that they are able to reject a null H_0 at the α = .05 level, and that the differences observed between means and proportions are large enough that they are confident they could not have occurred by sampling variation more than 5 percent of the time.

Z-TEST FOR A SINGLE SAMPLE PROPORTION

This test is used to determine whether a sample proportion or percentage (P_s) could have come from a known or assumed distribution of proportions with a mean of P_μ, or, stated differently, to determine whether a sample proportion or percentage is an estimate of, or could have come from, a known or assumed population proportion. This particular test should only be used for large sample sizes, where $N > 100$.

Example Eight percent of all students enrolled at the university fail courses. A survey of a random sample of 180 students enrolled in sociology classes reveals a failure rate of 5 percent. Is the proportion of failures in sociology classes significantly lower at the .05 level than that in the university as a whole?

1. *Hypotheses:*

   $H_0: P_s = P_\mu$

   $H_1: P_s < P_\mu$ (One-tailed, direction of lower is specified.)

2. *Formula:*

   $$Z = \frac{P_s - P_\mu}{\sqrt{P_\mu(1 - P_\mu)/N}} \text{ (See Section 10.)}$$

   Critical Z-value at α = .05 is -1.65.

3. *Calculation:*

   $$\text{obtained } Z = \frac{.05 - .08}{\sqrt{.08(1 - .08)/180}} = -1.49 \text{ (Change percentages to proportions.)}$$

4. *Decision:* Because obtained Z is less than critical Z ($-1.49 < -1.65$), the decision is: Fail to reject H_0.

5. *Discussion:* The percentage of failures in sociology classes is not significantly different from the percentage of failures in the entire university. The evidence does not support the idea that a smaller proportion of students fail sociology classes.

THE *t*-DISTRIBUTION

The Z-test could be used for large samples involving one sample mean (see Section 10). However, the statistician W. S. Gossett, while working for the Guinness Brewery in Dublin, Ireland, discovered that Z-scores and the standard normal curve are unreliable and inaccurate estimates of probability when sample sizes are small and the sample standard deviation (s) is used as an estimate of the unknown population standard deviation (σ). Gossett developed a different distribution, the *t*-distribution, as a substitute for the Z-distribution when N is small (usually when $N < 120$).

For small sample sizes the shape of the *t*-distribution is flatter than that of the Z-distribution, meaning that the areas under the *t*-curves differ from those under the Z-distribution. As N increases, the shape of the *t*-distribution becomes more like the Z-distribution, and when $N > 120$, the two distributions are identical.

Table II in Appendix D contains the critical values of *t* for one-tailed and two-tailed tests at various alpha levels. To determine the appropriate critical value of *t*, subtract 1 from N to obtain the degrees of freedom. For example, if $N = 20$, the critical value of *t* for a two-tailed test at $\alpha = .05$ has 19 degrees of freedom and a value of 2.093.

Note in Table 11.2, which is excerpted from Table II in Appendix D, that the critical *t*-values for small samples are larger than critical Z-scores, but as N increases, the critical *t*-value decreases, coming closer to critical Z-scores. For samples larger than 120, critical *t*- and Z-values are the same.

Table 11.2 Selected Critical Values of *t* and Z

N	d.f.	Critical *t*-Values One-Tailed $\alpha = .05$	$\alpha = .01$	Critical *t*-Values Two-Tailed $\alpha = .05$	$\alpha = .01$
5	4	2.015	3.365	± 2.571	± 4.032
20	19	1.729	2.539	± 2.093	± 2.861
∞	—	1.65	2.33	± 1.96	± 2.58
		Critical Z-Values			
		1.65	2.33	± 1.96	± 2.58

The formula for obtaining a *t*-value for a single sample mean is:

Formula   *t-Value for Single Sample Mean*

$$t = \frac{\bar{x} - \mu}{s/\sqrt{N - 1}} \text{ (with d.f. } = N - 1)$$

Note that this formula is identical to that for Z (see Section 10):

Formula   *Z-Value for Single Sample Mean*

$$Z = \frac{\bar{x} - \mu}{s/\sqrt{N - 1}}$$

A *t*-test must be used for small samples when the sample standard deviation (*s*) is used as an estimate of the population standard deviation (σ). Obtained *t*-values are calculated exactly the same way as Z-values are, and the critical values of *t* are the same as those for Z when N is large. For these reasons *t*-tests are always used when examining hypotheses concerning sample means.

t-TEST FOR A SINGLE SAMPLE MEAN

This test is used to determine whether a sample mean ($\bar{x}$) is an estimate of, or could have come from, a known or assumed population mean (μ), or could have come from a distribution of sample means with a mean of μ.

Example   A survey of a random sample of 31 Japanese Americans reveals an average of 13.0 years of education, with a standard deviation (*s*) of 1.7 years. Is this significantly different at the .05 level from the national average of 12.1 years?

1. *Hypotheses:*

    $H_0: \bar{x} = \mu$

    $H_1: \bar{x} \neq \mu$ (Two-tailed; direction of difference is not specified.)

2. *Formula:*

$$t = \frac{\bar{x} - \mu}{s/\sqrt{N - 1}}$$

Critical *t*-value at $\alpha = .05$, d.f. $N - 1 = 30$, is ± 2.042 (see Table II, Appendix D)

3. *Calculation:*

$$\text{obtained } t = \frac{13.0 - 12.1}{1.7/\sqrt{31 - 1}} = 2.90$$

4. *Decision:* Because obtained t is greater than critical t (2.90 > 2.042), the decision is: Reject H_0.

5. *Discussion:* The average educational attainment of Japanese Americans is significantly different from that of the overall American population.

Z-TEST FOR TWO SAMPLE PROPORTIONS

This test is used to determine whether two sample proportions are different (whether two sample proportions, which come from two independent samples, estimate or come from a common population proportion).

Example In a national random sample it is found that 65 percent of Democrats ($N = 326$) and 56 percent of Republicans ($N = 300$) think aid to the Contras in Nicaragua should be cut off. Is there a significant difference in opinion between the parties over this issue at the .05 and .01 levels?

1. *Hypotheses:*

$$H_0: P_1 = P_2$$
$$H_1: P_1 \neq P_2$$

2. *Formulas:* Obtain estimates of the overall population proportion (P_μ) and the standard deviation of the sampling distribution of the differences in sample proportions or the standard error of the difference between proportions ($\sigma_{P_1 - P_2}$) with the following formulas:

$$P_\mu = \frac{N_1 P_1 + N_2 P_2}{N_1 + N_2}$$

$$\sigma_{P_1 - P_2} = \sqrt{P_\mu(1 - P_\mu)} \, \sqrt{(N_1 + N_2)/(N_1)(N2)}$$

Then,

$$Z = \frac{P_{S_1} - P_{S_2}}{\sigma_{P_1 - P_2}}$$

Note: If both N_1 and N_2 are the same size, the following formula can be used instead of those above:

$$Z = \frac{P_{S_1} - P_{S_2}}{\sqrt{\dfrac{P_{S_1}(1 - P_{S_1})}{N_1} + \dfrac{P_{S_2}(1 - P_{S_2})}{N_2}}}$$

The denominator in the above formula is the standard error of the difference between proportions.
Critical Z-value at $\alpha = .05$ is ± 1.96.
Critical Z-value at $\alpha = .01$ is ± 2.58.

3. *Calculations:*

$$P_\mu = \frac{326(.65) + 300(.56)}{326 + 300} = .61$$

$$\sigma_{P_1 - P_2} = \sqrt{.61(1 - .61)} \quad \sqrt{326 + 300/(300)(326)} = .039$$

$$\text{obtained } Z = \frac{.65 - .56}{.039} = 2.31$$

4. *Decision:* At the .05 level, because the obtained Z of 2.31 is greater than the critical Z of 1.96, the decision is: Reject H_0. At the .01 level, because the obtained Z of 2.31 is less than the critical Z of 2.58, the decision is: Fail to Reject H_0.

5. *Discussion:* At the .05 level the conclusion is that a significant difference exists between the political parties on the issue of terminating aid to the Contras. However, at the .01 level no such claim can be made. Claims of significant results are obviously dependent on the alpha level chosen; and alpha levels should be set before research is conducted and results are analyzed. The level at which results are significant should be noted in research reports.

t-TEST FOR TWO SAMPLE MEANS

This test is used to determine whether two sample means are different (whether two sample means, which come from two independent samples, estimate or come from a common population mean).

Note that this *t*-test assumes that the variances are equal and uses the "pooled variance estimate" of the standard deviation of the sampling distribution or standard error of the difference between means.

Example   A social researcher is comparing driving under the influence (DUI) arrests in two police jurisdictions. A random sample of 25 city officers reveals an average of 27.0 DUI arrests per month, with a standard deviation (s) of 2.6; and a sample of 20 county deputies shows an average of 28.6 DUI arrests, with a standard deviation of 3.4. Is there a significantly lower average number of arrests for DUI in the city at the .05 level?

1. *Hypotheses:*

   H_0: $\mu_1 = \mu_2$ (Note that population symbols are used.)

   H_1: $\mu_1 < \mu_2$ (One-tailed; city mean is hypothesized to be lower.)

2. *Formula:*

$$ t = \frac{\bar{X}_1 - \bar{X}_2}{\sigma_{\bar{x}_1 - \bar{x}_2}} $$

where $\sigma_{\bar{x}_1 - \bar{x}_2}$, the standard error of the difference between the means, is calculated as follows:

$$ \sigma_{\bar{x}_1 - \bar{x}_2} = \sqrt{\frac{N_1 S_1^2 + N_2 S_2^2}{N_1 + N_2 - 2}} \sqrt{\frac{N_1 + N_2}{N_1 N_2}} $$

In this test the degrees of freedom $= N_1 + N_2 - 2$, and the critical t-value at $\alpha = .05$, d.f. $(25 + 20 - 2) = 43$, is -1.684 (see Table II, Appendix D).

3. *Calculation:*

$$ \text{obtained } t = \frac{27.0 - 28.6}{\sqrt{\frac{25(2.6)^2 + 20(3.4)^2}{25 + 20 - 2}} \sqrt{\frac{25 + 20}{25(20)}}} = -1.75 $$

4. *Decision:* Because obtained t is greater than critical t ($-1.75 > -1.684$), the decision is: Reject H_0.

5. *Discussion:* The average number of arrests for DUI appears to be significantly lower in the city than it is in the county.

The t-test for two sample means is used quite frequently in social research, and procedures are available in both SPSS/PC+ and STATPAC for using this test. Consider the following problem using variables from the CPS dataset: "Is there a difference at the .01 level between the ages of those who favor and those who oppose employee drug testing?" Here, the H_1: $\mu_1 \neq \mu_2$, and the critical $t = \pm 2.58$.

t-Tests for Two Sample Means Using SPSS/PC+

Instructions:
```
SPSS/PC:GET FILE='SPSSCPS'. [Enter]
        :SET PRINTER=ON. [Enter]
        :T-TEST GROUPS=DRUGEMP(1,2)/VARIABLES=AGE.
        [Enter]
```

Table 11.3 SPSS/PC+
Independent samples of DRUGEMP   Employee Drug Testing

Group 1: DRUGEMP EQ 1   Group 2: DRUGEMP EQ 2

t-test for: AGE   Age of Respondent

	Number of Cases	Mean	Standard Deviation	Standard Error
Group 1	285	47.9719	17.849	1.057
Group 2	224	38.3839	14.587	.975

F Value	2-Tail Prob.	Pooled Variance Estimate t Value	Degrees of Freedom	2-Tail Prob.	Separate Variance Estimate t Value	Degrees of Freedom	2-Tail Prob.
1.50	.002	6.51	507	.000	6.67	506.22	.000

t-Tests for Two Sample Means Using STATPAC

Instructions:

- Follow steps 1-10 in STATPAC ANALYSIS MANAGEMENT PROGRAMS in Appendix C
- Analysis type #6, "T-Test"
  Then, #2, "T-Test for independent groups"
- # of variable used to split the data into 2 groups = #16
- Code for Group 1 = 1/1
- Code for Group 2 = 2/2
- # of variable that will be analyzed = #75
- Select #6, "End task and write to disk"
- Execute now and start with Task 1

Table 11.4 STATPAC
T-test Position on drug testing by Age

....

Variable under analysis - AGE
Variable used to group cases - EMPLOYEE DRUG TESTING

Group 1   1/1/
1 = FAVOR
1 = FAVOR

....

Number of cases	= 285
Mean	= 47.97
Variance	= 317.47
Standard deviation	= 17.82
Standard error of the mean	= 1.06

Group 2   2/2/
2 = OPPOSE
2 = OPPOSE

....

Number of cases	= 224
Mean	= 38.38
Variance	= 211.83
Standard deviation	= 14.55
Standard error of the mean	= 0.97

T-Test statistics

....

Difference (Mean X − Mean Y)	= 9.588
Standard error of the difference	= 1.473
t-statistic	= 6.510
Degrees of freedom	= 507
Probability of t (One tailed test)	= 0.000
Probability of t (Two tailed test)	= 0.000

....

Looking at the SPSS/PC+ or STATPAC output, it can be seen that the mean age of those who favor mandatory drug testing for employees (Group 1) is 47.97 years and that the mean age of those who oppose drug testing (Group 2) is 38.38 years. The results of the t-test indicate that this difference is significant ($t = 6.51$, d.f. $= 507$, $p < .01$). Therefore, the decision is: Reject H_0. Results support the conclusion that there appears to be an age difference between those who favor and those who oppose employee drug testing.

t-TEST FOR BEFORE/AFTER OR PAIRED SAMPLES

This test is used when examining the difference between the scores of the same individuals in two situations (e.g., in experiments or in other situations where before and after measurements are obtained), or when pairs of comparable subjects that constitute matched, rather than independent, observations are examined, such as couples or twins.

Example Five randomly selected social workers take the state merit exam before and after taking a course on how to improve their scores. Their scores are listed in the chart below. Is there an improvement in their test scores after taking the course? Use the .01 level of significance. (Note: N is very small in this example for purposes of illustrating the computations.)

Individual	Before Course	After Course
A	63	76
B	60	74
C	71	80
D	62	64
E	77	76

1. *Hypotheses:*

$$H_0: d = 0 \ (d = \text{differences in scores})$$

$$H_1: d > 0$$

2. *Formula:*

$$t = \frac{\Sigma d}{\sqrt{\dfrac{N\Sigma d^2 - (\Sigma d)^2}{N - 1}}}$$

Critical t-value at $\alpha = .01$, d.f. $N - 1$ $(5 - 1 = 4)$, is 3.747.

3. *Calculation:*

$$\text{obtained } t = \frac{37}{\sqrt{\dfrac{5(451) - (37)^2}{4}}} = 2.49$$

Ind	d	d²
A	13	169
B	14	196
C	9	81
D	2	4
E	−1	1
	$\Sigma d = 37$	$\Sigma d^2 = 451$

4. *Decision:* Because obtained t is less than critical t (2.49 < 3.747), the decision is: Fail to reject H_0.

5. *Discussion:* There is not a significant improvement among the social workers in the test scores on the state exam after taking the course on how to score higher.

There are procedures in SPSS/PC+ and STATPAC for the t-test for paired samples. Because appropriate types of data for this test are not included in the CPS, examples of computer output for this test are not included in this text. However, the general instructions for running this procedure are as follows:

In SPSS/PC: *T-TEST PAIRS = VARLIST WITH VARLIST.*

In STATPAC: *Select Analysis type #6, "T-Test," then #1, "T-Test for matched pairs," and enter the numbers of the two variables to be compared. End task and write to disk, and execute starting with Task 1.*

F-TEST FOR VARIANCES

This test is used to determine whether two sample variances are different (or, whether two sample variances are independent estimates or come from the same population variance).

The F-distribution, another family of curves (see critical values of F in Table III in Appendix D), has degrees of freedom for the variance in the numerator and also degrees of freedom for the variance in the denominator of the formula used to compute the F ratio.

Example Two student groups have approximately the same GPA. However, a random sample of 15 Greeks shows a standard deviation of 1.17, and a random sample of 25 non-Greeks shows a standard deviation of .64. Is there more variance among Greek GPAs at the .01 level of significance?

1. *Hypotheses:*

H_0: $\sigma_1^2 = \sigma_2^2$ (The two population variances are equal.)

H_1: $\sigma_1^2 > \sigma_2^2$ (The H_1 is *always* one-tailed. Always hypothesize that the larger variance is greater than the smaller one.)

2. *Formula:*

$$F = \frac{s_1^2}{s_2^2}$$

(Always divide the larger s^2 by the smaller s^2. Obtained F must always be positive and > 1.)

Degrees of freedom: numerator $= N_1 - 1$
denominator $= N_2 - 1$

Critical F at $\alpha = .01$, d.f. $= 14, 24$, is 2.93 (see Table III, Appendix D).

3. *Calculation:*

$$\text{obtained } F = \frac{(1.17)^2}{(.64)^2} = 3.34$$

4. *Decision:* Because obtained F is greater than critical F $(3.34 > 2.93)$, the decision is: Reject H_0.

5. *Discussion:* There appears to be significantly more variation in GPA among Greeks than among non-Greeks.

ANOVA ONE-WAY TEST FOR THREE OR MORE SAMPLE MEANS

The Analysis of Variance (ANOVA) one-way test is used when testing the hypothesis that several (more than two) means are equal or that they all come from the same population.

Example A social psychological study reveals the following information on examination scores for random samples of students in three anxiety groups:

Group 1—low anxiety: $\bar{x}_1 = 84$, $s_1^2 = 10.1$, $N_1 = 10$
Group 2—med. anxiety: $\bar{x}_2 = 82$, $s_2^2 = 14.8$, $N_2 = 10$
Group 3—high anxiety: $\bar{x}_3 = 80$, $s_3^2 = 13.9$, $N_3 = 10$

Is there a significant difference among the groups at the .05 level?

1. *Hypotheses:*

$$H_0: \mu_1 = \mu_2 = \mu_3$$
$$H_1: \text{the means are not equal}$$

2. *Formula:*

$$F = \frac{s_B^2}{s_W^2}$$

where s_B^2 = the between-group variance or scatter among the sample means

s_W^2 = the within-group variance or dispersion of scores within each group

The following formulas are used when N for each group is the same and sample statistics ($\bar{x}$ and s) have been calculated.

$$s_B^2 = N\left[\frac{\Sigma \bar{x}^2 - \frac{(\Sigma \bar{x})^2}{K}}{K - 1}\right]$$

where K = the number of groups

N = the size of the sample for one group (because they are all equal)

$\bar{x}$ = the sample means

$$s_W^2 = \frac{\Sigma (s_j)^2}{K} \qquad \text{(Add all the variances and divide by } K.)$$

Degrees of freedom for the numerator = $K - 1$, and for the denominator = $N_T - K$. Here, degrees of freedom = 2 for the numerator ($3 - 1 = 2$) and 27 for the denominator ($30 - 3 = 27$). Critical F, at $\alpha = .05$, d.f. = 2, 27, is 3.35 (see Table III in Appendix D for critical values of F).

3. *Calculation:*

$$s_B^2 = 10\left[\frac{20{,}180 - \frac{(246)^2}{3}}{3 - 1}\right] = 40$$

$$s_W^2 = \frac{10.1 + 14.8 + 13.9}{3} = 12.93$$

$$\text{obtained } F = \frac{40}{12.93} = 3.09$$

4. *Decision:* Because obtained F is less than critical F (3.09 < 3.35), the decision is: Fail to reject H_0.

5. *Discussion:* The evidence does not suggest that there are any differences among the three anxiety groups in mean examination scores.

   If sample sizes for the groups being compared are not equal, however, then the following formulas must be used to calculate s_B^2 and s_W^2:

$$s_B^2 = \frac{\Sigma[N_i(\overline{x}_i - \overline{x}_T)^2]}{K - 1}$$

Subtract a sample mean for a group ($\overline{x}_i$) from the total mean of all the groups combined ($\overline{x}_T$), square the difference, and multiply by the sample size of the group. Do this for each group and sum together, and then divide by $K - 1$:

$$s_W^2 = \frac{\Sigma(N_i - 1)S_i}{N_T - K}$$

Multiply the sample variance for each group by its sample size minus 1, add together, and divide by the combined N of all groups minus the number of groups ($N_T - K$).

   Consider the following problem using variables from the CPS dataset: "Is there a difference at the .01 level among Republicans, Democrats, and Independents in the average number of years of education attained?" Here, there are three groups, so H_0: $\mu_1 = \mu_2 = \mu_3$. The critical F-value (d.f. = 2,562) at α = .01 is 4.66.

One-Way ANOVA Using SPSS/PC+

Instructions:

```
SPSS/PC:GET FILE= 'SPSSCPS'. [Enter]
        :SET PRINTER=ON. [Enter]
        :ONEWAY VARIABLES=GRADE BY POLPARTY (1,3)
        [Enter]
        :/OPTIONS=6 [Enter]
        :/STATISTICS=1. [Enter]
```

Table 11.5 SPSS/PC+

ONEWAY

Variable   GRADE   Years of School Completed
By Variable   POLPARTY Political Party Preference

Analysis of Variance

Source	D.F.	Sum of Squares	Mean Squares	F Ratio	F Prob.
Between Groups	2	185.1466	92.5733	8.9327	.0002
Within Groups	561	5813.8516	10.3634		
Total	563	5998.9982			

Page 6   SPSS/PC+   12/20/88
                                ONEWAY

Group	Count	Mean	Standard Deviation	Standard Error	95 Pct Conf Int for Mean
republic	151	13.5497	3.1298	.2547	13.0464 To 14.0529
democrat	281	12.4270	3.3916	.2023	12.0288 To 12.8253
independ	132	13.5985	2.9288	.2549	13.0942 To 14.1028
Total	564	13.0018	3.2643	.1375	12.7318 To 13.2718

Group	Minimum	Maximum
republic	3.0000	24.0000
democrat	2.0000	21.0000
independ	0.0	20.0000
Total	0.0	24.0000

One-Way ANOVA Using STATPAC

Instructions:

- Follow steps 1-10 concerning STATPAC in Appendix C
- Analysis type = #8 ANOVA
  Then #1 = one-way
- Is data already grouped—No
- Variable used to split data into groups—#86 for Polparty
- Codes: 1/1, 2/2, 3/3
- Enter − to end entries
- # of variable to be analyzed—#79 for Grade
- Select if variable #79 less than 99
- End task, write to disk and execute starting with Task 1

Table 11.6 STATPAC
Task number 1
Dependent variable - GRADE LEVEL

Anova Summary Table

Source of Variation	DF	Sum of Squares	Mean Squares	F	Significance Level
Between groups	2	185.147	92.573	8.933	0.000
Within groups	561	5813.852	10.363		
Total	563	5998.998			

Group Statistics

Group	Codes & Labels	N	Mean	SD
Group 1	1/1/ 1 = REPUBLICAN 1 = REPUBLICAN	151	13.550	3.130
Group 2	2/2/ 2 = DEMOCRAT 2 = DEMOCRAT	281	12.427	3.392
Group 3	3/3/ 3 = INDEPENDENT 3 = INDEPENDENT	132	13.598	2.929

T-Test Between Group Means (Values of p are for a two-tailed test)
Note: Statistics are only printed if p is less than or equal to .050.

t = 3.456	Group 1
p = .001	Group 2
t = 3.449	Group 2
p = .001	Group 3

As can be seen in Tables 11.5 and 11.6, results of the one-way ANOVA show that there are significant differences in mean educational attainment among members of the three political party preferences. ($F = 8.93$, d.f. $= 2, 561$, $p < .01$). Republicans and Independents have similar eduational levels, but the average educational attainment for Democrats is considerably lower than that for those of the other two political preferences.

One-Way ANOVA Worksheet

When none of the sample statistics ($\bar{x}$ or s) have been computed, ANOVA one-way can be calculated using the following worksheet procedure. N can be the same size or different sizes.

Example Four different methods of preparing students to take the ACT test are compared to see whether they differ in effectiveness. The raw data showing the ACT scores of students who prepared for the test under each method are shown below:

1. *Hypotheses:*

$$H_0: \mu_1 = \mu_2 = \mu_3 = \mu_4$$

$$H_1: \text{means are not equal}$$

	Method 1	Method 2	Method 3	Method 4	Row Totals
	$\frac{x_1}{32}$	$\frac{x_2}{23}$	$\frac{x_3}{27}$	$\frac{x_4}{26}$	
	33	32	34	17	
	36	20	31	30	
	34	19	22		
	32	32			
Σx	167	126	114	73	$\Sigma x_T = 480$
Σx^2	5,589	3,338	3,330	1,865	$\Sigma x_T^2 = 14,122$
N	5	5	4	3	$N_T = 17$
$(\Sigma x)^2$	27,889	15,876	12,996	5,329	
$(\Sigma x)^2/N$	5,577.8	3,175.2	3,249	1,776.3	$G = \dfrac{\Sigma(\Sigma x_j)^2}{N_1}$ $= 13,778.33$
$\bar{x}$	33.4	25.2	28.5	24.3	

2. *Formulas and Calculations:*

Sum of Squares Between:

$$SS_B = G - \frac{(\Sigma x_T)^2}{N_T} = 13{,}778.33 - \frac{(480)^2}{17} = 225.39$$

Sum of Squares Within:

$$SS_W = \Sigma x_T^2 - G = 14{,}122 - 13{,}778.33 = 343.67$$

Table 11.7 Summary Table for Summarizing and Reporting ANOVA

Variation	Sum of Squares	d.f.	Estimate of α^2	F-Ratio	Critical F
Between Group Means	$SS_B = 225.39$	$(k-1)$ 3	$s_B^2 = 75.13$	2.84	3.41
Within Group Means	$SS_W = 343.67$	$(N_T - k)$ 13	$s_W^2 = 26.44$		

3. *Decision:* Fail to reject H_0. Obtained F is less than critical F (2.84 < 3.41). There is no difference in effectiveness among the four methods.

Several cautions about what statistical tests of significance do and mean are appropriate as a conclusion to this section. For one, just because a difference is statistically significant does not necessarily mean that it is an important or meaningful difference from a practical or theoretical viewpoint. Very slight, and perhaps uninteresting or unimportant, differences will be statistically significant when N is large. Obviously, one sure way of obtaining statistically significant results, no matter how trivial or inconsequential the differences may be, is to take a large enough sample (see Sections 8 and 9).

Also, hypothesis testing by itself is not the complete or final way to test a hypothesis. There is an obvious need for replication of the findings with other independently drawn samples and for supplementary data that supports the results of particular statistical tests. Remember, hypothesis testing does not prove the alternative, or research, hypothesis (H_1) to be correct. Hypothesis testing only rejects or fails to reject the null hypothesis of no difference. When a null hypothesis is rejected, that is not the final answer to a question—it is only a partial answer, and the impetus for further inquiry and research. The research process is a continuing enterprise (see Section 1).

Exercise 11A:
Hypothesis Tests

For each problem follow the four-step hypothesis-testing procedure discussed in Section 11. The following should be provided for each question:

1. State the null (H_0) and research/alternative (H_1) hypotheses, using appropriate symbols and notations.
2. Select the appropriate test, and indicate what the critical value of the test statistic is at the indicated significance level (including degrees of freedom as appropriate).
3. Calculate the test statistic (show formulas and work).
4. Make the decision whether or not to reject the null hypothesis.

1. Forty-five percent of all adult Americans have never smoked cigarettes. In a random sample of 300 people in your community, it is found that 38 percent of them have never smoked. Is the proportion of never-smoked in your community significantly lower at the .05 level than the national never-smoked proportion?

H_0:

H_1:

Critical value of test statistic:

Calculation:

Decision:

2. Two drug treatment centers report similar average length of patient stays. However, random samples of 11 urban centers show a standard

deviation of 3.4, and random samples of 25 rural centers show a standard deviation of 2.2. Determine at the .05 level if there is greater variance among length of stay at urban centers.

H_0:

H_1:

Critical value of test statistic:

Calculation:

Decision:

3. A random sample of 15 students at your university had a mean ACT score of 17.6 with a sample standard deviation of 1.37. Is this significantly different from the national average of 18.5? Use the .01 level of significance.

H_0:

H_1:

Critical value of test statistic:

Calculation:

Decision:

4. A study conducted by the United Nations reveals the following information regarding number of years of education for random samples of women in three developing countries.

	Ethiopia	India	Nicaragua
$\bar{x}$	4.1	5.0	5.8
s^2	2.89	4.00	15.21
N	51	51	51

Is there a significant difference at the .05 level?

H_0:

H_1:

Critical value of test statistic:

Calculation:

Decision:

5. In a random sample of community residents it is found that 26 percent of the elderly ($N = 200$) and 18 percent of young adults ($N = 150$) are living alone. Are the elderly more likely to be living alone than young adults? Use the .05 level of significance.

H_0:

H_1:

Critical value of test statistic:

Calculation:

Decision:

6. A study of test-taking performance was conducted on a sample of male and female students. Males averaged 73 ($N = 10, s = 7.8$), while females averaged 65 ($N = 13, s = 8.7$). Did males score significantly higher than females on this test? Use the .05 level of significance.

H_0:

H_1:

Critical value of test statistic:

Calculation:

Decision:

7. Six real estate agents in a random sample take a test on house selling techniques before and after taking a course on sales techniques. The chart below shows the results.

	1	2	3	4	5	6
Before	63	77	60	62	71	82
After	76	76	74	64	80	81

Did the agents' scores improve significantly at the .05 level after taking the course?

H_0:

H_1:

Critical value of test statistic:

Calculation:

Decision:

Exercise 11B:
Hypothesis Tests

For each problem follow the four-step hypothesis-testing procedure discussed in Section 11. The following should be provided for each question:

1. State the null (H_0) and research/alternative (H_1) hypotheses, using appropriate symbols and notations.
2. Select the appropriate test, and indicate what the critical value of the test statistic is at the indicated significance level (including degrees of freedom as appropriate).
3. Calculate the test statistic (show formulas and work).
4. Make the decision whether or not to reject the null hypothesis.

1. In a national random survey it is found that 46 percent of Catholics ($N = 150$) and 43 percent of Protestants ($N = 185$) favor capital punishment. Are Catholics more likely to favor capital punishment than Protestants? Use the .05 level of significance.

H_0:

H_1:

Critical value of test statistic:

Calculation:

Decision:

2. Incomes of the elderly in two regions are being compared. Random samples of elderly in both regions reveal that the average income in the West is $7,000 ($N = 15$, $s = $1,000$) and average income in the East is $6,800 ($N = 17$, $s = 800). Is there a significant difference at the .05 level?

H_0:

H_1:

Critical value of test statistic:

Calculation:

Decision:

3. A study reveals the following information regarding average examination scores for random samples of students in three introductory courses.

	Sociology	English	History
$\bar{x}$	84	82	80
s^2	10.1	14.8	13.9
N	15	15	15

At the .05 level of significance is there a difference in the means for the students in the three courses?

H_0:

H_1:

Critical value of test statistic:

Calculation:

Decision:

4. Forty percent of all registered voters in the country usually fail to vote in general elections. In a random sample of 200 registered voters it is found that 32.5 percent of them did not vote in the last election. Is

the proportion of nonvoters in this last election significantly lower than the usual proportion of nonvoters? Use the .01 level of significance.

H_0:

H_1:

Critical value of test statistic:

Calculation:

Decision:

5. Eight students in a random sample participate in two reading programs. Their scores are presented below:

	1	2	3	4	5	6	7	8
New Program	2.4	1.8	3.6	3.0	2.5	1.7	5.0	3.0
Old Program	2.6	1.2	3.3	2.8	2.4	1.8	4.2	2.8

Are the students' scores significantly higher with the new program? Use the .01 level of significance.

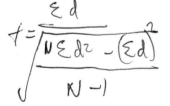

H_0:

H_1:

Critical value of test statistic:

Calculation:

Decision:

6. A random sample of 26 individuals who attended the first night game at Wrigley Field revealed an average of 13.0 years of education, with sample standard deviation of 1.8 years. Is this significantly higher than the national average of 12.0 years? Use the .01 level of significance.

   H_0:

   H_1:

   Critical value of test statistic:

   Calculation:

   Decision:

7. Two judges impose sentences of approximately the same duration. However, random samples of 30 convictions from Judge F show a standard deviation of 6.0 years and random samples of 25 convictions from Judge H show a standard deviation of 9.0 years. State the appropriate hypotheses, and determine at the .05 level of significance if there is more variance among Judge H's sentences.

   H_0:

   H_1:

   Critical value of test statistics:

   Calculation:

   Decision:

Exercise 11C:
One-way ANOVA

A researcher has investigated differences in hours spent watching TV for three social class groups. A random sample of 27 individuals reveals the following number of hours of TV viewed for individuals in each group. Complete the worksheet and determine at the .01 level of significance whether the three groups are similar or different in their average hours of TV viewed.

	Hours of TV Viewed								
I. Upper Class	20	5	8	10	12	22	30	10	18
II. Middle Class	22	30	12	40	18	42	31	27	43
III. Lower Class	45	30	35	24	36	60	55	28	32

H_0:

H_1:

	I	II	III	Totals
Σx				$\Sigma x_T =$
Σx^2				$\Sigma x_T^2 =$
N				$N_T =$
$(\Sigma x)^2$				
$(\Sigma x)^2/N$				$G =$

$SS_B =$

$SS_W =$

Source of Variation	Sum of Squares	d.f.	Estimate of σ^2	Obtained F	Critical F
Between Group Means	$SS_B =$				
Within Group Means	$SS_W =$				

Decision:

Exercise 11D:
Computer Applications

In the problems in this exercise use SPSS/PC+ or STATPAC to test hypotheses involving data from the CPS. For *t*-tests for two sample means and ANOVA problems the test statistic is computed and provided in the printed output. For Z-tests for single and two sample proportions, *t*-tests for a single sample mean, and F-tests for variances, use the Frequency, Descriptive Statistics, or Crosstab procedures to obtain the necessary proportions, means, standard deviations, and sample sizes, and then compute the appropriate test statistics as shown in Section 11.

For each problem state the H_0 and H_1 and the critical values of the test statistics. In your written analyses show all computations that were performed, examine the relevant statistics and the obtained value of the test statistic, and explain your decision of rejecting or failing to reject the H_0. All hypotheses should be examined at $\alpha = .01$. Printed computer outputs should be attached to your analyses.

1. *t-Test for Two Sample Means*
   Do those in favor of merging the school systems have a higher average number of years of school completed than those who oppose the school merger?
   (Groups = #11 MERGESCH(1,2), variable = #79 GRADE)

2. *ANOVA*
   Is there any significant difference in the average ages of those who think pornography is a serious problem, slight problem, or no problem?
   (Groups = #53 PORN(1,3), variable = #75 AGE)

3. *Z-Test for a Single Sample Proportion*
   Community officials believe that 50 percent of the county residents would be in favor of mandatory drug testing for high school athletes. Is the percentage of those CPS respondents in favor of such drug testing significantly higher than the officials' expectations?
   (Frequencies #17 DRUGHSAT)

4. *t-Test for a Single Sample Mean*
   The average educational attainment of adults in the state is 11.0

years. Is the educational attainment of CPS respondents significantly different?
(Frequencies or Descriptive Statistics #79 GRADE)

5. *Z-Test for Two Sample Proportions*
Is the percentage of city residents who favor establishing a bus service higher than the percentage of county residents who favor it?
(Crosstab #69 BUS by #4 RESIDE)

6. *F-Test for Variances*
Overall, average grades given the city and county school systems are similar. Is there greater variability in the grades given one school system compared to those given the other?
(Frequencies #30 BGSCHOOL, #31 WCSCHOOL)

7. *t-Test for Two Sample Means*
Is there a significant difference in the ages of those who are in favor of and those opposed to the establishment of a center for the elderly?
(Groups = #66 ELDERLY(1,2), variable = #75 AGE)

8. *ANOVA*
Is there a significant difference in the average number of years lived in the community between those who favor, oppose, or are uncertain about merging the city and county governments?
(Groups = #10 METROGOV(1,3), variable = #7 YRSLIVED)

9. *Z-Test for a Single Sample Proportion*
Some experts do not think that day-care services will be provided until more than two-thirds of the people want it. Is the percentage of those favoring day care in the CPS survey significantly higher than the two-thirds needed?
(Frequencies #62 DAYCARE)

10. *t-Test for a Single Sample Mean*
Average household size in the county is 2.73 per household. Is there a statistically significant difference between the county figure and the average household size in the CPS?
(Frequencies or Descriptive Statistics #77 HOUSESIZ)

11. *Z-Test for Two Sample Proportions*
Is the percentage of males who see sex discrimination as a serious problem significantly lower than the percentage of females who see sex discrimination as serious?
(Crosstab #49 SEXDISC by #74 SEX)

12. *t-Test for Two Sample Means*
Are those who support a new public swimming pool more likely to have a larger number of people under 18 in the household than those who oppose building the pool?
(Groups = #64 POOL(1,2), variable = #78 UNDER18)

Exercise 11E:
ANOVA

A researcher is interested in whether four groups differ in age at which death occurs. A random sample of 20 death certificates reveals the following ages at death for individuals in each group. Complete the worksheet and determine at the .01 level of significance whether the four groups are similar or different in age at death.

	Ages at Death					
I. Funeral Directors	75	89	72	53	74	
II. Clowns	37	57	83	49		
III. Symphony Conductors	94	62	69	67	51	
IV. College Presidents	71	84	93	85	64	60

H_0:

H_1:

	I	II	III	IV	Totals
Σx					$\Sigma x_T =$
Σx^2					$\Sigma x_T^2 =$
N					$N_T =$
$(\Sigma x)^2$					
$(\Sigma x)^2/N$					$G =$

$SS_B =$

$SS_W =$

Source of Variation	Sum of Squares	d.f.	Estimate of σ^2	Obtained F	Critical F
Between Group Means	$SS_B =$				
Within Group Means	$SS_W =$				

Decision:

12

Selected Nonparametric Statistics

Parametric statistics generally are applicable only to interval/ratio–level data. In this section several nonparametric, or distribution-free, statistics are covered. *Nonparametric statistics* make no assumptions about the shape of the population distribution that is sampled and are generally used with nominal- and ordinal-level data. Some nonparametric statistics have been discussed previously, such as the chi-square test of independence and measures of association for nominal and ordinal data (see Section 4). Sections 11 and 13 cover statistics and hypothesis tests that are parametric, or distribution-bound.

Note that each of the nonparametric statistics covered in this section has a parametric counterpart. The nonparametric statistics are used as an alternative to or a substitute for the parametric statistics when nominal- and ordinal-level data are analyzed or when assumptions about the shape of the distribution cannot be made.

Nonparametric Statistic	Parametric Counterpart
Spearman's rank order correlation coefficient, r_s	Pearson's correlation coefficient, r
chi-square goodness of fit test	t-test for single sample mean
Mann–Whitney U test	t-test for two sample means
Wilcoxon matched pairs/ signed ranks test	t-test for paired samples
Kruskal–Wallis H test	one-way ANOVA

SPEARMAN'S RANK ORDER CORRELATION

Spearman's correlation coefficient (r_s) is a measure of association for ordinal variables based on a comparison of the differences between ranks of individual cases on the two ordinal variables. The value of r_s is $+1.00$ when the rankings of the two variables match perfectly, and -1.00 when the rankings of the two variables are exactly opposite. As a measure of association for ordinal variables, r_s is very similar to gamma (see Section 4). Its parametric counterpart is Pearson's r (see Section 13).

Example   Consider the following hypothetical data for five individuals A–E regarding income level and the grade given to quality of community medical facilities. Here, both variables are measured at the ordinal level. (See the CPS Codebook in Appendix B. Income Level 1 = less $10,000, 2 = $10,000-20,000, etc., and Grade—Medical 1 = A, 2 = B, etc.)

	A	B	C	D	E
X (Income Level)	4	5	3	6	1
Y (Grade—Medical)	5	4	2	5	2

First, arrange the values of the X variable (Income) in descending order, keeping the corresponding value of Y (Grade—Medical) along with each value of X. Second, rank separately the X and Y variables, assigning the rank of 1 to the highest value. Where there are ties, give the average rank to all the cases that are tied. Third, obtain the difference between the ranks of X and Y. The sum of the differences should equal zero. Fourth, square each of the differences, and sum them. These steps are illustrated below:

Ind.	X	Y	Ind.	X Variable in Descending Order X	Y	Ranks X	Y	D	D²
A	4	5	D	6	5	1	1.5	−.5	.25
B	5	4	B	5	4	2	3.0	−1.0	1.00
C	3	2	A	4	5	3	1.5	1.5	2.25
D	6	5	C	3	2	4	4.5	.5	.25
E	1	2	E	1	2	5	4.5	−.5	.25
								$\Sigma D = 0$	$\Sigma D^2 = 4.00$

Spearman's correlation coefficient is calculated as follows:

$$r_s = 1 - \left[\frac{6\Sigma D^2}{N(N^2 - 1)} \right]$$

where D^2 = the square of the difference in rank of X and Y

N = the sample size

Therefore,

$$r_s = 1 - \left[\frac{6(4.0)}{5(5^2 - 1)} \right] = 1 - \left[\frac{24}{120} \right] = 1 - .20 = .80$$

The value of r_s obtained indicates a fairly strong and positive linear association between income level and grade given to medical facilities. In this instance, because higher grades were coded with lower numerical values, as income level goes up, grades given to medical facilities tend to go down. The interpretation of Spearman's r_s is the same as that for Pearson's r, except that with Spearman's r_s the relationship between ranks is examined. Spearman's r_s can be used for ordinal data and also for interval data that are not normally distributed.

CHI-SQUARE GOODNESS OF FIT TEST

The one-sample chi-square goodness of fit test is used when the categories of one discrete (nominal or ordinal) variable are involved. This test tells how well the categorical distribution of a variable in a sample fits the known or theoretical categorical distribution of a variable in a population. It can also be used to determine if there is a uniform distribution of sample data across all categories in a nominal or ordinal variable. It is analogous to the t-test for a sample mean for an interval/ratio–level variable.

The null hypothesis, H_0, is that there is no difference between the observed and expected distribution of the variable, and the alternative hypothesis, H_1, is that there is a difference. The formula for the chi-square goodness of fit test is the same as that for the chi-square test of independence (see Section 4).

Formula   *Chi-Square Goodness of Fit*

$$\chi^2 = \Sigma \left[\frac{(O - E)^2}{E} \right] \quad \text{or} \quad \chi^2 = \Sigma \left[\frac{(O)^2}{E} \right] - N_T$$

where O = the observed frequency in each category of the
variable

E = the expected frequency in each category of the
variable

N_T = total sample size

Degrees of freedom for the critical value of chi-square = $K - 1$, where K equals the number of categories of the variable (see Table IV, Appendix D for critical values of chi-square).

Example   Information on the political party preferences of CPS respondents revealed the following: Republicans = 154, Democrats = 291, and Independents = 134. It appears that respondents are more likely to be Democrats than Republicans or Independents. The one-sample chi-square goodness of fit test is appropriate to test the null hypothesis that there is no preference for a particular political party, or that party preference is evenly distributed. Here, the expected frequency of each of the categories of the variable POLPARTY is the same—193—and is determined by dividing N_T by K (579/3 = 193).

	Rep	Dem	Ind	Total
Observed	154	291	134	579
Expected	193	193	193	579

The value of chi-square is calculated as follows:

$$\chi^2 = \frac{(154 - 193)^2}{193} + \frac{(291 - 193)^2}{193} + \frac{(134 - 193)^2}{193} =$$

$$7.88 + 49.76 + 18.04 = 75.68$$

The critical value of chi-square at α = .01, with $K - 1$ or 2 degrees of freedom, equals 9.210 (see Table IV, Appendix D). Because the obtained chi-square value is greater than the critical value (75.68 > 9.21), the decision is: Reject H_0. Preferences for the political parties are not equally distributed. Respondents are more likely to be Democrats than Republicans or Independents.

To produce the same results using SPSS/PC+, enter the following command (nonparametric statistics are not available in STATPAC):

Chi-Square Goodness of Fit Using SPSS/PC+

Instructions:

`SPSS/PC: NONPAR TESTS CHISQUARE = POLPARTY (1,3). [Enter]`

(Note: The numbers in parentheses refer to the low and high values of the variable.)

Table 12.1 SPSS/PC+
Chi-square Test
POLPARTY Political Party Preference

	Category	Cases Observed	Expected	Residual
republican	1	154	193.00	−39.00
democratic	2	291	193.00	98.00
independent	3	134	193.00	−59.00
	Total	579		

Chi-Square	D.F.	Significance
75.679	2	.000

Example In this example, the same data about political party preference of CPS respondents as were in the previous example are used. However, in this instance a comparison of the sample distribution on this variable with some known or presumed distribution in the population is made. Suppose it is known that the breakdown of political party preferences in the population was 30 percent Republican, 50 percent Democrat, and 20 percent Independent. The chi-square goodness of fit test can again be used to test the null hypothesis that the distribution of preferences is not different or has not changed from what it has been in the population. Here, the expected frequencies for each party are determined by multiplying N by the proportion appropriate to that category (e.g., expected frequency for Republicans is 579(.30) = 173.7, for Democrats is 579(.50) = 289.5, and for Independents is 579(.20) = 115.8).

	Rep.	Dem.	Ind.	Total
Observed	154	291	134	579
Expected	173.7	289.5	115.8	579

The value of chi-square is calculated as follows:

$$\chi^2 = \frac{(154 - 173.7)^2}{173.7} + \frac{(291 - 289.5)^2}{289.5} + \frac{(134 - 115.8)^2}{115.8} =$$

$$2.23 + .01 + 2.86 = 5.10$$

The critical value of chi-square at $\alpha = .01$, with $K - 1$ or 2 degrees of freedom, is 9.21. Because the obtained chi-square value is less than the critical value (5.10 < 9.21), the decision is: Fail to reject H_0. There is no significant difference between the distribution of political party preferences in the sample and what they are or have been in the population. The SPSS/PC+ commands to produce these results are:

Chi-Square Goodness of Fit Using SPSS/PC+

Instructions:

```
SPSS/PC:NONPAR TESTS CHISQUARE=POLPARTY (1,3) [Enter]
       :/EXPECTED=173.7,289.5,115.8 [Enter]
```

(Note: If expected frequencies are not specified, it is assumed that all expected frequencies are equal.)

Table 12.2 SPSS/PC+
Chi-square Test
POLPARTY Political Party Preference

	Category	Cases Observed	Expected	Residual
republican	1	154	173.70	-19.70
democratic	2	291	289.50	1.50
independent	3	134	115.80	18.20
	Total	579		

Chi-Square	D.F.	Significance
5.102	2	.078

MANN–WHITNEY U TEST

The Mann–Whitney U test is an alternative to or substitute for the t-test for two sample means. The U test examines the hypothesis that two independent samples come from populations with the same distribution. The U test is appropriate when variables are measured at the ordinal level. However, because assumptions about the nature or shape of the distribution are not required, it can also be used for interval data that are not normally distributed.

Example A random sample of six men and five women are surveyed and asked to rate the president's performance. The data below show their ratings (10 = strongly approve, 1 = strongly disapprove). Do men and women residents differ in their ratings of the president's performance?

	Ratings of President					
Men	8	7	6	9	10	4
Women	3	4	1	9	8	

To compute the Mann–Whitney U test, combine the ratings from both samples and rank the entire combined set of scores, giving the highest score a rank of 1. In cases of ties, give the average rank to those cases that are tied, and then obtain the sum of the ranks for each sample or group in the analysis.

Ratings		Ranking	
Men	Women	Men	Women
8	3	4.5	10
7	4	6	8.5
6	1	7	11
9	9	2.5	2.5
10	8	1	4.5
4		8.5	
		$\Sigma R_m = \overline{29.5}$	$\Sigma R_w = \overline{36.5}$
$N_1 = 6$	$N_2 = 5$		

Then, obtain an estimate of U and U':

$$U = N_1 N_2 + N_1(N_1 + 1)/2 - \Sigma R_1$$

$$U' = N_1 N_2 - U \quad \text{or} \quad N_1 N_2 + N_2(N_2 + 1)/2 - \Sigma R_2$$

For the data above:

$$U = 6(5) + 6(6 + 1)/2 - 29.5 = 21.5$$

$$U' = 6(5) - 21.5 = 30 - 21.5 = 9.5$$

or

$$U' = 6(5) + 5(5 + 1)/2 - 36.5 = 9.5$$

Take the *smaller* value of U or U' and use in the following Z-test to test the hypotheses:

H_0: There is no difference by sex, or the ratings of men = the ratings of women

H_1: There is a difference by sex, or the ratings of men ≠ the ratings of women

$$Z = \frac{U - \mu_U}{\sigma_U}$$

where U = the smaller value of U or U'

μ_U = the mean of U, calculated by $\mu_U = (N_1)(N_2)/2$

σ_U = the standard deviation of U, calculated by:
$$\sigma_U = \sqrt{N_1 N_2 (N_1 + N_2 + 1)/12}$$

For the data above:

$$\mu_U = (6)(5)/2 = 15$$

$$\sigma_U = \sqrt{(6)(5)(6 + 5 + 1)/12} = \sqrt{(30)(12)/12} = 5.477$$

$$Z = \frac{9.5 - 15}{5.477} = -1.19$$

The critical value of Z at $\alpha = .01$, for a two-tailed test, is ± 2.58 (see Section 11 and Table I, Appendix D). Because obtained Z is less than critical Z $(-1.19 < \pm 2.58)$, the decision is: Fail to reject H_0. Men and women do not differ in their ratings of the performance of the president.

Consider the following problem from the CPS data where the Mann–Whitney U test is appropriate. The question is: Do city residents differ from county residents in their ratings of the quality of medical facilities in the community?

H_0: There is no difference, or ratings of city residents = ratings of county residents

H_1: There is a difference, or ratings of city residents $\neq$ ratings of county residents

To obtain the SPSS/PC+ output, enter the following statement:

Mann–Whitney U Test Using SPSS/PC+

Instructions:

SPSS/PC: NONPAR TEST M—W=MEDICAL BY RESIDE (1,2). [Enter]

Table 12.3 SPSS/PC+

Mann–Whitney U – Wilcoxon Rank Sum W Test

MEDICAL   Quality of Medical Facilities
by RESIDE   Place of Residence

Mean Rank	Cases	
295.89	343	RESIDE = 1 Bowling Green
307.80	258	RESIDE = 2 Warren County
	601	Total

		Corrected for Ties	
U	W	Z	2-tailed P
42493.0	79412.0	−.8879	.3746

The results of the Mann–Whitney U test reveal an obtained Z-value of −.8879 and a two-tailed probability of .3746. Therefore, at the alpha level of .05 the decision is: Fail to reject H_0. There is no significant difference between city and county residents in their ratings of the quality of medical facilities. Although with a sample of 600 cases the Mann–Whitney U test would be difficult and tedious to do by hand or calculator, it can easily be done with a large number of cases on a computer.

WILCOXON MATCHED PAIRS/SIGNED RANKS TEST

The Wilcoxon signed ranks test is the nonparametric alternative to the *t*-test for matched pairs. This test examines both direction and amount of change between ranks in two situations. Here, the Wilcoxon test will be used to reanalyze the data in Section 11 that was previously used to illustrate the *t*-test for before/after or paired situations; results with this less powerful nonparametric test can be compared to the *t*-test analysis (see Section 11).

Example The scores of five randomly selected individuals before and after taking a course are presented below:

	A	B	C	D	E
Before	63	60	71	62	77
After	76	74	80	64	76

First, obtain the differences (be sure to record sign of difference) between the before and after situations. Second, rank the differences, assigning the rank of 1 to the largest difference, regardless of sign. Third, obtain the sum of ranks for the positive differences and the sum of ranks for the negative differences:

	Before	After	Difference	Ranks	Ranks Positive	Ranks Negative
A	63	76	+13	2	2	
B	60	74	+14	1	1	
C	71	80	+9	3	3	
D	62	64	+2	4	4	
E	77	76	−1	5		5
					$\Sigma R+ = 10$	$\Sigma R- = 5$

The null hypothesis is that there is no difference between the before and after scores, or H_0: After = Before. The alternative hypothesis is that scores have improved in the after situation, or H_1: After > Before.

Calculate the obtained value of Z, using the following formula:

$$Z = \frac{v - \mu_v}{\sigma_v}$$

where v = the smaller of ΣR^+ or ΣR^-

$$\mu_v = N(N + 1)/4$$

$$\sigma_v = \sqrt{N(N + 1)(2N + 1)/24}$$

For the data above:

$$v = 5$$

$$\mu_v = 5(5 + 1)/4 = 7.5$$

$$\sigma_v = \sqrt{5(5 + 1)[2(5) + 1]/24} = 3.71$$

$$Z = \frac{5 - 7.5}{3.71} = \frac{-2.5}{3.71} = -.67$$

The critical Z value for a one-tailed test at α = .05 is -1.65 (see Section 11 and Table I, Appendix D). Because obtained Z is less than critical Z ($-.67 < 1.65$), the decision is: Fail to reject H_0. There is not a significant improvement in scores after taking the course. (The t-test in Section 11 resulted in a similar decision.)

Because appropriate types of before/after data for this test are not included in the CPS, examples of computer output for this test are not included here. However, the instructions to run this procedure in SPSS/PC+ are as follows:

```
SPSS/PC+:NONPAR TESTS WILCOXON=VARLIST WITH VARLIST.
[Enter]
```

where Varlist means variable names.

KRUSKAL–WALLIS *H* TEST

The Kruskal–Wallis *H* test is a nonparametric one-way analysis of variance by ranks for ordinal data for three or more samples. Although this procedure is appropriate for ordinal data, it can also be used as an alternative to the one-way ANOVA procedure discussed in Section 11 when the assumption of a normal distribution or the equality of variances assumption cannot be met.

The null hypothesis, H_0, is that all samples come from the same or identical populations. The alternative hypothesis, H_1, is that at least one sample is from a population that is not the same as the other populations. When N is large (each sample size greater than 5), the distribution of H is approximated by the chi-square distribution, with degrees of freedom $= K - 1$ (see Section 4).

The calculation of H is as follows:

$$H = \frac{12}{N(N + 1)} \left[\Sigma \left(\frac{R_i^2}{n_i} \right) \right] - 3(N + 1)$$

where N = the total sample size

n_i = the size of each sample

R_i^2 = the sum of the ranks for each sample, squared

Example   Consider data from the one-way ANOVA in Section 11 where ACT scores of 17 students who prepared for the test under four different methods are compared. (N is purposely small here to illustrate the computational procedures. However, in actual practice sample sizes (n_i) should each be greater than five for the H distribution to be approximated by the chi-square distribution.)

Method 1	Method 2	Method 3	Method 4
32	23	27	26
33	32	34	17
36	20	31	30
34	19	22	
32	32		

The procedure is to obtain a combined ranking of all the values in all the samples, by assigning the rank of 1 to the largest value and by giving the average rank to the values or cases that are tied (see below):

Method 1		Method 2		Method 3		Method 4	
Score	Rank	Score	Rank	Score	Rank	Score	Rank
32	6.5	23	13	27	11	26	12
33	4	32	6.5	34	2.5	17	17
36	1	20	15	31	9	30	10
34	2.5	19	16	22	14		
32	6.5	32	6.5				
$R_1 = 20.5$		$R_2 = 57.0$		$R_3 = 36.5$		$R_4 = 39.0$	

Check that

$$\Sigma R_i = N(N + 1)/2$$

$$\Sigma R_i = 20.5 + 57.0 + 36.5 + 39.0 = 153.0$$

$$N(N + 1)/2 = 17(17 + 1)/2 = 153$$

Then, calculate H as follows:

$$H = \frac{12}{17(17 + 1)}\left[\frac{(20.5)^2}{5} + \frac{(57)^2}{5} + \frac{(36.5)^2}{4} + \frac{(39)^2}{3}\right] - 3(17 + 1)$$

$$= .039[84.05 + 649.8 + 333.06 + 507.0] - 3(18)$$

$$= .039(1573.91) - 54$$

$$= 61.38 - 54$$

$$= 7.38$$

The critical value of chi-square at $\alpha = .05$, with d.f. $= K - 1 = 3$, is 7.815 (see Section 4 and Table IV, Appendix D). Because the obtained value of H is less than the critical chi-square value ($7.38 < 7.815$), the decision is: Fail to reject H_0. There appears to be no difference among the scores obtained through the four different methods of preparing for the test. (The one-way ANOVA in Section 11 produced similar results.)

Consider the following example from the CPS dataset where the Kruskal–Wallis H test is appropriate. A researcher is interested in knowing whether members of the various political party preferences differ in their rating of the seriousness of crime in the community.

The null hypothesis, H_0, is that there are no differences among Republicans, Democrats, and Independents in the perception of the seriousness of crime, or that all three samples come from an identical population. The alternative hypothesis, H_1, is that at least one political party differs from the others in the rating of the seriousness of crime, or that at least one sample is from a population that is not the same as the other populations.

To obtain the SPSS/PC+ output, enter the following statement:

Kruskal–Wallis **H** *Test Using SPSS/PC+*

Instructions:

SPSS/PC: NONPAR TESTS K−W=CRIME BY POLPARTY (1,3),

where (1,3) refers to the first and last categories of POLPARTY.

Table 12.4 SPSS/PC+

$$\text{Kruskal-Wallis 1-way ANOVA}$$

| CRIME | Seriousness of Crime |
| by POLPARTY | Political Party Preference |

	Mean Rank	Cases	
	298.34	154	POLPARTY = 1 republican
	280.61	291	POLPARTY = 2 democratic
	300.80	134	POLPARTY = 3 independent
		579	Total

			Corrected for Ties	
CASES	Chi-Square	Significance	Chi-Square	Significance
579	1.8574	.3951	2.3895	.3028

The result of the Kruskal–Wallis H test reveals an obtained value of 1.8574 or 2.3895 (corrected for ties). The critical value of chi-square at $\alpha = .05$, with d.f. $= K - 1 = 2$, is 5.991 (see Table IV, Appendix D). Because the obtained value of H is less than the critical chi-square (2.39 < 5.99), the decision is: Fail to reject H_0. CPS respondents who are members of the three political parties do not appear to differ in their perception of the seriousness of crime as a community problem.

Nonparametric statistics are important and useful when analyzing nominal and ordinal variables and when assumptions cannot be made about the nature of the population distribution. Decisions on whether to use the nonparametric statistics covered here and in Section 4 or the parametric statistics covered in Sections 11 and 13 are based on the types of variables involved and nature of the distribution of the population being studied.

Exercise 12A:
Spearman's Rank Order Correlation

Eight individuals gave the following ratings to the quality of the newspaper and the quality of cultural facilities (ratings of $1 = A, 2 = B, 3 = C, 4 = D, 5 = F$). Calculate Spearman's rank order correlation coefficient (r_s) for these data and discuss your result.

		Newspaper				Cultural Facilities	D	D^2
5	1	2	1.5	3		5	-1.5	2.25
1	1	2	1.5	3		2	-1.5	2.25
2	2	1	2	1		1	1	1
3	3	3	4.5	3		3	1.5	2.25
3	3	4	4.5	6		4	1.5	2.25
4	4	4	4	6		4	-2	4
5	5	5	7.5	7.5		5	0	
1	5	5	7.5	7.5		2	0	

Calculation:

					D	R
1	2	3	1.5	2.5	-1	
1	2	2	1.5	2.5	-1	
2	1	1	3	1	2	
3	3	4	4.5	4	.5	
3	4	5	4.5	5.5	-1	
6	4	4	6	5.5	.5	
7	5	5	7.5	7.5	0	
8	5	5	7.5	7.5	0	

$$r_s = 1 - \left[\frac{6\,(45)}{8\,(8^2 - 1)}\right]$$

Discussion:

$$= 1 - \frac{45}{8\,(63)} = 1 - \frac{6}{.91}$$

$$= .91$$

Exercise 12B:
Spearman's Rank Order Correlation

Five individuals made the following scores on two tests. Assume these data are not normally distributed. Calculate the Spearman's rank order correlation coefficient (r_s) for these data and discuss the result. (The same data are used in Exercise 13A to illustrate the parametric counterpart, Pearson's correlation coefficient, r.)

Test X	Test Y
10	3
20	15
30	17
2	5
25	4

Calculation:

X	Rank	Y	Rank	D	D²
2	5	1	3	3	-2	4
10	3	2	1	1	1
20	15	3	4	-1	1
25	4	4	2	2	4
30	17	5	5	0	0

$$r_s = 1 - \left[\frac{6 \Sigma D^2}{N(N^2-1)} \right] = 1 - \frac{6(10)}{5(25-1)} = \boxed{.5}$$

Discussion:

r_s indicates a positive linear association between the the test scores distribution of the two test scores

Exercise 12C:
Chi-Square Goodness of Fit Tests

a. Eighty students were randomly sampled and asked to indicate their choice among four major areas of study. Calculate the chi-square test for the data below to determine whether there is any preference at the .05 level of significance.

Major Area:	Science	Humanities	Education	Business
Choice:	20	17	15	28

H_0:

H_1:

Calculation:

Critical chi-square =

Decision:

b. Nationally, the breakdown of those favoring, opposing, or answering "don't know" about the issue of mandatory employee drug testing is: 35 percent favor, 40 percent oppose, and 25 percent don't know. Are the following results from CPS respondents similar to or different from the national breakdown? Use the chi-square test at the .01 level of significance.

	Favor	Oppose	Don't Know	Total
CPS respondents:	289	226	88	603

H_0:

H_1:

Calculation:

Critical chi-square =

Decision:

Exercise 12D:
Computer Applications

CPS respondents were asked to indicate their highest level of education. Data were grouped into the following categories: 1 = Not HS Grad, 2 = HS Grad/GED, 3 = Some Coll/Trade, and 4 = Coll Grad +. Conduct the nonparametric chi-square goodness of fit test on the variable DIPLOMA to determine at the .05 level of significance whether or not respondents are equally likely to be in each of the four educational categories. Attach your computer printout to the discussion on this sheet.

H_0:

H_1:

Obtained value of chi-square =

Critical value of chi-square =

d.f. =

α =

Decision:

Discussion:

Exercise 12E:
Mann–Whitney U Test

    A researcher obtained the following results from random samples of 11 white and 9 black respondents concerning their levels of education. Assuming that the data are not normally distributed, use the Mann–Whitney U test to determine whether there is a significant difference between whites and blacks at the .05 level. (Show all work, including calculations of ΣR_W, ΣR_B, estimates of U and U', μ_U and σ_U.)

					# Years of School						
White:	5	12	12	7	6	14	18	18	12	7	6
Black:	12	8	7	12	22	12	14	14	16		

H_0:

H_1:

Calculation:

Critical Z =

Decision:

Exercise 12F:
Computer Applications

In the CPS men and women were asked to give a grade to the quality of shopping facilities in the community. Use the nonparametric Mann–Whitney U test procedure to determine if men and women differ in their ratings of the quality of shopping facilities at the .05 level. Use "SELECT IF (SHOPPING LT 6)." to include only those who gave a grade to shopping. Attach your computer printout to the discussion on this sheet.

H_0:

H_1:

Obtained value of Z =

Critical value of Z =

α =

Decision:

Discussion:

Exercise 12G:
Wilcoxon Matched Pairs/Signed Ranks Test

A random sample of eight students participate in two reading programs. Their scores on a 50 item quiz are presented below. Use the Wilcoxon signed ranks test to determine if the students' scores are significantly higher at the .01 level of significance with the new program. (Show work, including $\Sigma R+$, $\Sigma R-$, v, μ_v, and σ_v.)

	1	2	3	4	5	6	7	8
New Program	24	18	36	30	25	17	50	30
Old Program	26	12	33	28	24	18	42	28

Calculation:

Obtained value of $Z =$

Critical value of $Z =$

Decision:

Discussion:

Exercise 12H:
Kruskal–Wallis H Test

A study assessing attitudes toward welfare was conducted on three samples of 10 respondents each. Group 1 is a middle-class sample, Group 2 is a sample of welfare clients, and Group 3 is an upper-class sample. The higher the score (on a scale of 1 to 10), the more favorable the attitude toward welfare. Use the Kruskal–Wallis H test to determine at the .05 level of significance whether the groups are similar or different in their attitudes toward welfare.

	Scores for Individuals in Each Group									
Group 1:	4	5	4	3	6	10	1	8	5	5
Group 2:	10	8	10	5	7	9	10	9	4	8
Group 3:	1	3	4	6	8	5	3	2	2	4

H_0:

H_1:

Calculation:

Obtained value of H =

Critical value of chi-square =

d.f. =

α =

Decision:

Discussion:

Exercise 121:
Computer Applications

CPS respondents of various educational levels were asked to rate the quality of the city schools on a scale of A = 1 to F = 5. Conduct the nonparametric Kruskal–Wallis one-way analysis of variance H test to determine at the .05 level if there are any differences among the four educational groups on the perception of the quality of the city schools. Use "SELECT IF (BGSCHOOL LT 6)." to eliminate DK responses. Attach your computer printout to the discussion on this sheet.

H_0:

H_1:

Obtained value of H =

Critical value of chi-square (corrected) =

d.f. =

α =

Decision:

Discussion:

13

Bivariate Association for Interval/Ratio–Level Variables

The questions of whether a relationship exists between two interval/ratio–level variables, how strong the association is, what the direction of the association is, and how good a predictor one variable is of the other, are the concerns of linear regression and correlation. The procedures of linear regression and correlation are interrelated and complement each other.

LINEAR REGRESSION

In a simple linear regression analysis, the best-fitting straight line that summarizes the linear relationship between values of individuals or things on two interval/ratio–level variables is obtained. Using the "least squares method," which minimizes the distance to all pairs of X, Y values, the line summarizes the relationship between a dependent variable, Y, and an independent variable, X. The equation for the best-fitting line then can be used to predict values of Y given particular values of X. The formula for the regression lines is:

Formula *Regression Line*

$$Y' = a + bX$$

where Y' = the predicted or estimated value of Y
 a = the Y intercept (the point where the line crosses the Y-axis on a scattergram, graphically depicting the values of X and Y)
 b = the slope (rise/run) of the line
 X = a value of the X variable

Scattergrams

As a first step in determining the nature of the relationship between the two variables, it is often helpful to construct a scatter diagram or *scattergram*, which graphically portrays the paired values of the two variables for each individual or case. Values of the X (independent) variable are placed on the horizontal axis, and values of the Y (dependent) variable on the vertical axis. Data points indicating the position of the paired X, Y values for each individual are then plotted on the graph. The pattern of the dots, or their "scatter," provides a good visual display of what the relationship is like.

Pearson's Correlation Coefficient

Pearson's correlation coefficient (r) is a measure of association that indicates the strength and direction of the relationship between interval/ratio–level variables X and Y on a scale of −1 to +1. When the value of r is positive, then the relationship between X and Y is a positive one—as values of one variable increase, values of the other variable generally increase. The magnitude of the value of r indicates the strength of the association (e.g., r = .20 indicates a somewhat weak, positive association, and r = .80 indicates a strong, positive association). If r = +1, the relationship between X and Y is positive and perfect—all data points when plotted on a scattergram fall on the positively sloping regression line, which runs upward from left to right. When the value of r is negative, then the relationship between X and Y is a negative one—as values of one variable increase, values of the other variable generally decrease. Again, the magnitude of r indicates the strength of the association (e.g., r = −.80 indicates a strong, negative association). A value of r = −1

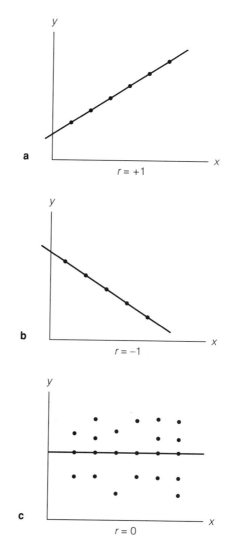

Figure 13.1 Regression lines showing (a) positive, (b) negative, and (c) no correlation

indicates a perfect, negative association—all data points when plotted on a scattergram fall on the negatively sloping regression line, which runs downward from left to right. When r = 0, there is no correlation, or linear relationship, between X and Y—the regression line runs horizontally and data points are scattered above and below it. Figure 13.1 depicts several types of correlation and regression lines on a scattergram.

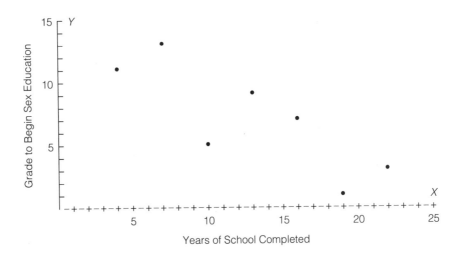

Figure 13.2 Scattergram of number of years of school completed (X) and suggested grade at which sex education should begin (Y)

Coefficient of Determination

The correlation coefficient squared (r^2), known as the *coefficient of determination*, indicates what proportion of the variation in Y is accounted for or explained by the variation in X, or how good a predictor X is of Y when the regression line is used. For example, if the correlation between X and Y is = .80, then $r^2 = (.80)^2 = .64$. This means that .64, or 64 percent, of the variability in Y is explained by the variability in X (the remaining 36 percent of the variability remains unexplained by X). Another way to interpret r^2 is to view it as the proportion of, or percent fewer, errors that are made by using X to predict Y in the regression line, as compared to making a prediction about Y when X is not used. The higher the value of r^2, the better X is as a predictor of Y.

Example Consider the following hypothetical data for seven individuals regarding years of education they have completed and the grade in school at which they think sex education should begin:

	A	B	C	D	E	F	G
X (Years of Education)	7	4	13	16	10	22	19
Y (Grade to Begin Sex Education)	13	11	9	7	5	3	1

Figure 13.2 shows that a negative association exists between respondents' years of education and grade at which they think sex education should begin. The pattern to the dots runs downward from left to right, meaning smaller values of X are paired with larger values of Y.

REGRESSION ANALYSIS

The values of the slope (b) and the Y intercept (a) must be calculated using the following formulas so that the regression line ($Y' = a + bX$) can be obtained and drawn on the scattergram, if desired.

Formulas   *Slope*

$$b = \frac{N\Sigma XY - (\Sigma X)(\Sigma Y)}{N\Sigma X^2 - (\Sigma X)^2}$$

where X = the value of the X variable for each case

Y = the corresponding value of the Y variable for each case

N = the number of cases

Y-Intercept

$$a = \overline{Y} - b(\overline{X})$$

where $\overline{Y}$ = the mean of the Y variable

$\overline{X}$ = the mean of the X variable

b = the slope

First, calculate the value of b; then use that value to obtain a. For the data in the example above, the following information is needed:

X	Y	XY	X²	Y²
7	13	91	49	169
4	11	44	16	121
13	9	117	169	81
16	7	112	256	49
10	5	50	100	25
22	3	66	484	9
19	1	19	361	1
$\Sigma X = 91$	$\Sigma Y = 49$	$\Sigma XY = 499$	$\Sigma X^2 = 1{,}435$	$\Sigma Y^2 = 455$

$$\bar{Y} = \frac{49}{7} = 7.0$$

$$\bar{X} = \frac{91}{7} = 13.0$$

$$S_X = 6.0$$

$$S_Y = 4.0$$

Slope

$$b = \frac{7(499) - (91)(49)}{7(1{,}435) - (91)^2}$$

$$= \frac{3{,}493 - 4{,}459}{10{,}045 - 8{,}281}$$

$$= \frac{-966}{1{,}764}$$

$$= -.547619$$

Y Intercept

$$a = 7.0 - (-.547619)(13)$$

$$= 7 + 7.119$$

$$= 14.119$$

The regression line then can be constructed as follows:

$$Y' = 14.119 - .547619(X)$$

As Figure 13.3 shows, the line intersects the Y axis slightly above the value of 14. And, for each unit of increase in X, there is slightly more than one-half a unit of decrease in Y.

CORRELATION ANALYSIS AND PREDICTION

Pearson's correlation coefficient (r) is calculated as follows:

Formula   *Pearson's Correlation Coefficient*

$$r = \frac{N\Sigma XY - (\Sigma X)(\Sigma Y)}{\sqrt{[N\Sigma X^2 - (\Sigma X)^2][N\Sigma Y^2 - (\Sigma Y)^2]}}$$

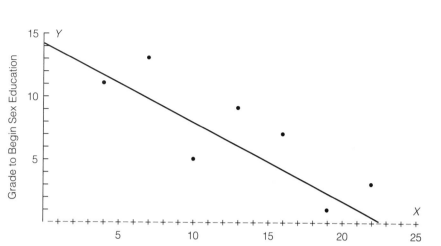

Figure 13.3 Scattergram of number of years of school completed (X) and suggested grade at which sex education should begin (Y), with regression line added

Using the information from the example on years of education and grade to begin sex education, we can calculate the following:

$$r = \frac{7(499) - (91)(49)}{\sqrt{[7(1,435) - (91)^2][7(455) - (49)^2]}} = \frac{-966}{\sqrt{(1,764)(784)}} = \frac{-966}{1,176} = -.8214$$

There is a strong negative association between the two variables: The more years of education respondents have, the earlier the grade at which they think sex education should begin.

The coefficient of determination, $r^2 = (-.8214)^2 = .67$, indicates that 67 percent of the variation in grade at which to begin sex education is explained by or accounted for by years of education completed (the remaining roughly one-third of the variability remains unexplained by years of education completed). The r^2 value of .6747 can also be interpreted as meaning that 67 percent fewer errors will be made using X in the regression equation to predict Y than would be made if X were ignored and $\overline{Y}$ were used to predict all the values of Y.

As a check on the calculations of r and b (slope of the regression line), the following formulas can be used. They will produce results that are identical to the formulas previously discussed. These formulas are somewhat easier to use but require that the means and standard deviations of X and Y be already available or else be calculated.

Formulas   *Pearson's Correlation Coefficient*   *Slope*

$$r = \frac{\dfrac{\Sigma XY}{N} - (\overline{X})(\overline{Y})}{(S_X)(S_Y)} \qquad\qquad b = r\frac{(S_Y)}{(S_X)}$$

Therefore,

$$r = \frac{\dfrac{499}{7} - (13)(7)}{(6)(4)} \qquad\qquad b = -.8214\frac{(4)}{(6)}$$

$$= -.8214 \qquad\qquad\qquad\qquad\quad = -.5476$$

TEST OF SIGNIFICANCE FOR *r*

There is also a *t*-test of significance to determine if the value of r, obtained from sample data, is greater than zero. The null and alternative hypotheses are:

$$H_0: r = 0$$

$$H_1: r > 1 \text{ (if r is positive)}$$

or

$$H_1: r < 1 \text{ (if r is negative)}$$

Note that H_1 is always a one-tailed alternative hypothesis (see Section 11). The *t*-test is calculated as follows:

Formula   *t-Test of Significance for* r

$$t = r\sqrt{\frac{N - 2}{1 - r^2}}$$

where r = Pearson's r

r^2 = the coefficient of determination

N = the sample size

The critical t has $N - 2$ degrees of freedom. The critical value of t at α = .05, for d.f. = 5, is -2.015, and at α = .01 is -3.365 (see Table II, Appendix D). Based on the figures obtained above:

$$t = -.8214 \sqrt{\frac{7 - 2}{1 - (-.8214)^2}} = -.8214 \sqrt{\frac{5}{.3253}} = -3.22$$

Using the hypothesis testing procedure discussed in Section 11, the decision would be as follows:

1. At the α = .05 level: Reject H_0. The obtained t of -3.22 is greater than the critical t of -2.015.

2. At the α = .01 level: Fail to reject H_0. The obtained value of -3.22 is less than the critical value of -3.365.

As can be seen above, even strong correlations may not be statistically significant when sample sizes are small. It should also be noted, however, that when sample sizes are large, even weak correlations will be statistically significant. There is an important distinction that must be made between a statistically significant result and a meaningful or important result. Just because a relationship between two variables is statistically significant does not mean it is an important or meaningful relationship. With large samples weak associations can be and often are statistically significant. Conversely, with small samples strong associations often may turn out not to be statistically significant.

Also, note that a correlation coefficient will have a low value if a relationship between X and Y exists but is not a linear one (e.g., some other type of curve or something other than a straight line). In situations of nonlinear relationships, correlation and linear regression are inappropriate and should not be used to describe such relationships. A scattergram is often helpful in detecting such nonlinear patterns.

PREDICTION AND ERROR

The regression line can be used to predict a value of Y, given a particular value of X. If one had no knowledge of the values of X and how they related to Y, then the best prediction or guess about any value of Y, knowing only the distribution of Y, would be $\overline{Y}$, the mean of Y. However, if there is an association between two variables (X and Y), then regression analysis allows better predictions of values of Y, given certain values of X. In the sex education example, if we know only the distribution of Y, grade to begin sex education, the prediction about a single value of Y would be 7.0, the mean of Y. However, using the regression line yields the following better estimates, or predictions, of Y:

$$\text{If } X = 6, Y' = 14.12 - .548(6) = 10.83.$$

For persons whose educational attainment was 6 years, the estimate or prediction of grade at which to begin sex education would be 10.83, or the eleventh grade:

$$\text{If } X = 12, Y' = 14.12 - .548(12) = 7.54.$$

For persons whose educational attainment was 12 years, the estimate or prediction of grade at which to begin sex education would be 7.54, or between the seventh and eighth grade.

How good a predictor or estimate X is of Y can be determined by the *error variance* and *standard error of the estimate*, measures that indicate how much the actual Y values differ from the regression line. The error variance of the best-fitting straight line, or the variance of the estimate, is calculated as follows:

Formula *Error Variance*

$$S^2_{Y \cdot X} = \frac{\Sigma (Y - Y')^2}{N - 2}$$

where $S^2_{Y \cdot X}$ = the variance of the estimate of Y for different values of X

$\Sigma(Y - Y')^2$ = the predicted values of Y subtracted from actual values of Y, squared, and summed

It is easier, however, to work with the following computational formula:

Formula *Error Variance*

$$S^2_{Y \cdot X} = S^2_Y - r^2(S^2_Y)$$

where r^2 = the correlation coefficient squared, or the coefficient of determination

S^2_Y = the variance of Y

Actually, to produce an unbiased estimate of $\sigma^2_{Y \cdot X}$, $N - 2$ should be used in the denominator of the variance formula instead of $N - 1$. When N is large, differences in results when using $N - 1$ instead of $N - 2$ will be inconsequential, however.

Here, we will use $N - 2$ and calculations from the previous seven-case example:

$$S^2_Y = \frac{\Sigma Y^2 - \dfrac{(\Sigma Y)^2}{N}}{N - 2} = \frac{455 - \dfrac{(49)^2}{7}}{5} = 22.4$$

The actual value of the sample variance using $N - 1$ is $S^2_Y = 18.67$.

$$S^2_{Y \cdot X} = 22.4 - (.8214)^2(22.4) = 7.2867$$

If the correlation is $+1$ or -1, then the error variance $= 0$. If the correlation is 0, then the error variance equals the variance of Y: $S^2_{Y \cdot X} = S^2_Y$. The stronger the correlation, the better X is as a predictor or estimator of Y, and the smaller the error variance will be.

The square root of the variance of the estimate is the *standard error of the estimate* $(S_{Y \cdot X})$:

$$S_{Y \cdot X} = \sqrt{S^2_{Y \cdot X}} = \sqrt{7.2867} = 2.699$$

Below are examples of the printed output of the regression and correlation analysis of Years of School Completed (GRADE) and Grade to Begin Sex Education (GRADESEX) from the CPS dataset.

Regression and Correlation Analysis Using SPSS/PC+

Instructions:

```
SPSS/PC:SET PRINTER=ON. [Enter]
        :GET FILE='SPSSCPS'. [Enter]
        :SELECT IF (GRADESEX LT 99). [Enter]
        :SELECT IF (GRADE LT 99). [Enter]
        :REGRESSION VARIABLES=GRADESEX,GRADE [Enter]
        :/DEPENDENT=GRADESEX [Enter]
        :/METHOD=ENTER GRADE [Enter]
        :/DESCRIPTIVES=ALL. [Enter]
```

Table 13.1   SPSS/PC+

....

```
                 ****MULTIPLE REGRESSION****
Listwise Deletion of Missing Data

              Mean     Std Dev   Variance    Label
GRADESEX      5.183    2.335     5.451       Grade to Begin Sex Education
GRADE        13.371    3.028     9.171       Years of School Completed

N of Cases = 447

Correlation, Covariance, 1-tailed Sig, Cross-Product:

              GRADESEX        GRADE
GRADESEX       1.000         -.180
               5.451         -1.275
                .999          .000
            2430.957       -568.452
GRADE          -.180         1.000
              -1.275         9.171
                .000          .999
            -568.452      4090.353

   Equation Number 1  Dependent Variable..  GRADESEX   Grade to Begin Sex
                                                        Education
```

Continued

Table 13.1 *Continued*

```
Beginning Block Number 1. Method: Enter   GRADE

Variable(s) Entered on Step Number
   1..  GRADE  Years of School Completed

Multiple R          .18027
R Square            .03250
Adjusted R Square   .03032
Standard Error      2.29898

Analysis of Variance
              DF     Sum of Squares    Mean Square
Regression     1        78.99991        78.99991
Residual     445      2351.95758         5.28530

F = 14.94711    Signif F = .0001

Equation Number 1   Dependent Variable..   GRADESEX   Grade to Begin Sex
                                                       Education

....................................... Variables in the Equation ...........................................

Variable           B        SE B       Beta         T       Sig T
GRADE         -.13897      .03595    -.18027     -3.866     .0001
(Constant)    7.04171      .49280                14.289     .0000

End Block Number   1   All requested variables entered.
```

Regression and Correlation Analysis Using STATPAC

Instructions:

- Follow steps 1–10 in Appendix C
- Analysis Type #5, Correlation and Regression
- X variable = #79 "Grade"
- Y variable = #23 "Gradesex"
- Options: #3 Select if Variable #79 less than value of 99 and Variable #23 less than value of 99, none.
- Select #6, End task and write to disk
- Execute now and start with Task 1

Table 13.2 STATPAC

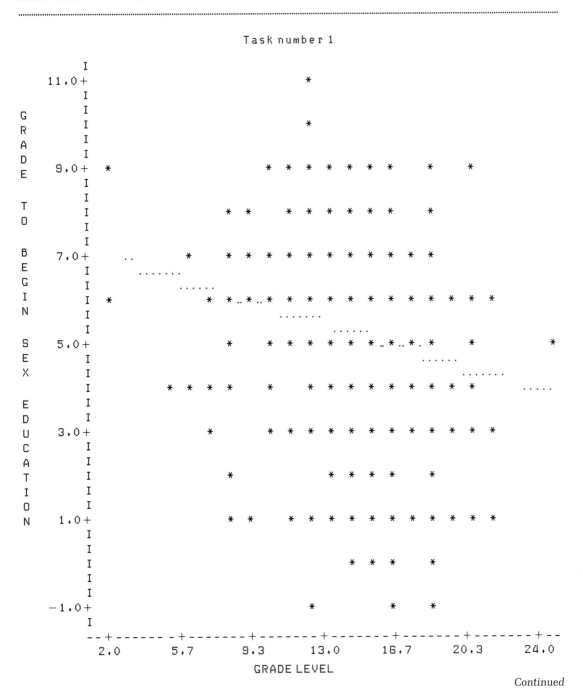

Task number 1

Continued

Table 13.2 *Continued*

```
Mean of X=13.37     Correlation Coefficient  =-0.180      Valid cases     = 447
S.D. of X=3.03      Degrees of freedom       =  445       Missing cases  = 126
Mean of Y=5.18      Slope of regression line =-0.139      Responses %     = 78
S.D. of Y=2.33      Y intercept              =  7.042

Regression equation: Y' = -0.139 X + 7.042
Standard error of estimate for regression = 2.294
t statistic for correlation coefficient   = 3.866
Significance of correlation coefficient   = 0.000
```

The relationship between Years of School Completed (X) and Grade at Which to Begin Sex Education (Y) for respondents in the CPS is a weak one. In both Table 13.1 and Table 13.2, it can be seen that the correlation is $-.18$, which indicates a weak, negative association between the two variables. The coefficient of determination is .03, indicating that only 3 percent of the variation in GRADESEX is explained by GRADE (97 percent remains unexplained by GRADE). Obviously, GRADE is not a very good predictor of GRADESEX, and using the regression equation, $Y' = 7.04 - .139X$, would not be much better than using $\bar{Y}$ (5.18). Note that the standard error of the estimate, $S_{Y \cdot X} = 2.29$, is only slightly lower than the standard deviation of GRADESEX, $S_Y = 2.33$. Therefore, there is very little improvement in using X to predict Y over not using it.

Despite having very little predictive ability, the t-test reveals that the correlation of $-.18$ is statistically significant. The obtained t-value $= -3.866$, $p < .01$ (the critical t at $\alpha = .01$, d.f. $= 445$, is -2.33; see Table II, Appendix D). Here is an instance of a weak and not very important or helpful association that is nonetheless statistically significant. Before dismissing educational attainment as a predictor, however, subsequent research might assess its combined effect along with other predictors in a multiple regression analysis (see Section 15).

A great deal of information about relationships between interval/ratio–level variables is obtained in regression and correlation analyses. The regression line summarizes the relationship between X and Y and can be used to estimate values of Y, given values of X. The standard error of the estimate indicates how good a predictor X is. The correlation coefficient describes the strength and direction of the relationship. The coefficient of determination indicates how much of the variation in Y is explained by X. And the t-test is used to determine if there is a statistically significant relationship, whether it be strong or weak, between the two variables.

Bivariate linear regression is an important first step in improving understanding and in making predictions. However, single-factor predictions have limited usefulness because usually more than one factor is involved in bringing about social phenomena (see the discussion of multiple causality in Section 14). Before final judgments are made about a predictor's worth, the predictor may be combined with other independent variables in a multiple regression analysis (see Section 15). Single and multiple regression procedures together may help provide a better picture of how independent variables predict outcomes. The goals of multivariate analyses for interval/ratio–level variables are similar to those in the process of elaboration in which additional variables are introduced to illuminate bivariate relationships between nominal and ordinal variables (see Section 14).

Exercise 13A:
Regression and Correlation

Five individuals scored as shown below on two tests. Based on that data, calculate and answer the following. Attach a sheet showing all work.

Test X:	10	20	30	2	25
Test Y:	3	15	17	5	4

1. The prediction formula for Y' (the best-fitting regression line).

   slope $b =$

   Y intercept $a =$

   $Y' =$

2. Using the regression line equation, predict Y' for $X = 16$.
3. What is the error variance of the estimate $(S^2_{Y \cdot X})$?
4. What is the standard error of the estimate $(S_{Y \cdot X})$?
5. What is the Pearson correlation coefficient (r)?
6. What is the coefficient of determination (r^2)?
7. Explain what the value of r^2 indicates.
8. Test to determine whether the correlation coefficient is significant at the .05 level.

   Hypotheses: H_0:

   H_1:

   critical t, $\alpha = .05$, d.f. = _____ is _____

   obtained $t =$

   Decision:

9. Discuss the nature of the relationship between X and Y.

Exercise 13B:
Regression and Correlation

The chart below shows how many hours per week seven students spend playing frisbee and what their grade point averages are. Based on the data shown, calculate and answer the following. Attach a sheet showing all work.

X (Hours Playing Frisbee):	2	8	10	12	16	6	4
Y (GPA):	3.50	2.50	2.25	1.75	.50	3.00	3.25

1. The prediction formula for Y' (the best-fitting regression line).

   slope $b =$

   Y intercept $a =$

   $Y' =$

2. Using the regression line equation, predict Y' for $X = 5$. Also, predict Y' for $X = 15$.

3. What is the error variance of the estimate $(S_{Y \cdot X}^2)$?

4. What is the standard error of the estimate $(S_{Y \cdot X})$?

5. What is the Pearson correlation coefficient (r)?

6. What is the coefficient of determination (r^2)?

7. Explain what the value of r^2 indicates.

8. Test to determine whether the correlation coefficient is significant at the .05 level.

   Hypotheses: H_0:

   H_1:

   critical t, $\alpha = .05$, d.f. = _____ is _____

   obtained $t =$

   Decision:

9. Discuss the nature of the relationship between X and Y.

Exercise 13C:
Computer Applications

Use SPSS/PC+ or STATPAC to obtain the regression and correlation statistics for (X) Years of School Completed (#79, GRADE) and (Y) Grade to Begin Drug Education (#25, GRADEDR). Select if both variables are less than 99. From your output, record and answer the following. Attach a copy of your output to this report.

1. The prediction formula for Y' (the best-fitting regression line).

   slope b =

   Y intercept a =

   Y' =

2. Using the regression line equation, predict Y' for $X = 10$. Also, predict Y' for $X = 16$.

3. What is the error variance of the estimate $(S^2_{Y \cdot X})$?

4. What is the standard error of the estimate $(S_{Y \cdot X})$?

5. What is the Pearson correlation coefficient (r)?

6. What is the coefficient of determination (r^2)?

7. Explain what the value of r^2 indicates.

8. Test to determine whether the correlation coefficient is significant at the .05 level.

   Hypotheses: H_0:

               H_1:

   critical t, α = .05, d.f. = _____ is _____

   obtained t =

   Decision:

9. Discuss the nature of the relationship between X and Y.

Exercise 13D:
Computer Applications

Use SPSS/PC+ or STATPAC to obtain the regression and correlation statistics for (X) Number of People Under 18 in the Household (#78, UNDER18) and (Y) Grade to Begin Sex Education or Drug Education (#23, GRADESEX or #25, GRADEDR). From your output, record and answer the following. Attach a copy of your output to this report.

1. The prediction formula for Y' (the best-fitting regression line).

   slope b =

   Y intercept a =

   Y' =

2. Using the regression line equation, predict Y' for $X = 1$. Also, predict Y' for $X = 3$.

3. What is the error variance of the estimate $(S^2_{Y \cdot X})$?

4. What is the standard error of the estimate $(S_{Y \cdot X})$?

5. What is the Pearson correlation coefficient (r)?

6. What is the coefficient of determination (r^2)?

7. Explain what the value of r^2 indicates.

8. Test to determine whether the correlation coefficient is significant at the .05 level.

   Hypotheses: H_0:

                 H_1:

   critical t, $\alpha = .05$, d.f. = _____ is _____

   obtained t =

   Decision:

9. Discuss the nature of the relationship between X and Y.

Exercise 13E:
Computer Applications

Use SPSS/PC+ or STATPAC to obtain the regression and correlation statistics for (X) Age (#75, AGE) and (Y) Years of School Completed (#79, GRADE). For the AGE variable, select if to include only those who are 25 and over and less than 65 years old. For GRADE, select if less than 99. From your output, record and answer the following. Attach a copy of your output to this report.

1. The prediction formula for Y' (the best-fitting regression line).

   slope $b =$

   Y intercept $a =$

   $Y' =$

2. Using the regression line equation, predict Y' for $X = 30$. Also, predict Y' for $X = 50$.

3. What is the error variance of the estimate ($S_{Y \cdot X}^2$)?

4. What is the standard error of the estimate ($S_{Y \cdot X}$)?

5. What is the Pearson correlation coefficient (r)?

6. What is the coefficient of determination (r^2)?

7. Explain what the value of r^2 indicates.

8. Test to determine whether the correlation coefficient is significant at the .05 level.

   Hypotheses: H_0:

                H_1:

   critical t, $\alpha = .05$, d.f. = _____ is _____

   obtained $t =$

   Decision:

9. Discuss the nature of the relationship between X and Y.

14

Elaboration of Bivariate Tables

A deterministic cause and effect model of human behavior guides the search for explanations in most social science research. *Determinism* assumes that social phenomena and observed differences between people or other units of analysis have causes, and that the factors or variables that are responsible for or account for such differences can be discovered.

CAUSE AND EFFECT

The variable whose variation results from something else is called the effect or *dependent variable*. A variable whose variation causes change in something else is called the cause or *independent variable*. Determinism means that the variation in the dependent variable is caused by variation in one or more independent variables (see Section 5). Most social research obtains evidence to test expected patterns of covariation between an independent or independent variables and a dependent variable (see Section 1). An *hypothesis* is the pattern or direction of covariation expected between an independent and a dependent variable. For example, it might be hypothesized that increased profit sharing among employees will increase firms' productivity, or that people's level of education will be positively related to their earned income (see Section 5).

Determinism does not necessitate a search for all the causes of the variation in something or for a complete understanding. There are many

395

Table 14.1 Earned Income by Level of Education (Hypothetical Data)

| | Level of Education | | |
Income	Some College or Less	College or More	Total
$30,000 or More	00.0	100.0	50.0
Less than $30,000	100.0	00.0	50.0
	100.0	100.0	100.0
	(N = 100)	(N = 100)	(N = 200)

chi-square = 200.00
p < .01, d.f. = 1
gamma = +1.00

causes of increased productivity or higher income. However, social researchers are interested in the most important causes; this search for the smallest number of the most important causes is called *parsimony*. Research has shown, for example, that level of education, years of experience, geographical mobility, and work performance are all important influences on earned income. Researchers know that complex phenomena in the social world are unlikely to have only one cause. In fact, single-cause explanations in social research are usually labeled *reductionistic*, and an explanation that involves only one cause may misrepresent or oversimplify complex reality. Instead, researchers contend that multiple causality, where several important causes work together to influence differences, operates.

Sufficient and Necessary Causes

Multiple causality means that no single cause will explain all the observed differences in a dependent variable. If one cause did explain all the variation in something, it would be both a necessary and a sufficient cause. A *sufficient cause* is one that always leads to something happening. If higher education level were a sufficient cause of higher earned income, all persons with more education would earn higher income. A *necessary cause* is one that must be present for something to result. If higher education level were a necessary cause of higher income, no persons with less education would earn higher income. If education were both a necessary and a sufficient cause, the influence of education on income would yield the results shown in Table 14.1.

Table 14.2 Total 1986 Family Income by Level of Education: Employed CPS Respondents Only

Total 1986 Family Income	Level of Education		Row Total
	Some College or Less	College Grad or More	
$30,000 or More	32.9	64.2	42.6
Less than $30,000	67.1	35.8	57.4
	100.0	100.0	100.0
	(N = 234)	(N = 106)	(N = 340)

chi-square (corrected) = 27.85
p < .01, d.f. = 1
gamma = + .57

The hypothetical results in Table 14.1 indicate that higher education level is a necessary cause of higher income. There are no instances in which people having less education earn higher income—the less education/higher-income cell is empty. The hypothetical results in Table 14.1 also indicate that higher education level is a sufficient cause of earning higher income. In all the cases of more education people earn higher income—the more education/lower-income cell is empty. The complete pairing of more education/higher income and less education/ lower income illustrates what a necessary and sufficient cause would be: one that is *perfectly* associated with differences in a dependent variable.

This ideal situation is never found in the real world. Among employed CPS respondents, for example, the relationship between education and family income, shown in Table 14.2, differs considerably from the perfect relationship in Table 14.1. Results reported in Table 14.2 show that a much larger percentage of employed people with a college degree or more education (64.2 percent) than employed people with less education (32.9 percent) have family incomes of $30,000 or more. Among employed people the relationship between level of education and family income is statistically significant at the .01 level (chi-square corrected = 27.85, p < .01, d.f. = 1). There is a moderate, positive relationship between level of education and family income among employed people (gamma = +.57). Level of education has substantial influence on family income.

However, higher education level is neither a sufficient nor a necessary cause of higher family income among employed people in the CPS.

Having a college degree or more education is not a sufficient cause of higher family income because 35.8 percent of employed people with more education have family incomes less than $30,000. Higher education level is also not a necessary cause of higher income because 32.9 percent of the employed people with less than a college degree have family incomes over $30,000. The example illustrates the idea that important causes found in social research are not perfect or complete causes.

Nomothetic or Probabilistic Explanations

Level of education in the previous example illustrates the type of cause that would be included, along with other important causes, in a nomothetic explanation of income differences. A *nomothetic* or *probabilistic explanation* is an explanation involving causes that explain most but not all the differences observed in a dependent variable. The strength of a nomothetic or probabilistic explanation lies in the fact that it works most of the time, not that it works every time. Social researchers do not expect, and never find, complete explanations.

CRITERIA FOR CAUSALITY

Three requirements must be met before X can be considered to be a cause of Y. First, X must exist before or must precede Y in time or in the typical sequence by which things occur. This logical ordering of the independent before the dependent variable is called *asymmetry*. For instance, it is logical to consider level of education completed as a cause of earned income, because people complete their education before entering an occupation.

Second, X and Y must covary, that is, be associated or correlated. The relationship between X and Y should be statistically significant, and the covariation should be reasonably large rather than trivial. This second standard for establishing cause is called *covariation*, which should be demonstrable through bivariate measures of association for either nominal, ordinal, or categorized interval/ratio variables (see Section 4). For example, for employed people in the CPS the covariation between level of education and family income was found to be statistically significant, and the relationship was positive and moderate (see Table 14.2).

Third, the Y by X relationship must be found to be nonspurious, or not false. A *spurious*, or false, *relationship* is one that involves observed covariation between X and Y, but this covariation results because a third variable, C, causes the variation in both X and Y; this C variable is called an *antecedent variable.*

Many spurious relationships exist in everyday life. A classic example of a spurious relationship is the observed relationship between storks and the birth rate. The idea that storks bring babies may once have been held; today, however, it is obvious that storks are not part of the human reproductive process and that more storks do not cause the birth rate to increase. In rural areas in years past there were more storks, and in rural areas the birth rate was higher. Rural residence was an antecedent variable that influenced both the number of storks and the birth rate. As another example, although lower-class people save less money than do middle-class people, being in the lower class does not automatically make one a poor money manager. Instead, it is the absence of extra money, as an antecendent variable, that results in both low social status and lack of savings. This second example of a spurious relationship may be illustrated in the following diagram:

In summary, three conditions must be met before X can be a cause of Y: (1) X must precede Y, (2) X and Y must covary, and (3) the Y by X relationship must not be spurious.

ELABORATION PROCEDURES AND OUTCOMES

In a bivariate table or a crosstabulation, the basic relationship between two variables is examined (see Section 4). The introduction of an additional variable or variables during data analysis often is desirable for the purpose of elaboration—that is, for clarifying the original relationship. In the simplest type of elaboration, the effect of the presence of a third variable on the bivariate relationship is examined.

In an elaboration the third variable is introduced as a *control variable.* After the original bivariate table has been obtained and assessed, the data are divided into subgroups according to categories of the control variable, and bivariate tables are obtained and assessed for each subgroup. The original table, without the control for the third variable, is the complete table and contains the *zero-order association* between the two variables. The tables for each subgroup are the partial tables and contain the *first-order* or *partial associations.*

Elaboration is used (1) to ascertain if an independent variable X is a cause of a dependent variable Y, (2) to determine under what conditions of a third variable, C, the Y by X relationship holds, and (3) to discover if the link between X and Y depends on the presence of C. A third variable added as a control may reveal one of the following outcomes:

1. No change occurs in the original relationship between X and Y.
2. A spurious relationship exists between X and Y. If the Y by X relationship disappears or is considerably diminished within each category of the control variable, then the relationship may be spurious, as in the following diagram:

3. An *intervening relationship*, where the control variable, C, intervenes between X and Y, may exist. If the Y by X relationship disappears or is considerably diminished within each category of the control variable, then the control variable may be an intervening variable (see the diagram below). The statistical outcome for spurious and intervening relationships is the same. Determination of whether a relationship is spurious or intervening is a matter of theoretical judgment or temporal sequencing, not a matter of statistics.

$$X \longrightarrow C \longrightarrow Y$$

4. A *conditional* or *interactive relationship*, where the relationships between X and Y in the partial tables differ from each other and from the original bivariate table, may exist. For example, as illustrated in the diagram below, the relationship between X and Y (a) may hold in only one category of the control variable and not in the other or (b) may be different or the opposite in each category of the control variable. In these situations the control variable specifies the conditions under which the relationship between X and Y holds.

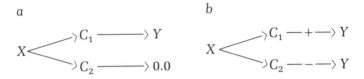

The results in Table 14.2 show a sizable and statistically significant relationship between family income and level of education among employed people in the CPS. In the case of the family income (Y) by level of

Table 14.3 Total 1986 Family Income by Respondent's Level of Education, by Migration Status of Employed CPS Respondents

Total 1986 Family Income	Migrants* Level of Education			Nonmigrants* Level of Education		
	Some College or Less	College or More	Total	Some College or Less	College or More	Total
$30,000 or More	31.6	62.8	43.3	35.5	75.0	40.9
Less than $30,000	68.4	37.2	56.7	64.5	25.0	59.1
	100.0	100.0	100.0	100.0	100.0	100.0
	(N = 158)	(N = 94)	(N = 252)	(N = 76)	(N = 12)	(N = 88)

χ^2 (corrected) = 22.0 χ^2 (corrected) = 5.15
$p < .01$, d.f. = 1 $p < .05$, d.f. = 1
gamma = +.57   gamma = +.69

*Nonmigrants are those who have lived in the community all their lives. Migrants are those who have not lived in the community all their lives. See variable #6, LIVEWC.

education (X) relationship among employed people in the CPS, a variable that might affect the original relationship is migration status. Migrants who are employed may be both better educated and better payed, making migration status an antecedent variable that is related to both X and Y; this would make the original relationship spurious. Migration status might also intervene in the family income (Y) by level of education (X) relationship among employed people in the CPS. Better-educated people may be more likely to move, which in turn would explain why they also have higher-paying jobs. Migration status might also be a variable that specifies the family income (Y) by level of education (X) relationship among employed people in the CPS. It may be that the family income by level of education relationship holds for employed migrants but not for employed nonmigrants, or holds differently for migrants and nonmigrants.

1. No Change in the Original Relationship

The crosstabulations within each category of the control variable, migration status, are presented in Table 14.3. These partial tables are compared to each other and to the complete bivariate table (Table 14.2). As

Table 14.4 Rating of the Quality of Cultural Facilities by
Income Level (Hypothetical Data)

| | Income Level | | |
	Low (Under $30,000)	High ($30,000 or More)	Total
Rating of Cultural Facilities			
A or B	55.0	33.3	42.0
C, D, F	45.0	66.7	58.0
	100.0	100.0	100.0
	(N = 200)	(N = 300)	(N = 500)

gamma = −.42

can be seen in these tables, the income by education relationship does
not diminish within either migration status category. In both migrant
and nonmigrant groups the income by education relationship is statistically significant and nearly as large or larger than it was among all
employed CPS respondents (compare results in Tables 14.2 and 14.3).
Consequently, the income by education relationship is *not* considered
to be spurious or false. (Caution needs to be exercised in interpreting
results, however, given the small number of cases in the nonmigrant
with college or more category.) It can also be concluded that the link
between income and education does not depend on migration as an intervening variable. Furthermore, because the relationship holds under
both conditions of the third variable, this means that migration status is
a variable that does not appear to specify or limit the conditions under
which the income by education relationship holds. Because the relationship between education and income is the same in the partial tables
as it is in the complete table, the control variable, migration status, appears to be unrelated to or does not account for the relationship.

2. A Spurious Relationship

In Table 14.4 hypothetical data showing a relationship between income
level and rating of the quality of cultural facilities in a community are
presented. Gamma of −.42 indicates a moderate, negative association
between income and grade given to cultural facilities. People with low
incomes are more likely to give an A or B grade to cultural facilities than
are high income people (55 percent versus 33 percent).

Table 14.5 Rating of the Quality of Cultural Facilities by Income Level, by Educational Level (Hypothetical Data)

		Level of Education					
		Some College or Less—			College or More—		
		Income			Income		
Ratings of Cultural Facilities		Low	High	Total	Low	High	Total
A or B		74.1	74.3	74.1	20.0	19.6	19.7
C, D, F		25.9	25.7	25.9	80.0	80.4	80.3
		100.0	100.0	100.0	100.0	100.0	100.0
	(N)	(135)	(70)	(205)	(65)	(230)	(295)
		gamma = .006			gamma = −.01		

However, when educational level is introduced as a control (see partial tables in Table 14.5), the relationship disappears. Gamma is .006 for those with some college or less, and −.01 for those who have completed college or more. A lower educational level is associated with higher grades being given to cultural facilities. Slightly over 74 percent of those with some college or less gave cultural facilities an A or B rating, but only 20 percent of college graduates rated cultural facilities as above average. Also, educational level is positively associated with income level. Only 34 percent (70 out of 205) of those at the lower educational level are in the higher-income category, compared to the 78 percent (230 out of 295) of college graduates who have high incomes. In this instance the original relationship is spurious. Educational level is an antecedent variable that affects both income and the rating of the quality of cultural facilities.

3. An Intervening Relationship

The same hypothetical data (i.e., the same numbers and percentages) that are in Tables 14.4 and 14.5 will be used here with a different set of variables in order to illustrate the situation where an intervening variable is the appropriate interpretation. Remember that the statistical results for spurious and intervening variables are the same.

Table 14.6 Income Level by Sex of Respondent (Hypothetical Data)

	Sex of Respondent		
Total 1986 Family Income	Male	Female	Total
$30,000 or More	55.5	33.3	42.0
Less than $30,000	45.5	66.7	58.0
	100.0	100.0	100.0
	(N = 200)	(N = 300)	(N = 500)

gamma = −.42

Table 14.7 Income Level by Sex of Respondent, by Educational Level (Hypothetical Data)

	Level of Education					
	Some College or Less			College or More		
Total 1986 Family Income	Male	Female	Total	Male	Female	Total
$30,000 or More	20.0	19.6	19.7	74.1	74.3	74.1
Less than $30,000	80.0	80.4	80.3	25.9	25.7	25.9
	100.0	100.0	100.0	100.0	100.0	100.0
(N)	(65)	(230)	(295)	(135)	(70)	(205)
		gamma = −.01			gamma = .006	

In Table 14.6 data appear to indicate a difference between men and women in terms of income levels. A higher percentage of men have high incomes than do women (55 percent versus 33 percent), and gamma of −.42 indicates a moderate association. However, when educational attainment is introduced as a control, the differences disappear (see partial tables in Table 14.7). Here, it makes sense to view educational level as an intervening variable. Sex of respondent influences educational level attained, and then educational level affects income level. Males are more likely to be college graduates than are women (67 percent—135 out of 200—versus 23 percent—70 out of 300); and, in turn, those who complete college, both male and female, are more likely to have higher income levels (74 percent) than those who do not go to or finish college (20 percent).

Table 14.8 Position on Mandatory Drug Testing of Employees by CPS Respondent's Perception of the Seriousness of Adult Drug Use

| | Drug Use Among Adults | | |
Mandatory Drug Testing of Employees	Slight or No Problem	Serious Problem	Total
Favor	45.6	62.7	55.7
Oppose	54.4	37.3	44.3
	100.0	100.0	100.0
	(N = 171)	(N = 249)	(N = 420)

chi-square (corrected) = 11.24
p < .01, d.f. = 1.
gamma = +.33

4. A Conditional Relationship

Consider the actual data from the CPS survey that are presented in Table 14.8. Here, there seems to be support for an hypothesis expecting a positive relationship between the perception of drug use among adults as serious and support for mandatory employee drug testing. Two-thirds of those who see drug use among adults as serious favor mandatory employee drug testing, compared to 45.6 percent of those who see adult drug use as a slight or no problem being in favor of drug testing (gamma = +.33).

However, when income level is introduced as a control, as can be seen in the partial tables in Table 14.9, the relationship only holds, and in fact is more pronounced, for those with incomes below $30,000 (gamma = +.50). For those earning $30,000 or more, the relationship between perceived seriousness of adult drug use and mandatory employee drug testing disappears (gamma = −.004). The comparisons of the partial tables with each other and with the complete bivariate table reveal an interactive relationship among these variables. Low-income people are more likely to favor mandatory employee drug testing than are high-income people (61.8 percent versus 44.1 percent); and for people with low incomes there is an association between seeing adult drug use as serious and favoring mandatory drug testing. For people with high incomes the association does not hold.

The SPSS/PC+ and STATPAC instructions that produced Tables 14.8 and 14.9 are provided next.

Table 14.9 Position on Mandatory Drug Testing of Employees
by CPS Respondent's Perception of the Seriousness of Adult
Drug Use, by Income Level

| | | Income Level | | | | | |
| | | Under $30,000 | | | $30,000 and over | | |
Mandatory Drug Testing of Employees		Slight/ No Prob	Serious Prob	Total	Slight/ No Prob	Serious Prob	Total
Favor		46.4	72.1	61.8	44.3	44.0	44.1
Oppose		53.6	27.9	38.2	55.7	56.0	55.9
		100.0	100.0	100.0	100.0	100.0	100.0
	(N)	(110)	(165)	(275)	(61)	(84)	(145)

χ^2 (corrected) = 17.48
p < .01, d.f. = 1
gamma = + .50

χ^2 (corrected) = 0.00
(not significant)
gamma = − .004

Elaboration of Bivariate Tables Using SPSS/PC+

Instructions:

```
SPSS/PC:GET FILE='SPSSCPS'. [Enter]
        :SET PRINTER=ON. [Enter]
        :SELECT IF (DRUGADUL LT 4). [Enter]
        :RECODE DRUGADUL (1=2)(2,3=1). [Enter]
        :VALUE LABELS DRUGADUL 1'Slight/no'
         2'Serious'. [Enter]
        :SELECT IF (DRUGEMP LT 3). [Enter]
        :SELECT IF (INCOME LT 7). [Enter]
        :RECODE INCOME (1 THRU 3=1)(4 THRU 6=2).
         [Enter]
        :VALUE LABELS INCOME 1'Under $30000' 2'$30000
         Plus'. [Enter]
        :CROSSTABS TABLES=DRUGEMP BY DRUGADUL [Enter]
        :/DRUGEMP BY DRUGADUL BY INCOME [Enter]
        :/OPTIONS=4 [Enter]
        :/STATISTICS=ALL. [Enter]
```

Elaboration of Bivariate Tables Using STATPAC

Instructions:

- Follow steps 1–10 in Appendix C
- Analysis type #4 "Crosstabs and chi-square analysis"
  First variable (X) = #47 for DRUGADUL
  Second variable (Y) = #16 for DRUGEMP
- Options: #3 Select if variable #47 "less than" (4), and #3 Select if variable #16 "less than" (3), 0 "none"
- Options: #1 Recode variable #47, Recode Statement: $(1 = 2)(2 - 3 = 1)$
- Select #6 "End task and write to disk"

Note that the instructions above produce the original bivariate table. To obtain the partial tables, add additional tasks. Repeat steps 1–3 that produced the bivariate table, and select if #85 income "less than" (4) to produce the partial table for the "Under $30,000" income category. Repeat steps 1–3 again and select if #85 income "greater than" (3) and "less than" (7) to produce the partial table for the "$30,000 and over" category.

Researchers conduct elaboration in order to make sure that the relationships they have found are genuine, to determine the conditions under which relationships do and do not exist, and to more fully understand how an independent variable causes a dependent variable. Elaboration is an important technique in crosstabulation analyses involving three or more variables. Analogous analyses for interval/ratio–level variables are techniques such as multiple regression (see Section 15).

Exercise 14A:
Multiple Causality and Elaboration

Clearly and concisely answer each of the following questions. Be sure to provide a *specific example* to illustrate each answer.

1. What is a sufficient cause?

2. What is covariation?

3. What is an antecedent variable?

4. What is a control variable?

5. What is an intervening relationship?

6. What is a conditional or interactive relationship?

7. Describe the outcomes in partial tables when no change occurs in an original relationship.

Exercise 14B:
Multiple Causality and Elaboration

Clearly and concisely answer each of the following questions. Be sure to include a *specific example* in each answer.

1. What is a necessary cause?

2. What is asymmetry?

3. What is a control variable?

4. What is a spurious or false relationship?

5. What is a conditional relationship?

6. Describe the outcomes in partial tables when an intervening relationship is found.

7. What is the difference between an intervening relationship and a spurious relationship?

Exercise 14C:
Causality, Elaboration, and Bivariate Tables

Clearly and concisely answer each of the following questions. Include a *specific example* in answers to questions 1, 2, and 3.

1. What is parsimony?

2. What is a probabilistic explanation?

3. What is nonspuriousness?

4. Explain how you could use income level ("higher" versus "lower") as an antecedent variable to show that the relationship between the neighborhood racial composition ("majority white" versus "majority black") and the crime rate ("high" versus "low") is spurious. Make clear what the percentage outcomes would look like in the original bivariate table and in each of the two partial tables. Note: You do not have to include any frequency figures in your tables; include just the percentages.

Exercise 14D:
Causality, Elaboration, and Bivariate Tables

Clearly and concisely answer each of the following questions. Be sure to include a *specific example* of your own as you answer questions 1 through 3.

1. What is determinism?

2. What is reductionism?

3. What would a "perfect" relationship be?

4. Explain how you could use type of occupation ("majority male" versus "majority female") as an antecedent variable to show that the relationship between sex ("male" versus "female") and income ("higher" versus "lower") is spurious. Make clear what the percentage outcomes would look like in the original bivariate table and in each of the two partial tables. Note: You do not have to include any frequency figures in your tables; include just the percentages.

Exercise 14E:
Bivariate and Partial Tables

Construct the tables requested below, and discuss what the tables show.

1. Using *percentages only* construct an original bivariate table and two partial tables to illustrate the following elaboration outcome: The variable urbanization ("urban" versus "rural") intervenes between level of education ("less than college" versus "some college or more") and income ("higher" versus "lower"). Note: Assume that there is a positive relationship between level of education and income in the original bivariate table.

2. Using *percentages only* construct an original bivariate table and two partial tables to illustrate the following elaboration outcome: There is a positive relationship between level of education ("less than college" versus "some college or more") and income ("higher" versus "lower"). However, the relationship holds for men but not for women.

Exercise 14F:
Elaboration and Bivariate Tables

Study the data in Table 14.10 and then answer the following questions or complete the activities indicated.

Table 14.10   Income Level by Sex, by Respondent's Occupation

		Type of Occupation			
		Clerical or Service		Professional and Managerial	
		Sex		Sex	
Income		Women	Men	Women	Men
$30,000 or More		22.5	24.0	61.7	65.2
Less than $30,000		77.5	76.0	38.3	34.8
		100.0	100.0	100.0	100.0
	(N)	(240)	(50)	(60)	(250)
		gamma = +.04		gamma = +.08	

1. Construct the original bivariate table in which the relationship of income level by sex is reported. Attach the table and a discussion of it to this sheet.

2. What type of elaboration outcome does the example illustrate? Why?

3. Draw a diagram that represents the elaboration outcome you think the example illustrates.

Exercise 14G:
Elaboration and Bivariate Tables

Study the data in Table 14.11 and then answer the following questions or complete the acitvities indicated.

Table 14.11 Income by Level of Education, by Sex

| | Women | | Men | |
| | Education | | Education | |
Income	H.S. or Less	Some College or More	H.S. or Less	Some College or More
$30,000 or More	37.5	40.0	40.0	71.4
Less than $30,000	62.5	60.0	60.0	28.6
	100.0	100.0	100.0	100.0
(N)	(200)	(100)	(125)	(175)
	gamma = +.05		gamma = +.58	

1. Construct the original bivariate table in which the relationship of income level by education is reported. Attach the table and a discussion of it to this sheet.

2. What type of elaboration outcome does the example illustrate? Why?

3. Draw a diagram that represents the elaboration outcome you think the example illustrates.

421

Exercise 14H:
Computer Applications

Following the steps in Section 14 dealing with Tables 14.8 and 14.9, use either SPSS/PC+ or STATPAC to obtain the tables requested below. Include this page with your printout and discussion. Then answer the questions or complete the activities indicated.

1. Obtain an original bivariate table reporting the INCOME BY DI-PLOMA relationship where INCOME is recoded as "$30,000 or less" versus "more than $30,000" and DIPLOMA is recoded as "some college or less" versus "college graduate or more."

2. Now obtain the two partial tables that report the INCOME by DI-PLOMA relationship, controlling for SEX.

3. Describe the results in the tables.

4. What type of elaboration outcome have you found? Why?

5. Draw a diagram that explains the type of elaboration outcome you have found.

Exercise 14I:
Computer Applications

Following the steps in Section 14 dealing with Tables 14.8 and 14.9, use either SPSS/PC+ or STATPAC to obtain the tables requested below. Include this page with your printout and discussion. Then answer the questions or complete the activities indicated.

1. Obtain an original bivariate table reporting the DRUGADUL by DIPLOMA relationship. DRUGADUL should be recoded as "serious" versus "no problem or slight problem" and DIPLOMA should be recoded as "high school or less" versus "some college or more."

2. Now obtain the two partial tables that report the DRUGADUL by DIPLOMA relationship, controlling for SEX.

3. Describe the results in the tables.

4. What type of elaboration have you found? Why?

5. Draw a diagram that explains the type of elaboration outcome you think you have found.

15

Multiple Regression

Multiple regression is an extension of simple linear regression and correlation analysis (see Section 13). In the simple regression equation $(Y' = a + bX)$ values of one independent variable (X) are used to estimate or predict the values of a dependent variable (Y). In bivariate correlation analysis the zero-order correlation (or Pearson's r) indicates the size and direction of the linear association between X and Y, and the coefficient of determination (r^2) indicates the proportion of the variation in Y accounted for by X.

INTRODUCTION TO MULTIPLE REGRESSION

In a *multiple regression* several independent variables $(X_1, X_2, X_3 \ldots X_k)$ are used to predict the values of a dependent variable (Y). Including additional independent variables usually provides a better prediction of Y than just one independent variable can provide. The goal of multiple regression is to account for more of the variance in Y by examining the joint contributions of several independent variables.

In multiple regression analysis the *multiple correlation coefficient* (R) indicates the total correlation between the combination of *all* the independent variables $(X_i$'s) and the dependent variable (Y). R^2, the *coefficient of multiple determination*, tells what proportion of the total variation in Y is explained jointly by or associated jointly with all of the independent variables. For example, a multiple R^2 of .60 means that 60 percent of the variance in a dependent variable (Y) is accounted for or explained by a certain set of independent variables $(X_1 \ldots X_k)$.

The general form of the multiple regression prediction equation is as follows:

Formula *Multiple Regression Prediction*

$$Y' = a + b_1X_1 + b_2X_2 + b_3X_3 + \ldots b_kX_k$$

where Y' = the predicted or estimated value of Y

a = the Y intercept

X_i = the independent variables $(i = 1, 2 \ldots k)$

b_i = the partial slope of each independent variable (i.e., the amount of change in Y for each unit of change in X_i, holding the other independent variables constant). These b_i's are also known as the *unstandardized regression coefficients*. They show the amount of change in Y that results from one X_i, after the influence of other X_i's has been removed $(i = 1, 2 \ldots k)$.

k = the number of independent variables.

Usually, the multiple correlation coefficient (R) is greater than any of the zero-order correlations between each of the independent variables and the dependent variable. This is because the joint power of several independent variables to explain variance in Y is greater than a single independent variable's ability to explain variance in Y.

BETA COEFFICIENTS OR WEIGHTS

The unstandardized form of the multiple regression equation—$Y' = a + b_1X_1 + b_2X_2 + b_3X_3 + \ldots b_kX_k$—can be used to predict values of the dependent variable (Y). When this is done, actual values of each independent variable (X_i) are placed into the formula and multiplied by their respective b values; the sum of the products for all the independent variables and the intercept value equals the predicted value of Y.

However, the unstandardized multiple regression equation does not allow the direct comparison of the relative importance or contribution of each independent variable in accounting for variance in Y. This is because the various independent variables have been measured in different units, some perhaps in thousands of dollars, some in years, and others on a 5- or 10-point index (see Sections 7 and 8).

In order to be able to compare directly and meaningfully the relative importance of all independent variables in explaining variance in Y, social researchers often use the standardized form of the multiple regression equation:

Formula   *Multiple Regression (Standardized Form)*

$$Z_y' = b_1^* Z_1 + b_2^* Z_2 + b_3^* Z_3 + \ldots b_k^* Z_k$$

where b_i^* = a *beta weight* or beta coefficient (i.e., a conversion of b_i values to standardized Z-score form: $b_i^* = b_i(S_i/S_y)$

Z_i = the Z-scores of the independent variables (i = 1, 2 . . . k)

k = the number of independent variables

Calculation and display of both b_i and b_i^* values for each independent variable are provided in most multiple regression computer programs, including SPSS/PC+ and STATPAC. The unstandardized values of b are based on the actual units used to measure each X, which may be, and usually are, quite dissimilar; hence, the b_i values are not comparable to one another. This makes conclusions about how important each independent variable is in explaining Y an artificial product of measurement rather than a reflection of explanatory importance.

The standardized beta weights or beta coefficients (b_i^*'s) are all converted into the same units of measurement and thus *are* directly comparable to one another. The sizes of the b_i^*'s indicate the relative importance of each independent variable. The larger the absolute value of the beta weight or beta coefficient, the more important the contribution of an independent variable, X_i, is in an explanation of variance in the dependent variable (Y).

TESTS OF SIGNIFICANCE FOR REGRESSION STATISTICS

There are t-tests that determine if the beta weight or beta coefficient for a given independent variable (b_i^*) is significantly different from zero (H_1: $b_i^* \neq 0$). The null hypothesis tested is that the standardized b value for each predictor is unrelated to the dependent variable (H_0: $b_i^* = 0$). If a b_i^* is statistically significant, then it may be concluded that an independent variable contributes to the prediction of the variance in the dependent variable. A level of probability of .05 or less (e.g., .01 or .001) is used to test whether b_i^*'s are statistically significant (see Section 11). An F-test of significance is used to determine if R^2 is significant. In a multiple regression analysis an assessment of which independent variables have statistically significant associations with the dependent variable, as well as an assessment of whether or not the joint association between all predictors and the dependent variable is significantly different from zero, can be made (see Section 11).

The key considerations in a multiple regression analysis are the following:

1. r_{XY}'s—the zero-order correlations between each independent variable and the dependent variable
2. b_i's—the partial slopes of each independent variable (i.e., the amount of change in Y for each unit of change in X_i, holding the other independent variables constant)
3. b_i^*'s—the beta weights or beta coefficients (i.e., the standardized b values showing which independent variables account for the greatest amounts of variance in Y)
4. t-tests of significance to determine whether or not the b_i^*'s are statistically significant at a given level of probability ($p < .05$)
5. R^2—the coefficient of multiple determination (i.e., the proportion of total variation in Y explained jointly by all the independent variables)
6. An F-test to determine whether R^2 is statistically significant at a given level of probability ($p < .05$)

APPLICATIONS OF MULTIPLE REGRESSION

Because the calculation of multiple regression outcomes by hand or calculator is a very lengthy and tedious process, only computer procedures for obtaining the outputs for multiple regression analysis will be covered in this text. Attention will be directed toward describing and interpreting typical computer output when a multiple regression is done. Most multiple regression analyses, especially when sample sizes exceed 300 and when four or more independent variables are used, must rely on computer analysis of results. Using variables from the CPS, multiple regression will be used to find out which of several independent variables are the best predictors of the variable INCOME (total family income). The independent variables considered in an explanation of variance in family income are:

1. GRADE: years of schooling completed, 1–24
2. EMPLOYED: being employed, 1 = yes, 0 = no
3. RACE: 1 = white, 0 = nonwhite
4. HOMETYPE: 1 = own home, 0 = rent
5. HOUSESIZ: number of people in household, 1–11
6. MARITAL: 1 = married, 0 = not married
7. AGE: years of age, 18–64
8. SEX: 1 = male, 0 = female

INCOME, the dependent variable, was measured as an ordinal variable with six categories: 1 = less than \$10,000, 2 = \$10,000–20,000, 3 = \$20,000–30,000, 4 = \$30,000–40,000, 5 = \$40,000–50,000, and 6 = \$50,000 or more. The six values of INCOME represent a total family income index in this example. Social researchers often use ordinal indexes as if they were interval/ratio measures in multiple regression. The variables EMPLOYED, RACE, HOMETYPE, MARITAL, and SEX are all categorical variables that are recoded in the way researchers typically use such variables in a multiple regression. Each has been recoded as a dichotomy, where a value of "1" has been assigned to the condition (e.g., "being employed" or "being married" or "owning a home") that is expected to be related to the dependent variable. All other categories of these variables have been assigned a value of "0." In multiple regression such recoded variables are called "dummy" or "indicator" variables.

Stepwise Multiple Regression

The type of multiple regression used in the present example to illustrate SPSS/PC+ procedures is called *stepwise multiple regression*. In this procedure the computer output lists the independent variables step by step in a descending order of predictive power, with the independent variable that explains the greatest amount of the variance in the dependent variable listed in the first step. In subsequent steps additional independent variables are added to the regression equation output. Output in each step includes (1) the unstandardized regression coefficients (b_i's); (2) the standardized regression coefficients or beta weights (b_i^*'s); (3) the t-tests for the significance of each independent variable; (4) the coefficient of multiple determination (R^2) indicating the total variation in the dependent variable explained as each predictor is added; and (5) the F-test for the significance of the coefficient of multiple determination.

The computer output for stepwise multiple regression ceases when predictors or independent variables no longer have standardized regression coefficients or beta weights that are statistically significant at a predetermined level of probability, usually $p < .05$. Therefore, the last step in the output will include in the regression equation all the independent variables that have statistically significant beta weights and will exclude all those predictors that do not. By using stepwise regression, a researcher is thereby able to identify the relative importance of all predictors and include only the statistically meaningful ones in the overall explanation of variance in a dependent variable. This final equation, composed of all meaningful predictors, is often called a "regression model." A *model* is an equation representing the "best" combination of independent variables that jointly explain the most variation in the dependent variable.

Stepwise Multiple Regression Using SPSS/PC+

The following SPSS/PC+ commands would be used to obtain a stepwise regression in which GRADE, EMPLOYED, RACE, HOMETYPE, HOUSESIZ, MARITAL, AGE, and SEX are used to explain total variation in INCOME.

Instructions:

```
SPSS/PC+:GET FILE='SPSSCPS', [Enter]
        :SET PRINTER=ON, [Enter]
        :SELECT IF (INCOME LT 7), [Enter]
        :SELECT IF (GRADE LT 99), [Enter]
        :SELECT IF (EMPLOYED LT 3), [Enter]
        :RECODE EMPLOYED (1=1) (2=0), [Enter]
        :SELECT IF (RACE LT 4), [Enter]
        :RECODE RACE (1=1)(2,3=0), [Enter]
        :RECODE HOMETYPE (1=1)(2=0), [Enter]
        :RECODE MARITAL (1=1)(2 thru 6=0), [Enter]
        :SELECT IF (AGE LT 65), [Enter]
        :RECODE SEX (1=1)(2=0), [Enter]
```

```
:REGRESSION VARIABLES=INCOME,GRADE,EMPLOYED,
 [Enter]
:RACE,HOMETYPE,HOUSESIZ,MARITAL,AGE,SEX
 [Enter]
:/DESCRIPTIVES=CORR
:/DEPENDENT=INCOME
:/METHOD=STEPWISE,
```

Table 15.1 SPSS/PC+
****MULTIPLE REGRESSION

Listwise Deletion of Missing Data
N of Cases = 457
Correlation:

	INCOME	GRADE	EMPLOYED	RACE	HOMETYPE	HOUSESIZ	MARITAL
INCOME	1.000	.332	.152	.188	.339	.185	.335
GRADE	.332	1.000	.265	.074	−.039	−.062	−.030
EMPLOYED	.152	.265	1.000	.064	−.047	−.019	−.068
RACE	.188	.074	.064	1.000	.253	−.032	.181
HOMETYPE	.339	−.039	−.047	.253	1.000	.151	.393
HOUSESIZ	.185	−.062	−.019	−.032	.151	1.000	.406
MARITAL	.335	−.030	−.068	.181	.393	.406	1.000
AGE	.141	−.196	−.098	.070	.369	−.177	.308
SEX	.103	.087	.129	.002	−.033	−.040	−.001

Page 5 SPSS/PC+
****MULTIPLE REGRESSION****

	AGE	SEX
INCOME	.141	.103
GRADE	−.196	.087
EMPLOYED	−.098	.129
RACE	.070	.002
HOMETYPE	.369	−.033
HOUSESIZ	−.177	−.040
MARITAL	.308	−.001
AGE	1.000	−.009
SEX	−.009	1.000

Continued

Table 15.1 *Continued*

Page 6 SPSS/PC+
****MULTIPLE REGRESSION****

Equation Number 1 Dependent Variable.. INCOME Total Family Income

Beginning Block Number 1. Method: Stepwise

Variable(s) Entered on Step Number
   1.. HOMETYPE Own or Rent Housing

Multiple R	.33884
R Square	.11481
Adjusted R Square	.11286
Standard Error	1.47054

Analysis of Variance

	DF	Sum of Squares	Mean Square
Regression	1	127.61717	127.61717
Residual	455	983.93644	2.16250

F = 59.01378 Signif F = .0000

Page 7 SPSS/PC+
****MULTIPLE REGRESSION****

Equation Number 1 Dependent Variable..

Variables in the Equation

Variable	B	SE B	Beta	T	Sig T
HOMETYPE	1.14409	.14893	.33884	7.682	.0000
(Constant)	2.42553	.12384		19.586	.0000

Variables not in the Equation

Variable	Beta In	Partial	Min Toler	T	Sig T
GRADE	.34567	.36713	.99850	8.410	.0000
EMPLOYED	.16869	.17910	.99775	3.879	.0001
RACE	.10936	.11245	.93593	2.411	.0163
HOUSESIZ	.13739	.14436	.97721	3.108	.0020
MARITAL	.23854	.23317	.84577	5.109	.0000
AGE	.01812	.01790	.86350	.381	.7031
SEX	.11415	.12126	.99890	2.603	.0095

Continued

Table 15.1 *Continued*

SPSS/PC+
                                  ****MULTIPLE REGRESSION****

Equation Number 1 Dependent Variable.. INCOME Total Family Income

Variable(s) Entered on Step Number

   2.. GRADE   Years of School Completed

Multiple R	.48386
R Square	.23412
Adjusted R Square	.23074
Standard Error	1.36936

Analysis of Variance

	DF	Sum of Squares	Mean Square
Regression	2	260.23438	130.11719
Residual	454	851.31923	1.87515

F = 69.39019   Signif F = 0.0

SPSS/PC+
                                  ****MULTIPLE REGRESSION****

Equation Number 1   Dependent Variable..   INCOME   Total Family Income

Variables in the Equation

Variable	B	SE B	Beta	T	Sig T
HOMETYPE	1.18925	.13879	.35221	8.569	.0000
GRADE	.18638	.02216	.34567	8.410	.0000
(Constant)	-.09916	.32160		-.308	.7580

Variables not in the Equation

Variable	Beta In	Partial	Min Toler	T	Sig T
EMPLOYED	.08323	.09162	.92825	1.958	.0508
RACE	.07886	.08684	.92883	1.855	.0642
HOUSESIZ	.15769	.17784	.97407	3.846	.0001
MARITAL	.24486	.25727	.84506	5.666	.0000
AGE	.09428	.09818	.83059	2.100	.0363
SEX	.08504	.09676	.99111	2.069	.0391

Continued

Table 15.1 *Continued*

SPSS/PC+
                                    ****MULTIPLE REGRESSION****

Equation Number 1 Dependent Variable..   INCOME   Total Family Income

Variable(s) Entered on Step Number

   3..   MARITAL   Marital Status

Multiple R	.53368
R Square	.28481
Adjusted R Square	.28007
Standard Error	1.32473

Analysis of Variance

	DF	Sum of Squares	Mean Square
Regression	3	316.58266	105.52755
Residual	453	794.97095	1.75490

F = 60.13299   Signif F = 0.0

SPSS/PC+
                                    ****MULTIPLE REGRESSION****

Equation Number 1   Dependent Variable..   INCOME   Total Family Income

Variables in the Equation

Variable	B	SE B	Beta	T	Sig T
HOMETYPE	.86505	.14594	.25620	5.927	.0000
GRADE	.18840	.02144	.34942	8.786	.0000
MARITAL	.79720	.14069	.24486	5.666	.0000
(Constant)	-.41487	.31607		-1.313	.1900

Variables not in the Equation

Variable	Beta In	Partial	Min Toler	T	Sig T
EMPLOYED	.09536	.10849	.84335	2.320	.0208
RACE	.05761	.06536	.80970	1.393	.1644
HOUSESIZ	.08288	.08945	.72309	1.909	.0569
AGE	.04880	.05162	.77695	1.099	.2724
SEX	.08189	.09642	.84414	2.059	.0400

Continued

Table 15.1 *Continued*

Page 12

SPSS/PC+
****MULTIPLE REGRESSION****

Equation Number 1 Dependent Variable.. INCOME Total Family Income

Variable(s) Entered on Step Number

    4..   EMPLOYED   Employment Status

Multiple R	.54151
R Square	.29323
Adjusted R Square	.28697
Standard Error	1.31836

Analysis of Variance

	DF	Sum of Squares	Mean Square
Regression	4	325.94036	81.48509
Residual	452	785.61325	1.73808

F = 46.88218   Signif F = 0.0

Page 13

SPSS/PC+
****MULTIPLE REGRESSION****

Equation Number 1   Dependent Variable..   INCOME   Total Family Income

Variables in the Equation

Variable	B	SE B	Beta	T	Sig T
HOMETYPE	.87030	.14526	.25775	5.991	.0000
GRADE	.17488	.02212	.32434	7.905	.0000
MARITAL	.81374	.14019	.24994	5.804	.0000
EMPLOYED	.33118	.14273	.09536	2.320	.0208
(Constant)	−.48665	.31606		−1.540	.1243

Variables not in the Equation

Variable	Beta In	Partial	Min Toler	T	Sig T
RACE	.05176	.05896	.80906	1.254	.2104
HOUSESIZ	.08046	.08732	.72079	1.861	.0633
AGE	.05175	.05504	.77692	1.171	.2423
SEX	.07265	.08551	.84302	1.823	.0690

Continued

Table 15.1 *Continued*

....

SPSS/PC+
                                   ****MULTIPLE REGRESSION****

Equation Number 1 Dependent Variable.. INCOME Total Family Income
End Block Number 1 PIN = .050 Limits reached.

....

Discussion of Stepwise Multiple Regression Results

The first part of the SPSS/PC+ output is a table or matrix of zero-order correlations between all the variables in the stepwise multiple regression analysis. Such a matrix is used in two ways. First, as can be seen in the INCOME column, the independent variables most related to IN-COME are GRADE, HOMETYPE, and MARITAL. These are the first indications that these predictors may be relatively more important than the others in explaining variation in family income. Second, examination of the zero-order correlation matrix indicates that certain predictors are related to one another. For example, the correlation between HOUSESIZ and MARITAL = .406 and the correlation between MARITAL and HOMETYPE = .393. These are the first indications that some independent variables will be excluded from the final regression equation, or regression model, because they are related to other predictors. Remember, the regression analysis will be determining the separate importance of each independent variable in the best combination or model of predictors of variance in family income.

Step 1 of the regression output indicates that the best single predictor of family income is HOMETYPE. Its beta weight = .33884, and it is statistically significant ($p < .01$). The coefficient of determination (R^2) for this variable alone is .11481, indicating that slightly over 11 percent of the variance in INCOME is accounted for by HOMETYPE. The R^2 for HOMETYPE alone is also statistically significant ($p < .01$).

In step 2 another predictor of family income, GRADE (or years of schooling completed) is added to the regression equation. Its beta weight = .34567, and it is statistically significant ($p < .01$). The multiple coefficient of determination (R^2), when both HOMETYPE and GRADE are included in the regression equation, is .23412, indicating that over 23 percent of the total variance in family income is accounted for by the combination of the separate influences of HOMETYPE and GRADE. The R^2 for the combination of HOMETYPE and GRADE is statistically significant ($p < .01$). Each of the best two predictors explains somewhat more than 11 percent of the variance in total family income, based on the steps of increase in R^2 (11.5 percent + 11.9 percent = 23.4 percent).

The third-best predictor of total family income, entered on step 3 of the analysis, is MARITAL (or being married). Its beta weight = .24486, and it is statistically significant (p < .01). The multiple coefficient of determination (R^2) for the combination of HOMETYPE, GRADE and MARITAL is .28481, indicating that somewhat more than 28 percent of the variance in total family income is accounted for by the combination of the separate influences of the three best predictors. The R^2 is statistically significant (p < .01). The addition of a third independent variable, MARITAL, adds slightly more than 5 percent additional explained variance in total family income based on the stepwise increase in R^2 (11.5 percent + 11.9 percent + 5.1 percent = 28.5 percent).

In step 4 the final statistically significant predictor of total family income, EMPLOYED, is added. Its beta weight = .09536, and it is statistically significant (p < .05). The multiple coefficient of determination (R^2), when all four statistically meaningful predictors are included in the regression equation, is .29323, indicating that somewhat over 29 percent of the variance in total family income has been accounted for by HOMETYPE, GRADE, MARITAL, and EMPLOYED. The R^2 for the combination of all the meaningful predictors is statistically significant (p < .01). The fourth, and final, predictor, EMPLOYED, contributes less than 1 percent of additional explained variation in total family income based on the stepwise increase in R^2 (11.5 percent + 11.9 percent + 5.1 percent + .8 percent = 29.3 percent).

You should notice that in the final regression equation, or model, the final statistical calculations show that the predictor with the largest beta weight is GRADE = .32434, meaning that the relative contribution of years of schooling is greater than that of the other variables in explaining the variation in family income. The next two predictors are of nearly equal importance—beta's of HOMETYPE = .25775 and MARITAL = .24994. The least important predictor is EMPLOYED with a beta weight of .09536. RACE, HOUSESIZ, AGE, and SEX were not statistically significant and are not included in the final equation.

The equation or model, useful in predicting Y', total family income values, would be as follows:

$$Y' = -.48665 + .87030(X_H) + .17488(X_G) + .81374(X_M) + .33118(X_E)$$

Each of the unstandardized regression coefficients is obtained from the "B" column on the final step of the regression output, and the intercept value (−.48665) is the "constant" in the variable column.

Forced-Entry Multiple Regression Using STATPAC

The multiple regression procedure in STATPAC is the same as the "METHOD = ENTER" procedure in SPSS/PC+. This method is a forced-entry type. All independent variables are entered in a single step. The following STATPAC commands would be used to obtain a multiple regression analysis using the same variables.

Note that the STATPAC routine does not include a stepwise procedure. All predictors are included in the analysis, and the researcher selects meaningful predictors based on those which turn out to be statistically significant at a predetermined level of probability ($p < .05$ or beyond). (SPSS/PC+ has an option called "Enter" that produces results identical to those of STATPAC. The only change in SPSS/PC+ commands previously given in this section to use the enter option is to change the final command to /METHOD = ENTER.)

Instructions:

- Follow steps 1–10 in Appendix C
- Analysis type = #7 Multiple linear regression
- Dependent variable = #85 Income
- Independent variables: #79 Grade
  - #83 Employed
  - #82 Race
  - #81 Hometype
  - #77 Housesiz
  - #76 Marital
  - #75 Age
  - #74 Sex
- Select if #85 LT 7 and #79 LT 99
  - and #83 LT 3 and #82 LT 4
  - and #75 LT 65, none.
- Recode #83 (1 = 1)(2 = 0)
  - and #82 (1 = 1)(2 = 0)(3 = 0)
  - and #81 (1 = 1)(2 = 0)
  - and #76 (1 = 1)(2 = 0)(3 = 0)(4 = 0)(5 = 0)(6 = 0)
  - and #74 (1 = 1)(2 = 0), none.
- Select #6—End task and write to disk
- Execute now and start with task 1

Table 15.2 STATPAC
Multiple Regression

Variables in the equation-Descriptive statistics

Var.	Variable label	Mean	Standard Dev.
DV	INCOME	3.2166	1.5613
IV1	GRADE LEVEL	13.3786	2.8957
IV2	EMPLOYED	0.7199	0.4495
IV3	RACE	0.9322	0.2517
IV4	OWN OR RENT	0.6915	0.4624
IV5	NUMBER OF PEOPLE IN HOUSEHOLD	2.8950	1.4196
IV6	MARITAL STATUS	0.6433	0.4795
IV7	AGE	38.1685	12.6794
IV8	SEX	0.4223	0.4945

Regression Statistics

Coefficient of multiple determination = 0.3148
Coefficient of multiple correlation   = 0.5611
Standard error of multiple estimate   = 1.3039

F-Ratio   = 25.7293
Degrees of freedom = 8 & 448
Probability of chance = 0.0000

Number of valid cases   = 457
Number of missing cases = 39
Response percent   = 92.14%

Regression coefficients

Constant = −1.6939

Var.	Coeff.	Beta	F-ratio	Prob.	Std. Error
IV1	0.1833	0.3400	66.322	0.000	0.0225
IV2	0.2849	0.0820	4.001	0.043	0.1424
IV3	0.4274	0.0689	2.793	0.091	0.2557
IV4	0.7340	0.2174	22.592	0.000	0.1544
IV5	0.1428	0.1298	7.717	0.006	0.0514
IV6	0.5503	0.1690	11.726	0.001	0.1607
IV7	0.0125	0.1017	4.616	0.030	0.0058
IV8	0.2398	0.0760	3.688	0.052	0.1249

Continued

Table 15.2 *Continued*

		DV	IV1	IV2	IV3	IV4	IV5	IV6	IV7
				Multiple Regression					
				Simple correlation matrix					
IV1	I	0.332							
IV2	I	0.152	0.265						
IV3	I	0.188	0.074	0.064					
IV4	I	0.339	−0.039	−0.047	0.253				
IV5	I	0.185	−0.062	−0.019	−0.032	0.151			
IV6	I	0.335	−0.030	−0.068	0.181	0.393	0.406		
IV7	I	0.141	−0.196	−0.098	0.070	0.369	−0.177	0.308	
IV8	I	0.103	0.087	0.129	0.002	−0.033	−0.040	−0.001	−0.009

Discussion of Forced-Entry Multiple Regression Results

The first part of the STATPAC output includes the descriptive statistics on all variables, the regression coefficients for all independent variables and their statistical significance, and the coefficient of multiple determination results. The second part of the STATPAC output includes the zero-order correlation matrix of all variables.

Output from the STATPAC multiple regression results indicates that the statistically meaningful predictors of total family income may be arranged in this order based upon the absolute value of the beta weights: GRADE (.3400), HOMETYPE (.2174), MARITAL (.1690), HOUSESIZ (.1298), AGE (.1017), and EMPLOYED (.0820). The order and power of the independent variables in explaining variance in total family income in the STATPAC results is similar to that produced by the SPSS/PC+ stepwise procedure, except that STATPAC orders HOUSESIZ and AGE before EMPLOYED. HOUSESIZ did not appear in the stepwise final equation, but it was the variable closest to being statistically significant among those excluded by the stepwise procedures.

Though the STATPAC procedures indicate that both HOUSESIZ and AGE should be retained as meaningful predictors, the total variance explained by the inclusion of these additional predictors does not increase R^2 much more than when only GRADE, HOMETYPE, MARITAL, and EMPLOYED were included in the stepwise procedure. (In both STATPAC and SPSS/PC+, Enter the value of R^2 is .3148. In SPSS/PC+,

Table 15.3 Multiple Regression Analysis of Predictor
Variables on Total Family Income

Predictor	Total Family Income (beta)
Grade level	.3400**
Employed (1 = employed)	.0820*
Race (1 = white)	.0689
Home ownership (1 = own)	.2174**
Household size	.1298**
Marital status (1 = married)	.1690**
Age	.1017*
Sex (1 = male)	.0760
	R^2 = .3148**

* $p < .05$ ** $p < .01$

stepwise R^2 = .29323.) Both regression approaches indicate that the combination of the separate importance of statistically significant predictors explains about 30 percent of the variance in total family income.

Using information concerning the unstandardized regression coefficients from the STATPAC output, the multiple regression equation that would be used to predict values of total family income (Y'), based upon STATPAC or SPSS/PC+ Enter procedures, would be:

$$Y' = -1.6939 + .1833(\text{IV1}) + .2849(\text{IV2}) + .4274(\text{IV3})$$
$$+ .7340(\text{IV4}) + .1428(\text{IV5}) + .5503(\text{IV6})$$
$$+ .0125(\text{IV7}) + .2398(\text{IV8})$$

Studies that have employed multiple regression often report the regression results in a summary table such as Table 15.3. And a research report would include a discussion similar to that below.

Example Results in Table 15.3 indicate that of the eight predictors used to explain the variation in family income, six were statistically significant (at $p < .05$). An examination of the beta coefficients shows that the best predictors of family income, all of which are positively associated with family income, are grade level, home ownership, marital status, household size, age, and employment, listed in order of importance. Race and sex are not related to and do not help explain family income. Jointly, or in combination, the independent variables explain or account for slightly over 31 percent of the variation in total family income ($R^2 = .3148$).

CONCLUSION

The example discussed in this section makes clear three very important and powerful uses of multiple regression analysis. First, researchers can decide which among many independent variables are the most important influences on a dependent variable. Second, researchers can determine which particular order of independent variables should be considered when a multivariate explanation of a dependent variable is considered. And, finally, once a "best" or "final" regression equation has been calculated, researchers can use it to predict values of a dependent variable. For these reasons, regression procedures are one of the most powerful and widely used multivariate methods in social research.

Exercise 15A:
Computer Applications

Use the CPS dataset and run the following multiple regression analysis using either the SPSS/PC+ stepwise procedure or the STATPAC or SPSS/PC+ forced-entry procedure. The dependent variable should be #23 GRADESEX; here, select if (GRADESEX LT 99). Independent variables should include #79 GRADE (Select if LT 99), #74 SEX (1 = male, 0 = female), #82 RACE (Select if LT 4 and Recode 1 = white, 0 = black and other), #78 UNDER18, #77 HOUSESIZ, #85 INCOME (Select if LT 7), #25 GRADEDR (Select if LT 99), #75 AGE (Select if LT 65), #76 MARITAL (Recode married = 1, all others = 0). Attach your printout to this report and answer the following questions:

1. What is the value of the multiple correlation coefficient (R)?

2. Examine the *t*-tests for significance, and list the independent variables that are significantly related (at least at the $p < .05$ level) to #23 GRADESEX.

3. Examine the beta weights, and arrange the statistically significant independent variables in order of relative importance in explaining Y, from the most to the least important predictor:

Independent Variables   *Beta Weights*

4. Use the values of the b coefficients to construct the multiple regression equation:

   $Y' =$

5. Examine R^2. What proportion of the variation in Grade to Begin Sex Education is explained jointly by the independent variables?

6. Discussion:

Exercise 15B:
Computer Applications

Use the CPS dataset and run the following multiple regression analysis using either the SPSS/PC+ stepwise procedure or the STATPAC or SPSS/PC+ forced-entry procedure. The dependent variable should be #35 CULTURAL; here, select if (CULTURAL LT 6). Independent variables should include #79 GRADE (Select if LT 99), #75 AGE, #7 YRSLIVED, #85 INCOME (Select if LT 7), #36 NEWSPAP (Select if LT 6). Attach your printout to this report and answer the following questions:

1. What is the value of the multiple correlation coefficient (R)?

2. Examine the *t*-tests for significance, and list the independent variables that are significantly related (at least at the $p < .05$ level) to #35 CULTURAL.

3. Examine the beta weights, and arrange the statistically significant independent variables in order of their relative importance in explaining *Y*, from the most to the least important predictor:

Independent Variables   *Beta Weights*

447

4. Use the values of the b coefficients to construct the multiple regression equation:

$Y' =$

5. Examine R^2. What proportion of the variation in Quality of Cultural Facilities is explained jointly by the independent variables?

6. Discussion:

Exercise 15C:
Computer Applications

Use the CPS dataset and run a multiple regression analysis using either the SPSS/PC+ stepwise procedure or the forced-entry procedure in STATPAC or SPSS/PC+.

Select your dependent variable: _____

Select at least five independent variables. Remember that if variables are not interval/ratio types, they should be collapsed into dichotomous "dummy"/"indicator" variables as was done in the example in Section 15. Record your variables here:

1.

2.

3.

4.

5.

Attach your printout to this report and answer the following questions:

1. What is the value of the multiple correlation coefficient (R)?

2. Examine the t-tests for significance, and list the independent variables that are significantly related (at least at the $p < .05$ level) to the dependent variable.

3. Examine the beta weights, and arrange the statistically significant independent variables in order of relative importance in explaining the dependent variable, from the most to the least important predictor:

Independent Variables   *Beta Weights*

4. Use the values of the b coefficients to construct the multiple regression equation:

$Y' =$

5. Examine R^2. What proportion of the variation in your dependent variable is explained jointly by the independent variables?

6. Discussion:

A

Instructions for Computer Installation and Operation of the CPS

The CPS dataset can be used with either SPSS/PC+ or STATPAC on the IBM PC/XT or compatible computers. The CPS can also be used with SPSS[x] on mainframe computers. Instructions for installing the CPS in the various systems are provided below.

On the enclosed floppy diskette, entitled Community Preference Survey (CPS), are four files:

```
1. CPSDATA        64256
2. CPSCODE         6144
3. SPSSCPS        69704
4. SPSSCPS.POR   117589
```

A. STATPAC

If you have STATPAC in a directory on the hard drive, all you need to do to use the CPS is copy "CPSCODE" and "CPSDATA" to the STATPAC directory. Place the CPS disk in Drive A and copy these files with the following DOS commands:

```
COPY A:CPSCODE C:CPSCODE/V [Enter]
COPY A:CPSDATA C:CPSDATA/V [Enter]
```

If you are using STATPAC with two floppy drives, all you need to do to use the CPS is have your working copy of the CPS disk in Drive B and enter B:CPSCODE when prompted by STATPAC for the codebook filename and B:CPSDATA when prompted for the data filename. Analysis control files can be added to your working copy of the CPS disk.

B. SPSS/PC+

To add the CPS file to the SPSS directory, do the following:

1. Place the CPS disk in Drive A.
2. Copy SPSSCPS file with the following DOS command:

```
COPY A:SPSSCPS C:SPSSCPS/V. [Enter]
```

Then, you are ready to use the file SPSSCPS.

C. SPSS^X

To add the CPS file to SPSS^X, do the following:

1. Transfer the CPS data file from a PC to the mainframe via modem by using Kermit or some other file transfer program to import the export file 'SPSSCPS.POR'.
2. Use the IMPORT FILE command for the file 'A:SPSSCPS.POR'.

Once the transfer is completed, you are ready to use the file SPSSCPS on SPSS^X.

D. DIFFERENCES BETWEEN SPSS/PC+ and SPSS^X

All of the instructions and examples in the text pertain to SPSS/PC+. Users of SPSS^X will have to make some modifications in order to perform the analyses. However, it should be noted that in most cases command structures and syntax are similar in the two systems. Some of the more important differences are pointed out below. For further and more detailed discussions, the SPSS^X User's Guide should be consulted.

The biggest and most basic difference in syntax between the two systems involves the use of command terminators at the end of command lines. Because SPSS/PC+ is an interactive system, each command must be terminated with a period. SPSS^x is a batch system and does not require command terminators, or periods, at the end of each command. Therefore, the periods that appear at the end of command lines in SPSS/ PC+ instructions in this text and exercises should not be included when using SPSS^x.

A comparison of SPSS/PC+ commands used in this book and similarities and differences in SPSS^x is made below.

SPSS/PC+ Command	*SPSS^x Command*
GET FILE = 'SPSSCPS'.	FILE HANDLE SPSSCPS/ GET FILE = SPSSCPS*
SET PRINTER = ON	Not needed. Directions for routing printed output are provided in system instructions.
CORRELATION	PEARSON CORR
CROSSTABS	No change for General mode.
DESCRIPTIVES	CONDESCRIPTIVES
FINISH	Same
FREQUENCIES	Same
NPAR TESTS	Same
ONEWAY	Same
RECODE	Same
REGRESSION	Same
SELECT IF	Same
T-TEST	Same
VALUE LABELS	Same

*Note: The file specifications on the FILE HANDLE command differ from one computer to another and may be unnecessary on some systems. The handle that SPSS^x will accept is the DD name supplied in the job control language (JCL).

B

Community Preference Survey (CPS) Codebook

STATPAC Variable #	SPSSPC Var. Name	Variable Description	Values
2	INTID	Interviewer ID #	01–11 (2 col)
3	WCQUAL	Warren Co Place to Live	1 = Good, 2 = Fair, 3 = Poor, 4 = DK
4	RESIDE	Residence	1 = BG, 2 = WC, 3 = DK
5	BORNWC	Born in W.C.	1 = Yes, 2 = No, 3 = DK
6	LIVEWC	Lived in W.C. all life	1 = Yes, 2 = No, 3 = DK
7	YRSLIVED	Yrs Lived in W.C.	# yrs, 00–91 (2 col)
8	PAST5YRS	Change in WC Past 5 years	1 = Better, 2 = Worse, 3 = Same, 4 = DK
9	NEXT5YRS	Change in WC Next 5 years	1 = Better, 2 = Worse, 3 = Same, 4 = DK
10	METROGOV	Metropolitan Government	Variables #10–22 and #24 have the values:
11	MERGESCH	Merge School Systems	1 = Favor
12	NUDEDAN	Ordinance Banning Nude Dancing	2 = Oppose 3 = Uncertain

STATPAC Variable #	SPSSPC Var. Name	Variable Description	Values
13	COMMAIR	Commuter Airline Service	
14	CONVCENT	Build Convention Center	
15	MEASTEL	Measured Telephone Service	
16	DRUGEMP	Employee Drug Testing	
17	DRUGHSAT	Drug Testing HS Athletes	
18	SEATBELT	Mandatory Seatbelt Use	
19	NOSMOKE	No Smoking Areas in Work	
20	BANSHOP	Ban New Shopping Centers	
21	LEASHLAW	Leash Law in City— Dogs	
22	SEXEDUC	Sex Educ in Schools	
24	DRUGEDUC	Drug Educ in Schools	
23	GRADESEX	Grade to Begin Sex Educ	(2 col)
25	GRADEDR	Grade to Begin Drug Educ	(2 col)
26	CITYGOV	Quality of City Government	Variables #26–40 have values:
27	COUNGOV	Quality County Government	1 = A 2 = B
28	POLICE	Quality Police Protection	3 = C 4 = D
29	FIRE	Quality Fire Protection	5 = F
30	BGSCHOOL	Quality BG City Schools	6 = DK

STATPAC Variable #	SPSSPC Var. Name	Variable Description	Values
31	WCSCHOOL	Quality WC County Schools	
32	WKU	Quality of W.K.U.	
33	MEDICAL	Quality Medical Facilities	
34	SHOPPING	Quality Shopping Facilities	
35	CULTURAL	Quality Cultural Facilities	
36	NEWSPAP	Quality of Newspaper	
37	CH13	Quality Ch. 13, WBKO-TV	
38	CHCOMM	Quality of Chamber of Commerce	
39	PLANZON	Qual. Planning/Zoning Com.	
40	PARKSREC	Quality Parks and Recreation	
41	CRIME	Seriousness of Crime	Problems asked in Variables #41–56 have values
42	DRINKING	Seriousness Minors Drinking	1 = Serious
43	SMOKING	Seriousness Smoking Youths	2 = Slight
44	DRUGELEM	Seriousness Drug— Elementary	3 = No Problem 4 = DK
45	DRUGHS	Seriousness Drugs— High School	
46	DRUGCOLL	Seriousness Drugs— College	
47	DRUGADUL	Seriousness Drugs— Adults	
48	RACEDISC	Seriousness Race Discrim.	
49	SEXDISC	Seriousness Sex Discrim.	

STATPAC Variable #	SPSSPC Var. Name	Variable Description	Values
50	WATERPOL	Seriousness Water Pollution	
51	POLLBIRD	Seriousness Bird Pollution	
52	ILLIT	Seriousness of Illiteracy	
53	PORN	Seriousness of Pornography	
54	ROADS	Seriousness Road Conditions	
55	UNEMP	Seriousness of Unemployment	
56	POVERTY	Seriousness of Poverty	
57	RAPECRIS	Expand Rape Crisis Services	Projects Asked in Variables #57–70 have values: 1 = Yes 2 = No 3 = DK
58	CHILABUS	Need More Child Abuse Serv.	
59	HOPELESS	Need Services for Homeless	
60	DRREHAB	Need Drug Rehab Services	
61	INDUSTRY	Need Attract New Industry	
62	DAYCARE	Need Day Care Services	
63	REVDOWN	Need Revitalize Downtown	
64	POOL	Need New Public Swimming Pool	
65	GOLF	Need New 18 Hole Golf Course	
66	ELDERLY	Need Center for Elderly	
67	I65EXIT	Need I-65 Exit Cemetery Rd.	

STATPAC Variable #	SPSSPC Var. Name	Variable Description	Values
68	LOOP	Need City Traffic Loop	
69	BUS	Need City Bus Service	
70	COMMCOLL	Need WKU Community College	
71	CITYTAX	City Taxes	1 = High, 2 = Right, 3 = Low, 4 = DK
72	WCTAX	County Taxes	1 = High, 2 = Right, 3 = Low, 4 = DK
73	NEWTAX	Willing To Support New Tax	1 = Yes, 2 = No, 3 = DK
74	SEX	Sex	1 = Male, 2 = Female
75	AGE	Age	18–91 (2 col)
76	MARITAL	Marital Status	1 = Married, 2 = Single, 3 = Divorce, 4 = Widow, 5 = Separated, 6 = Cohab, 7 = DK
77	HOUSESIZ	#People in Household	01–20 (2 col)
78	UNDER18	#Under 18 in Household	00–12 (2 col)
79	GRADE	Grade Level	00–24 (2 col)
80	DIPLOMA	Highest Diploma	1 = No HS Grad, 2 = HS Grade/GED, 3 = Some Coll/Trade, 4 = Coll Grad +, 5 = DK
81	HOMETYPE	Own or Rent	1 = own, 2 = rent, 3 = DK
82	RACE	Race	1 = white, 2 = black, 3 = other, 4 = DK
83	EMPLOYED	Employed	1 = Yes, 2 = No, 3 = DK
84	OCCUP	Occupation	Not Coded

STATPAC Variable #	SPSSPC Var. Name	Variable Description	Values
85	INCOME	Family Income	1 = less $10,000, 2 = $10,000–20,000, 3 = $20,000–30,000, 4 = $30,000–40,000, 5 = $40,000–50,000, 6 = $50,000, 9 = DK
86	POLPARTY	Political Party	1 = Rep, 2 = Dem, 3 = Ind, 4 = Other, 5 = DK
87	REGVOTER	Registered Voter	1 = Yes, 2 = No, 3 = DK
88	AREA	Area Living in	Not Coded

STATPAC Codebook filename = CPSCODE

STATPAC Datafile filename = CPSDATA

In SPSSPC access the CPS data file with the command:

```
GET FILE = 'SPSSCPS'.
```

C
STATPAC Analysis
Management Programs

In order to do any statistical analyses of a data file and its associated codebook, an analysis control file needs to be created. This file provides instructions for the statistical analysis of data.

1. From the Main Menu select #3, Analysis.

2. From the Analysis Management Menu select #1, Create a New Analysis Control File.

3. First, you will be asked for the filename of the control file. Enter a new filename (eight-character max.), preceded by the appropriate drive specification. If STATPAC is on hard disk, store on floppy in Drive A. Example: A: TASK 1. If STATPAC is on Drive A, store on floppy in Drive B. Example: B: TASK 2.

4. The program will then ask you to enter the filenames of the codebook to be used in the analysis. Enter the CPSCODE (hard disk) or B: CPSCODE (if using two disk drives).

5. Then you will be asked for the name of the data file to be used in the analysis. Enter CPSDATA (for hard disk) or B: CPSDATA (if using two floppy disks).

6. *Page Heading.* What you enter here will be printed at the top of each page for all analyses in this control file. It may be up to 63 characters in length.

7. *Task Title.* What you enter here will be the heading for the table (up to 63 characters).

8. You will then be given a menu to select the *type of analysis* to be performed. The analysis types include:
   a. #2 Frequency Distribution
   b. #3 Descriptive Statistics
   c. #4 Crosstabs and Chi-Square Analysis
   d. #5 Correlation and Linear Regression
   e. #6 T-Test
   f. #7 Multiple Regression
   g. #8 Analysis of Variance

9. Information for each type of analysis is entered generally in the following sequence:
   a. Select the type of analysis to be performed.
   b. Identify the variable numbers (from your codebook) to be analyzed.
   c. Select special options (e.g., on some analyses you may wish to recode, select, or compute).
   d. Write the task to the task control file and floppy disk.

10A. *#2 Frequency Distribution and #3 Descriptive Statistics*
   a. The program will ask for the variable number (#) to be analyzed. Type in number of the variable and ENTER.
   b. *Options.* If no recodes, selects, or computes are needed, select #6, End Task and Write to Disk. This will save your task on the floppy disk in drive A.
   c. *Additional Tasks (Y/N)?* If there are additional tasks to be included on this file, they can be added now. If not, type in N and ENTER.
   d. You will be asked if you want to execute the file now (Y/N)? If you select Y, you will be asked to enter the number of the first task to be executed. If you have only one task on the file or want to start with the first of several tasks, enter 1. Be sure your printer is turned on and the switch is at the correct letter. After a minute or so your analysis will be printed on the printer. If you select N, you will return to the menu. The analysis can be run at a later time.
   e. To run an already saved analysis control file, select #5, Execute an Analysis from the Analysis Management Menu, and when prompted, enter the name of the control file to be executed. Be sure to include the Drive A specification. Example: A: Task 1. Then, enter the number of the first task to be executed. Enter 1 if you want the first or only task on the file.

f. *Outputs*

i. *Frequency Analysis.* Provides a table showing number, percent and cumulative percentage for each of the variables. It will also print a crude bar graph and pie chart (optional).

ii. *Descriptive Statistics.* Calculates and prints range, mean, median, mode, variance, standard deviation, standard error, and 95 and 99 percent confidence intervals. This should only be used for interval- and ratio-level data.

10B. *#4 CROSSTABS and Chi Square Analysis + #5 CORRELATION and REGRESSION*

a. The program asks for two variable numbers to be entered. The first variable will be the variable on the X axis—the *independent* variable (in a crosstab it is the variable across the top of the table). The second variable will be the variable on the Y axis—the *dependent* variable (in a crosstab it is the variable down the side of the table).

b. *Options.* If recodes or select is needed, they are selected here. If not, select #6, End Task and Write to Disk.

c. Then, steps c–e outlined in instruction 10A on frequency distributions are followed.

d. *Outputs*

i. *CROSSTABS.* Presents a table with cell frequencies, row percentage, column percentage, total percentage, and the following statistics: chi-square, probability of chance, phi or Cramer's V, contingency coefficient.

ii. *Correlation and Regression.* Produces a scattergram and the following statistics: means and standard deviations of X and Y, correlation coefficient, slope and Y intercept of regression line equation, standard error of estimate, and t-test of the correlation coefficient.

10c. *#6 T-Test*

Two types are available: #1 T-test for Matched Pairs and #2 T-test for Independent Groups. #1 is for when you have data on before and after or pretest and posttest situations. You will *not use* option #1 here. #2 is for examining differences between two groups on a particular variable. This is the test you may use if your dependent variable is continuous (at least ordinal, preferably interval or ratio). Only the procedure for option #2 is explained here.

a. First, enter the variable number that will be split into two groups.

b. Enter codes for Group 2: Enter the number of the appropriate value label.

c. Enter codes for Group 2: Enter the number of the appropriate value label. Example: If GENDER was coded 1 = Male and 2 = Female and you wanted to examine the differences between males and females on some variable, the code for Group 1 would be 1, and the code for Group 2 would be 2.

d. Enter the number of the variable that will be analyzed: Enter the number of the dependent variable.

e. Options: Again, if no recodes or selects are needed, enter #6 to end and write to disk.

f. Then, steps c–e outlined in instruction 10A are followed.

g. Output: Means, variances, standard deviations of the dependent variable for both groups, and *t*-test statistics, including probability.

10D. *#7 Multiple Regression and #8 Analysis of Variance*
See the STATPAC manual for these.

D
Statistical Tables

TABLE I Z-SCORES AND AREAS UNDER THE NORMAL CURVE

Fractional parts of the total area (10,000) under the normal curve, corresponding to distances between the mean and ordinates that are Z standard deviation units from the mean.

Z	.00	.01	.02	.03	.04	.05	.06	.07	.08	.09
0.0	0000	0040	0080	0120	0159	0199	0239	0279	0319	0359
0.1	0398	0438	0478	0517	0557	0596	0636	0675	0714	0753
0.2	0793	0832	0871	0910	0948	0987	1026	1064	1103	1141
0.3	1179	1217	1255	1293	1331	1368	1406	1443	1480	1517
0.4	1554	1591	1628	1664	1700	1736	1772	1808	1844	1879
0.5	1915	1950	1985	2019	2054	2088	2123	2157	2190	2224
0.6	2257	2291	2324	2357	2389	2422	2454	2486	2518	2549
0.7	2580	2612	2642	2673	2704	2734	2764	2794	2823	2852
0.8	2881	2910	2939	2967	2995	3023	3051	3078	3106	3133
0.9	3159	3186	3212	3238	3264	3289	3315	3340	3365	3389
1.0	3413	3438	3461	3485	3508	3531	3554	3577	3599	3621
1.1	3643	3665	3686	3718	3729	3749	3770	3790	3810	3830
1.2	3849	3869	3888	3907	3925	3944	3962	3980	3997	4015
1.3	4032	4049	4066	4083	4099	4115	4131	4147	4162	4177
1.4	4192	4207	4222	4236	4251	4265	4279	4292	4306	4319
1.5	4332	4345	4357	4370	4382	4394	4406	4418	4430	4441
1.6	4452	4463	4474	4485	4495	4505	4515	4525	4535	4545
1.7	4554	4564	4573	4582	4591	4599	4608	4616	4625	4633
1.8	4641	4649	4656	4664	4671	4678	4686	4693	4699	4706
1.9	4713	4719	4726	4732	4738	4744	4750	4758	4762	4767
2.0	4773	4778	4783	4788	4793	4798	4803	4808	4812	4817
2.1	4821	4826	4830	4834	4838	4842	4846	4850	4854	4857
2.2	4861	4865	4868	4871	4875	4878	4881	4884	4887	4890
2.3	4893	4896	4898	4901	4904	4906	4909	4911	4913	4916
2.4	4918	4920	4922	4925	4927	4929	4931	4932	4934	4936
2.5	4938	4940	4941	4943	4945	4946	4948	4949	4951	4952
2.6	4953	4955	4956	4957	4959	4960	4961	4962	4963	4964
2.7	4965	4966	4967	4968	4969	4970	4971	4972	4973	4974
2.8	4974	4975	4976	4977	4977	4978	4979	4980	4980	4981
2.9	4981	4982	4983	4984	4984	4984	4985	4985	4986	4986
3.0	4986.5	4987	4987	4988	4988	4988	4989	4989	4989	4990
3.1	4990.0	4991	4991	4991	4992	4992	4992	4992	4993	4993
3.2	4993.129									
3.3	4995.166									
3.4	4996.631									
3.5	4997.674									
3.6	4998.409									
3.7	4998.922									
3.8	4999.277									
3.9	4999.519									
4.0	4999.683									
4.5	4999.966									
5.0	4999.997133									

TABLE II   CRITICAL VALUES OF *t*

Degrees of Freedom (d.f.)	Level of Significance for One-Tailed Test					
	.10	.05	.025	.01	.005	.0005
	Level of Significance for Two-Tailed Test					
	.20	.10	.05	.02	.01	.001
1	3.078	6.314	12.706	31.821	63.657	636.619
2	1.886	2.920	4.303	6.965	9.925	31.598
3	1.638	2.353	3.182	4.541	5.841	12.941
4	1.533	2.132	2.776	3.747	4.604	8.610
5	1.476	2.015	2.571	3.365	4.032	6.859
6	1.440	1.943	2.447	3.143	3.707	5.959
7	1.415	1.895	2.365	2.998	3.499	5.405
8	1.397	1.860	2.306	2.896	3.355	5.041
9	1.383	1.833	2.262	2.821	3.250	4.781
10	1.372	1.812	2.228	2.764	3.169	4.587
11	1.363	1.796	2.201	2.718	3.106	4.437
12	1.356	1.782	2.179	2.681	3.055	4.318
13	1.350	1.771	2.160	2.650	3.012	4.221
14	1.345	1.761	2.145	2.624	2.977	4.140
15	1.341	1.753	2.131	2.602	2.947	4.073
16	1.337	1.746	2.120	2.583	2.921	4.015
17	1.333	1.740	2.110	2.567	2.898	3.965
18	1.330	1.734	2.101	2.552	2.878	3.922
19	1.328	1.729	2.093	2.539	2.861	3.883
20	1.325	1.725	2.086	2.528	2.845	3.850
21	1.323	1.721	2.080	2.518	2.831	3.819
22	1.321	1.717	2.074	2.508	2.819	3.792
23	1.319	1.714	2.069	2.500	2.807	3.767
24	1.318	1.711	2.064	2.492	2.797	3.745
25	1.316	1.708	2.060	2.485	2.787	3.725
26	1.315	1.706	2.056	2.479	2.779	3.707
27	1.314	1.703	2.052	2.473	2.771	3.690
28	1.313	1.701	2.048	2.467	2.763	3.674
29	1.311	1.699	2.045	2.462	2.756	3.659
30	1.310	1.697	2.042	2.457	2.750	3.646
40	1.303	1.684	2.021	2.423	2.704	3.551
60	1.296	1.671	2.000	2.390	2.660	3.460
120	1.289	1.658	1.980	2.358	2.617	3.373
∞	1.282	1.645	1.960	2.326	2.576	3.291

Tables 1 & 2: Fisher & Yates': *Statistical Tables for Biological, Agricultural and Medical Research* published by Longman Group UK Ltd., London (previously published by Oliver and Boyd Ltd., Edinburgh) and by permission of the authors and publishers.

TABLE III CRITICAL VALUES OF F

.05 Level in Roman Type, .01 Level in Boldface

Degrees of Freedom for the Numerator

df (denom)	1	2	3	4	5	6	7	8	9	10	11	12	14	16	20	24	30	40	50	75	100	200	500	∞
1	161 / 4,052	200 / 4,999	216 / 5,403	225 / 5,625	230 / 5,764	234 / 5,859	237 / 5,928	239 / 5,981	241 / 6,022	242 / 6,056	243 / 6,082	244 / 6,106	245 / 6,142	246 / 6,169	248 / 6,208	249 / 6,234	250 / 6,261	251 / 6,286	252 / 6,302	253 / 6,323	253 / 6,334	254 / 6,352	254 / 6,361	254 / 6,366
2	18.51 / 98.49	19.00 / 99.00	19.16 / 99.17	19.25 / 99.25	19.30 / 99.30	19.33 / 99.33	19.36 / 99.36	19.37 / 99.37	19.38 / 99.39	19.39 / 99.40	19.40 / 99.41	19.41 / 99.42	19.42 / 99.43	19.43 / 99.44	19.44 / 99.45	19.45 / 99.46	19.46 / 99.47	19.47 / 99.48	19.47 / 99.48	19.48 / 99.49	19.49 / 99.49	19.49 / 99.49	19.50 / 99.50	19.50 / 99.50
3	10.13 / 34.12	9.55 / 30.82	9.28 / 29.46	9.12 / 28.71	9.01 / 28.24	8.94 / 27.91	8.88 / 27.67	8.84 / 27.49	8.81 / 27.34	8.78 / 27.23	8.76 / 27.13	8.74 / 27.05	8.71 / 26.92	8.69 / 26.83	8.66 / 26.69	8.64 / 26.60	8.62 / 26.50	8.60 / 26.41	8.58 / 26.35	8.57 / 26.27	8.56 / 26.23	8.54 / 26.18	8.54 / 26.14	8.53 / 26.12
4	7.71 / 21.20	6.94 / 18.00	6.59 / 16.69	6.39 / 15.98	6.26 / 15.52	6.16 / 15.21	6.09 / 14.98	6.04 / 14.80	6.00 / 14.66	5.96 / 14.54	5.93 / 14.45	5.91 / 14.37	5.87 / 14.24	5.84 / 14.15	5.80 / 14.02	5.77 / 13.93	5.74 / 13.83	5.71 / 13.74	5.70 / 13.69	5.68 / 13.61	5.66 / 13.57	5.65 / 13.52	5.64 / 13.48	5.63 / 13.46
5	6.61 / 16.26	5.79 / 13.27	5.41 / 12.06	5.19 / 11.39	5.05 / 10.97	4.95 / 10.67	4.88 / 10.45	4.82 / 10.29	4.78 / 10.15	4.74 / 10.05	4.70 / 9.96	4.68 / 9.89	4.64 / 9.77	4.60 / 9.68	4.56 / 9.55	4.53 / 9.47	4.50 / 9.38	4.46 / 9.29	4.44 / 9.24	4.42 / 9.17	4.40 / 9.13	4.38 / 9.07	4.37 / 9.04	4.36 / 9.02
6	5.99 / 13.74	5.14 / 10.92	4.76 / 9.78	4.53 / 9.15	4.39 / 8.75	4.28 / 8.47	4.21 / 8.26	4.15 / 8.10	4.10 / 7.98	4.06 / 7.87	4.03 / 7.79	4.00 / 7.72	3.96 / 7.60	3.92 / 7.52	3.87 / 7.39	3.84 / 7.31	3.81 / 7.23	3.77 / 7.14	3.75 / 7.09	3.72 / 7.02	3.71 / 6.99	3.69 / 6.94	3.68 / 6.90	3.67 / 6.88
7	5.59 / 12.25	4.74 / 9.55	4.35 / 8.45	4.12 / 7.85	3.97 / 7.46	3.87 / 7.19	3.79 / 7.00	3.73 / 6.84	3.68 / 6.71	3.63 / 6.62	3.60 / 6.54	3.57 / 6.47	3.52 / 6.35	3.49 / 6.27	3.44 / 6.15	3.41 / 6.07	3.38 / 5.98	3.34 / 5.90	3.32 / 5.85	3.29 / 5.78	3.28 / 5.75	3.25 / 5.70	3.24 / 5.67	3.23 / 5.65
8	5.32 / 11.26	4.46 / 8.65	4.07 / 7.59	3.84 / 7.01	3.69 / 6.63	3.58 / 6.37	3.50 / 6.19	3.44 / 6.03	3.39 / 5.91	3.34 / 5.82	3.31 / 5.74	3.28 / 5.67	3.23 / 5.56	3.20 / 5.48	3.15 / 5.36	3.12 / 5.28	3.08 / 5.20	3.05 / 5.11	3.03 / 5.06	3.00 / 5.00	2.98 / 4.96	2.96 / 4.91	2.94 / 4.88	2.93 / 4.86
9	5.12 / 10.56	4.26 / 8.02	3.86 / 6.99	3.63 / 6.42	3.48 / 6.06	3.37 / 5.80	3.29 / 5.62	3.23 / 5.47	3.18 / 5.35	3.13 / 5.26	3.10 / 5.18	3.07 / 5.11	3.02 / 5.00	2.98 / 4.92	2.93 / 4.80	2.90 / 4.73	2.86 / 4.64	2.82 / 4.56	2.80 / 4.51	2.77 / 4.45	2.76 / 4.41	2.73 / 4.36	2.72 / 4.33	2.71 / 4.31
10	4.96 / 10.04	4.10 / 7.56	3.71 / 6.55	3.48 / 5.99	3.33 / 5.64	3.22 / 5.39	3.14 / 5.21	3.07 / 5.06	3.02 / 4.95	2.97 / 4.85	2.94 / 4.78	2.91 / 4.71	2.86 / 4.60	2.82 / 4.52	2.77 / 4.41	2.74 / 4.33	2.70 / 4.25	2.67 / 4.17	2.64 / 4.12	2.61 / 4.05	2.59 / 4.01	2.56 / 3.96	2.55 / 3.93	2.54 / 3.91
11	4.84 / 9.65	3.98 / 7.20	3.59 / 6.22	3.36 / 5.67	3.20 / 5.32	3.09 / 5.07	3.01 / 4.88	2.95 / 4.74	2.90 / 4.63	2.86 / 4.54	2.82 / 4.46	2.79 / 4.40	2.74 / 4.29	2.70 / 4.21	2.65 / 4.10	2.61 / 4.02	2.57 / 3.94	2.53 / 3.86	2.50 / 3.80	2.47 / 3.74	2.45 / 3.70	2.42 / 3.66	2.41 / 3.62	2.40 / 3.60
12	4.75 / 9.33	3.88 / 6.93	3.49 / 5.95	3.26 / 5.41	3.11 / 5.06	3.00 / 4.82	2.92 / 4.65	2.85 / 4.50	2.80 / 4.39	2.76 / 4.30	2.72 / 4.22	2.69 / 4.16	2.64 / 4.05	2.60 / 3.98	2.54 / 3.86	2.50 / 3.78	2.46 / 3.70	2.42 / 3.61	2.40 / 3.56	2.36 / 3.49	2.35 / 3.46	2.32 / 3.41	2.31 / 3.38	2.30 / 3.36
13	4.67 / 9.07	3.80 / 6.70	3.41 / 5.74	3.18 / 5.20	3.02 / 4.86	2.92 / 4.62	2.84 / 4.44	2.77 / 4.30	2.72 / 4.19	2.67 / 4.10	2.63 / 4.02	2.60 / 3.96	2.55 / 3.85	2.51 / 3.78	2.46 / 3.67	2.42 / 3.59	2.38 / 3.51	2.34 / 3.42	2.32 / 3.37	2.28 / 3.30	2.26 / 3.27	2.24 / 3.21	2.22 / 3.18	2.21 / 3.16

Degrees of Freedom for the Denominator

TABLE III CONTINUED

Degrees of Freedom for the Numerator

	1	2	3	4	5	6	7	8	9	10	11	12	14	16	20	24	30	40	50	75	100	200	500	∞
14	4.60 / 8.86	3.74 / 6.51	3.34 / 5.56	3.11 / 5.03	2.96 / 4.69	2.85 / 4.46	2.77 / 4.28	2.70 / 4.14	2.65 / 4.03	2.60 / 3.94	2.56 / 3.86	2.53 / 3.80	2.48 / 3.70	2.44 / 3.62	2.39 / 3.51	2.35 / 3.43	2.31 / 3.34	2.27 / 3.26	2.24 / 3.21	2.21 / 3.14	2.19 / 3.11	2.16 / 3.06	2.14 / 3.02	2.13 / 3.00
15	4.54 / 8.68	3.68 / 6.36	3.29 / 5.42	3.06 / 4.89	2.90 / 4.56	2.79 / 4.32	2.70 / 4.14	2.64 / 4.00	2.59 / 3.89	2.55 / 3.80	2.51 / 3.73	2.48 / 3.67	2.43 / 3.56	2.39 / 3.48	2.33 / 3.36	2.29 / 3.29	2.25 / 3.20	2.21 / 3.12	2.18 / 3.07	2.15 / 3.00	2.12 / 2.97	2.10 / 2.92	2.08 / 2.89	2.07 / 2.87
16	4.49 / 8.53	3.63 / 6.23	3.24 / 5.29	3.01 / 4.77	2.85 / 4.44	2.74 / 4.20	2.66 / 4.03	2.59 / 3.89	2.54 / 3.78	2.49 / 3.69	2.45 / 3.61	2.42 / 3.55	2.37 / 3.45	2.33 / 3.37	2.28 / 3.25	2.24 / 3.18	2.20 / 3.10	2.16 / 3.01	2.13 / 2.96	2.09 / 2.98	2.07 / 2.86	2.04 / 2.80	2.02 / 2.77	2.01 / 2.75
17	4.45 / 8.40	3.59 / 6.11	3.20 / 5.18	2.96 / 4.67	2.81 / 4.34	2.70 / 4.10	2.62 / 3.93	2.55 / 3.79	2.50 / 3.68	2.45 / 3.59	2.41 / 3.52	2.38 / 3.45	2.33 / 3.35	2.29 / 3.27	2.23 / 3.16	2.19 / 3.08	2.15 / 3.00	2.11 / 2.92	2.08 / 2.86	2.04 / 2.79	2.02 / 2.76	1.99 / 2.70	1.97 / 2.67	1.96 / 2.65
18	4.41 / 8.28	3.55 / 6.01	3.16 / 5.09	2.93 / 4.58	2.77 / 4.25	2.66 / 4.01	2.58 / 3.85	2.51 / 3.71	2.46 / 3.60	2.41 / 3.51	2.37 / 3.44	2.34 / 3.37	2.29 / 3.27	2.25 / 3.19	2.19 / 3.07	2.15 / 3.00	2.11 / 2.91	2.07 / 2.83	2.04 / 2.78	2.00 / 2.71	1.98 / 2.68	1.95 / 2.62	1.93 / 2.59	1.92 / 2.57
19	4.38 / 8.18	3.52 / 5.93	3.13 / 5.01	2.90 / 4.50	2.74 / 4.17	2.63 / 3.94	2.55 / 3.77	2.48 / 3.63	2.43 / 3.52	2.38 / 3.43	2.34 / 3.36	2.31 / 3.30	2.26 / 3.19	2.21 / 3.12	2.15 / 3.00	2.11 / 2.92	2.07 / 2.84	2.02 / 2.76	2.00 / 2.70	1.96 / 2.63	1.94 / 2.60	1.91 / 2.54	1.90 / 2.51	1.88 / 2.49
20	4.35 / 8.10	3.49 / 5.85	3.10 / 4.94	2.87 / 4.43	2.71 / 4.10	2.60 / 3.87	2.52 / 3.71	2.45 / 3.56	2.40 / 3.45	2.35 / 3.37	2.31 / 3.30	2.28 / 3.23	2.23 / 3.13	2.18 / 3.05	2.12 / 2.94	2.08 / 2.86	2.04 / 2.77	1.99 / 2.69	1.96 / 2.63	1.92 / 2.56	1.90 / 2.53	1.87 / 2.47	1.85 / 2.44	1.84 / 2.42
21	4.32 / 8.02	3.47 / 5.78	3.07 / 4.87	2.84 / 4.37	2.68 / 4.04	2.57 / 3.81	2.49 / 3.65	2.42 / 3.51	2.37 / 3.40	2.32 / 3.31	2.28 / 3.24	2.25 / 3.17	2.20 / 3.07	2.15 / 2.99	2.09 / 2.88	2.05 / 2.80	2.00 / 2.72	1.96 / 2.63	1.93 / 2.58	1.89 / 2.51	1.87 / 2.47	1.84 / 2.42	1.82 / 2.38	1.81 / 2.36
22	4.30 / 7.94	3.44 / 5.72	3.05 / 4.82	2.82 / 4.31	2.66 / 3.99	2.55 / 3.76	2.47 / 3.59	2.40 / 3.45	2.35 / 3.35	2.30 / 3.26	2.26 / 3.18	2.23 / 3.12	2.18 / 3.02	2.13 / 2.94	2.07 / 2.83	2.03 / 2.75	1.98 / 2.67	1.93 / 2.58	1.91 / 2.53	1.87 / 2.46	1.84 / 2.42	1.81 / 2.37	1.80 / 2.33	1.78 / 2.31
23	4.28 / 7.88	3.42 / 5.66	3.03 / 4.76	2.80 / 4.26	2.64 / 3.94	2.53 / 3.71	2.45 / 3.54	2.38 / 3.41	2.32 / 3.30	2.28 / 3.21	2.24 / 3.14	2.20 / 3.07	2.14 / 2.97	2.10 / 2.89	2.04 / 2.78	2.00 / 2.70	1.96 / 2.62	1.91 / 2.53	1.88 / 2.48	1.84 / 2.41	1.82 / 2.37	1.79 / 2.32	1.77 / 2.28	1.76 / 2.26
24	4.26 / 7.82	3.40 / 5.61	3.01 / 4.72	2.78 / 4.22	2.62 / 3.90	2.51 / 3.67	2.43 / 3.50	2.36 / 3.36	2.30 / 3.25	2.26 / 3.17	2.22 / 3.09	2.18 / 3.03	2.13 / 2.93	2.09 / 2.85	2.02 / 2.74	1.98 / 2.66	1.94 / 2.58	1.89 / 2.49	1.86 / 2.44	1.82 / 2.36	1.80 / 2.33	1.76 / 2.27	1.74 / 2.23	1.73 / 2.21
25	4.24 / 7.77	3.38 / 5.57	2.99 / 4.68	2.76 / 4.18	2.60 / 3.86	2.49 / 3.63	2.41 / 3.46	2.34 / 3.32	2.28 / 3.21	2.24 / 3.13	2.20 / 3.05	2.16 / 2.99	2.11 / 2.89	2.06 / 2.81	2.00 / 2.70	1.96 / 2.62	1.92 / 2.54	1.87 / 2.45	1.84 / 2.40	1.80 / 2.32	1.77 / 2.29	1.74 / 2.23	1.72 / 2.19	1.71 / 2.17
26	4.22 / 7.72	3.37 / 5.53	2.98 / 4.64	2.74 / 4.14	2.59 / 3.82	2.47 / 3.59	2.39 / 3.42	2.32 / 3.29	2.27 / 3.17	2.22 / 3.09	2.18 / 3.02	2.15 / 2.96	2.10 / 2.86	2.05 / 2.77	1.99 / 2.66	1.95 / 2.58	1.90 / 2.50	1.85 / 2.41	1.82 / 2.36	1.78 / 2.28	1.76 / 2.25	1.72 / 2.19	1.70 / 2.15	1.69 / 2.13

Degrees of Freedom for the Denominator

TABLE III CONTINUED

Degrees of Freedom for the Numerator

	1	2	3	4	5	6	7	8	9	10	11	12	14	16	20	24	30	40	50	75	100	200	500	∞
27	4.21 / 7.68	3.35 / 5.49	2.96 / 4.60	2.73 / 4.11	2.57 / 3.79	2.46 / 3.56	2.37 / 3.39	2.30 / 3.26	2.25 / 3.14	2.20 / 3.06	2.16 / 2.98	2.13 / 2.93	2.08 / 2.83	2.03 / 2.74	1.97 / 2.63	1.93 / 2.55	1.88 / 2.47	1.84 / 2.38	1.80 / 2.33	1.76 / 2.25	1.74 / 2.21	1.71 / 2.16	1.68 / 2.12	1.67 / 2.10
28	4.20 / 7.64	3.34 / 5.45	2.95 / 4.57	2.71 / 4.07	2.56 / 3.76	2.44 / 3.53	2.36 / 3.36	2.29 / 3.23	2.24 / 3.11	2.19 / 3.03	2.15 / 2.95	2.12 / 2.90	2.06 / 2.80	2.02 / 2.71	1.96 / 2.60	1.91 / 2.52	1.87 / 2.44	1.81 / 2.35	1.78 / 2.30	1.75 / 2.22	1.72 / 2.18	1.69 / 2.13	1.67 / 2.09	1.65 / 2.06
29	4.18 / 7.60	3.33 / 5.42	2.93 / 4.54	2.70 / 4.04	2.54 / 3.73	2.43 / 3.50	2.35 / 3.33	2.28 / 3.20	2.22 / 3.08	2.18 / 3.00	2.14 / 2.92	2.10 / 2.87	2.05 / 2.77	2.00 / 2.68	1.94 / 2.57	1.90 / 2.49	1.85 / 2.41	1.80 / 2.32	1.77 / 2.27	1.73 / 2.19	1.71 / 2.15	1.68 / 2.10	1.65 / 2.06	1.64 / 2.03
30	4.17 / 7.56	3.32 / 5.39	2.92 / 4.51	2.69 / 4.02	2.53 / 3.70	2.42 / 3.47	2.34 / 3.30	2.27 / 3.17	2.21 / 3.06	2.16 / 2.98	2.12 / 2.90	2.09 / 2.84	2.04 / 2.74	1.99 / 2.66	1.93 / 2.55	1.89 / 2.47	1.84 / 2.38	1.79 / 2.29	1.76 / 2.24	1.72 / 2.16	1.69 / 2.13	1.66 / 2.07	1.64 / 2.03	1.62 / 2.01
32	4.15 / 7.50	3.30 / 5.34	2.90 / 4.46	2.67 / 3.97	2.51 / 3.66	2.40 / 3.42	2.32 / 3.25	2.25 / 3.12	2.19 / 3.01	2.14 / 2.94	2.10 / 2.86	2.07 / 2.80	2.02 / 2.70	1.97 / 2.62	1.91 / 2.51	1.86 / 2.42	1.82 / 2.34	1.76 / 2.25	1.74 / 2.20	1.69 / 2.12	1.67 / 2.08	1.64 / 2.02	1.61 / 1.98	1.59 / 1.96
34	4.13 / 7.44	3.28 / 5.29	2.88 / 4.42	2.65 / 3.93	2.49 / 3.61	2.38 / 3.38	2.30 / 3.21	2.23 / 3.08	2.17 / 2.97	2.12 / 2.89	2.08 / 2.82	2.05 / 2.76	2.00 / 2.66	1.95 / 2.58	1.89 / 2.47	1.84 / 2.38	1.80 / 2.30	1.74 / 2.21	1.71 / 2.15	1.67 / 2.08	1.64 / 2.04	1.61 / 1.98	1.59 / 1.94	1.57 / 1.91
36	4.11 / 7.39	3.26 / 5.25	2.86 / 4.38	2.63 / 3.89	2.48 / 3.58	2.36 / 3.35	2.28 / 3.18	2.21 / 3.04	2.15 / 2.94	2.10 / 2.86	2.06 / 2.78	2.03 / 2.72	1.98 / 2.62	1.93 / 2.54	1.87 / 2.43	1.82 / 2.35	1.78 / 2.26	1.72 / 2.17	1.69 / 2.12	1.65 / 2.04	1.62 / 2.00	1.59 / 1.94	1.56 / 1.90	1.55 / 1.87
38	4.10 / 7.35	3.25 / 5.21	2.85 / 4.34	2.62 / 3.86	2.46 / 3.54	2.35 / 3.32	2.26 / 3.15	2.19 / 3.02	2.14 / 2.91	2.09 / 2.82	2.05 / 2.75	2.02 / 2.69	1.96 / 2.59	1.92 / 2.51	1.85 / 2.40	1.80 / 2.32	1.76 / 2.22	1.71 / 2.14	1.67 / 2.08	1.63 / 2.00	1.60 / 1.97	1.57 / 1.90	1.54 / 1.86	1.53 / 1.84
40	4.08 / 7.31	3.23 / 5.18	2.84 / 4.31	2.61 / 3.83	2.45 / 3.51	2.34 / 3.29	2.25 / 3.12	2.18 / 2.99	2.12 / 2.88	2.07 / 2.80	2.04 / 2.73	2.00 / 2.66	1.95 / 2.56	1.90 / 2.49	1.84 / 2.37	1.79 / 2.29	1.74 / 2.20	1.69 / 2.11	1.66 / 2.05	1.61 / 1.97	1.59 / 1.94	1.55 / 1.88	1.53 / 1.84	1.51 / 1.81
42	4.07 / 7.27	3.22 / 5.15	2.83 / 4.29	2.59 / 3.80	2.44 / 3.49	2.32 / 3.26	2.24 / 3.10	2.17 / 2.96	2.11 / 2.86	2.06 / 2.77	2.02 / 2.70	1.99 / 2.64	1.94 / 2.54	1.89 / 2.46	1.82 / 2.35	1.78 / 2.26	1.73 / 2.17	1.68 / 2.08	1.64 / 2.02	1.60 / 1.94	1.57 / 1.91	1.54 / 1.85	1.51 / 1.80	1.49 / 1.78
44	4.06 / 7.24	3.21 / 5.12	2.82 / 4.26	2.58 / 3.78	2.43 / 3.46	2.31 / 3.24	2.23 / 3.07	2.16 / 2.94	2.10 / 2.84	2.05 / 2.75	2.01 / 2.68	1.98 / 2.62	1.92 / 2.52	1.88 / 2.44	1.81 / 2.32	1.76 / 2.24	1.72 / 2.15	1.66 / 2.06	1.63 / 2.00	1.58 / 1.92	1.56 / 1.88	1.52 / 1.82	1.50 / 1.78	1.48 / 1.75
46	4.05 / 7.21	3.20 / 5.10	2.81 / 4.24	2.57 / 3.76	2.42 / 3.44	2.30 / 3.22	2.22 / 3.05	2.14 / 2.92	2.09 / 2.82	2.04 / 2.73	2.00 / 2.66	1.97 / 2.60	1.91 / 2.50	1.87 / 2.42	1.80 / 2.30	1.75 / 2.22	1.71 / 2.13	1.65 / 2.04	1.62 / 1.98	1.57 / 1.90	1.54 / 1.86	1.51 / 1.80	1.48 / 1.76	1.46 / 1.72
48	4.04 / 7.19	3.19 / 5.08	2.80 / 4.22	2.56 / 3.74	2.41 / 3.42	2.30 / 3.20	2.21 / 3.04	2.14 / 2.90	2.08 / 2.80	2.03 / 2.71	1.99 / 2.64	1.96 / 2.58	1.90 / 2.48	1.86 / 2.40	1.79 / 2.28	1.74 / 2.20	1.70 / 2.11	1.64 / 2.02	1.61 / 1.96	1.56 / 1.88	1.53 / 1.84	1.50 / 1.78	1.47 / 1.73	1.45 / 1.70

Degrees of Freedom for the Denominator

TABLE III CONTINUED

Degrees of Freedom for the Numerator

	1	2	3	4	5	6	7	8	9	10	11	12	14	16	20	24	30	40	50	75	100	200	500	∞
50	4.03 / 7.17	3.18 / 5.06	2.79 / 4.20	2.56 / 3.72	2.40 / 3.41	2.29 / 3.18	2.20 / 3.02	2.13 / 2.88	2.07 / 2.78	2.02 / 2.70	1.98 / 2.62	1.95 / 2.56	1.90 / 2.46	1.85 / 2.39	1.78 / 2.26	1.74 / 2.18	1.69 / 2.10	1.63 / 2.00	1.60 / 1.94	1.55 / 1.86	1.52 / 1.82	1.48 / 1.76	1.46 / 1.71	1.44 / 1.68
55	4.02 / 7.12	3.17 / 5.01	2.78 / 4.16	2.54 / 3.68	2.38 / 3.37	2.27 / 3.15	2.18 / 2.98	2.11 / 2.85	2.05 / 2.75	2.00 / 2.66	1.97 / 2.59	1.93 / 2.53	1.88 / 2.43	1.83 / 2.35	1.76 / 2.23	1.72 / 2.15	1.67 / 2.06	1.61 / 1.96	1.58 / 1.90	1.52 / 1.82	1.50 / 1.78	1.46 / 1.71	1.43 / 1.66	1.41 / 1.64
60	4.00 / 7.08	3.15 / 4.98	2.76 / 4.13	2.52 / 3.65	2.37 / 3.34	2.25 / 3.12	2.17 / 2.95	2.10 / 2.82	2.04 / 2.72	1.99 / 2.63	1.95 / 2.56	1.92 / 2.50	1.86 / 2.40	1.81 / 2.32	1.75 / 2.20	1.70 / 2.12	1.65 / 2.03	1.59 / 1.93	1.56 / 1.87	1.50 / 1.79	1.48 / 1.74	1.44 / 1.68	1.41 / 1.63	1.39 / 1.60
65	3.99 / 7.04	3.14 / 4.95	2.75 / 4.10	2.51 / 3.62	2.36 / 3.31	2.24 / 3.09	2.15 / 2.93	2.08 / 2.79	2.02 / 2.70	1.98 / 2.61	1.94 / 2.54	1.90 / 2.47	1.85 / 2.37	1.80 / 2.30	1.73 / 2.18	1.68 / 2.09	1.63 / 2.00	1.57 / 1.90	1.54 / 1.84	1.49 / 1.76	1.46 / 1.71	1.42 / 1.64	1.39 / 1.60	1.37 / 1.56
70	3.98 / 7.01	3.13 / 4.92	2.74 / 4.08	2.50 / 3.60	2.35 / 3.29	2.23 / 3.07	2.14 / 2.91	2.07 / 2.77	2.01 / 2.67	1.97 / 2.59	1.93 / 2.51	1.89 / 2.45	1.84 / 2.35	1.79 / 2.28	1.72 / 2.15	1.67 / 2.07	1.62 / 1.98	1.56 / 1.88	1.53 / 1.82	1.47 / 1.74	1.45 / 1.69	1.40 / 1.62	1.37 / 1.56	1.35 / 1.53
80	3.96 / 6.96	3.11 / 4.88	2.72 / 4.04	2.48 / 3.56	2.33 / 3.25	2.21 / 3.04	2.12 / 2.87	2.05 / 2.74	1.99 / 2.64	1.95 / 2.55	1.91 / 2.48	1.88 / 2.41	1.82 / 2.32	1.77 / 2.24	1.70 / 2.11	1.65 / 2.03	1.60 / 1.94	1.54 / 1.84	1.51 / 1.78	1.45 / 1.70	1.42 / 1.65	1.38 / 1.57	1.35 / 1.52	1.32 / 1.49
100	3.94 / 6.90	3.09 / 4.82	2.70 / 3.98	2.46 / 3.51	2.30 / 3.20	2.19 / 2.99	2.10 / 2.82	2.03 / 2.69	1.97 / 2.59	1.92 / 2.51	1.88 / 2.43	1.85 / 2.36	1.79 / 2.26	1.75 / 2.19	1.68 / 2.06	1.63 / 1.98	1.57 / 1.89	1.51 / 1.79	1.48 / 1.73	1.42 / 1.64	1.39 / 1.59	1.34 / 1.51	1.30 / 1.46	1.28 / 1.43
125	3.92 / 6.84	3.07 / 4.78	2.68 / 3.94	2.44 / 3.47	2.29 / 3.17	2.17 / 2.95	2.08 / 2.79	2.01 / 2.65	1.95 / 2.56	1.90 / 2.47	1.86 / 2.40	1.83 / 2.33	1.77 / 2.23	1.72 / 2.15	1.65 / 2.03	1.60 / 1.94	1.55 / 1.85	1.49 / 1.75	1.45 / 1.68	1.39 / 1.59	1.36 / 1.54	1.31 / 1.46	1.27 / 1.40	1.25 / 1.37
150	3.91 / 6.81	3.06 / 4.75	2.67 / 3.91	2.43 / 3.44	2.27 / 3.14	2.16 / 2.92	2.07 / 2.76	2.00 / 2.62	1.94 / 2.53	1.89 / 2.44	1.85 / 2.37	1.82 / 2.30	1.76 / 2.20	1.71 / 2.12	1.64 / 2.00	1.59 / 1.91	1.54 / 1.83	1.47 / 1.72	1.44 / 1.66	1.37 / 1.56	1.34 / 1.51	1.29 / 1.43	1.25 / 1.37	1.22 / 1.33
200	3.89 / 6.76	3.04 / 4.71	2.65 / 3.88	2.41 / 3.41	2.26 / 3.11	2.14 / 2.90	2.05 / 2.73	1.98 / 2.60	1.92 / 2.50	1.87 / 2.41	1.83 / 2.34	1.80 / 2.28	1.74 / 2.17	1.69 / 2.09	1.62 / 1.97	1.57 / 1.88	1.52 / 1.79	1.45 / 1.69	1.42 / 1.62	1.35 / 1.53	1.32 / 1.48	1.26 / 1.39	1.22 / 1.33	1.19 / 1.28
400	3.86 / 6.70	3.02 / 4.66	2.62 / 3.83	2.39 / 3.36	2.23 / 3.06	2.12 / 2.85	2.03 / 2.69	1.96 / 2.55	1.90 / 2.46	1.85 / 2.37	1.81 / 2.29	1.78 / 2.23	1.72 / 2.12	1.67 / 2.04	1.60 / 1.92	1.54 / 1.84	1.49 / 1.74	1.42 / 1.64	1.38 / 1.57	1.32 / 1.47	1.28 / 1.42	1.22 / 1.32	1.16 / 1.24	1.13 / 1.19
1000	3.85 / 6.66	3.00 / 4.62	2.61 / 3.80	2.38 / 3.34	2.22 / 3.04	2.10 / 2.82	2.02 / 2.66	1.95 / 2.53	1.89 / 2.43	1.84 / 2.34	1.80 / 2.26	1.76 / 2.20	1.70 / 2.09	1.65 / 2.01	1.58 / 1.89	1.53 / 1.81	1.47 / 1.71	1.41 / 1.51	1.36 / 1.54	1.30 / 1.44	1.26 / 1.38	1.19 / 1.28	1.13 / 1.19	1.08 / 1.11
∞	3.84 / 6.64	2.99 / 4.60	2.60 / 3.78	2.37 / 3.32	2.21 / 3.02	2.09 / 2.80	2.01 / 2.64	1.94 / 2.51	1.88 / 2.41	1.83 / 2.32	1.79 / 2.24	1.75 / 2.18	1.69 / 2.07	1.64 / 1.99	1.57 / 1.87	1.52 / 1.79	1.46 / 1.69	1.40 / 1.59	1.35 / 1.52	1.28 / 1.41	1.24 / 1.36	1.17 / 1.25	1.11 / 1.15	1.00 / 1.00

Degrees of Freedom for the Denominator

Table 3 reprinted by permission of the Biometrika Trustees.

TABLE IV CRITICAL VALUES OF CHI-SQUARE

df	.99	.98	.95	.90	.80	.70	.50	.30	.20	.10	.05	.02	.01	.001
1	.03157	.03628	.00393	.0158	.0642	.148	.455	1.074	1.642	2.706	3.841	5.412	6.635	10.827
2	.0201	.0404	.103	.211	.446	.713	1.386	2.408	3.219	4.605	5.991	7.824	9.210	13.815
3	.115	.185	.352	.584	1.005	1.424	2.366	3.665	4.642	6.251	7.815	9.837	11.341	16.268
4	.297	.429	.711	1.064	1.649	2.195	3.357	4.878	5.989	7.779	9.488	11.668	13.277	18.465
5	.554	.752	1.145	1.610	2.343	3.000	4.351	6.064	7.289	9.236	11.070	13.388	15.086	20.517
6	.872	1.134	1.635	2.204	3.070	3.828	5.348	7.231	8.558	10.645	12.592	15.033	16.812	22.457
7	1.239	1.564	2.167	2.833	3.822	4.671	6.346	8.383	9.803	12.017	14.067	16.622	18.475	24.322
8	1.646	2.032	2.733	3.490	4.594	5.527	7.344	9.524	11.030	13.362	15.507	18.168	20.090	26.125
9	2.088	2.532	3.325	4.168	5.380	6.393	8.343	10.656	12.242	14.684	16.919	19.679	21.666	27.877
10	2.558	3.059	3.940	4.865	6.179	7.267	9.342	11.781	13.442	15.987	18.307	21.161	23.209	29.588
11	3.053	3.609	4.575	5.578	6.989	8.148	10.341	12.899	14.631	17.275	19.675	22.618	24.725	31.264
12	3.571	4.178	5.226	6.304	7.807	9.034	11.340	14.011	15.812	18.549	21.026	24.054	26.217	32.909
13	4.107	4.765	5.892	7.042	8.634	9.926	12.340	15.119	16.985	19.812	22.362	25.472	27.688	34.528
14	4.660	5.368	6.571	7.790	9.467	10.821	13.339	16.222	18.151	21.064	23.685	26.873	29.141	36.123
15	5.229	5.985	7.261	8.547	10.307	11.721	14.339	17.322	19.311	22.307	24.996	28.259	30.578	37.697
16	5.812	6.614	7.962	9.312	11.152	12.624	15.338	18.418	20.465	23.542	26.296	29.633	32.000	39.252
17	6.408	7.255	8.672	10.085	12.002	13.531	16.338	19.511	21.615	24.769	27.587	30.995	33.409	40.790
18	7.015	7.906	9.390	10.865	12.857	14.440	17.338	20.601	22.760	25.989	28.869	32.346	34.805	42.312
19	7.633	8.567	10.117	11.651	13.716	15.352	18.338	21.689	23.900	27.204	30.144	33.687	36.191	43.820
20	8.260	9.237	10.851	12.443	14.578	16.266	19.337	22.775	25.038	28.412	31.410	35.020	37.566	45.315
21	8.897	9.915	11.591	13.240	15.445	17.182	20.337	23.858	26.171	29.615	32.671	36.343	38.932	46.797
22	9.542	10.600	12.338	14.041	16.314	18.101	21.337	24.939	27.301	30.813	33.924	37.659	40.289	48.268
23	10.196	11.293	13.091	14.848	17.187	19.021	22.337	26.018	28.429	32.007	35.172	38.968	41.638	49.728
24	10.856	11.992	13.848	15.659	18.062	19.943	23.337	27.096	29.533	33.196	36.415	40.270	42.980	51.179
25	11.524	12.697	14.611	16.473	18.940	20.867	24.337	28.172	30.675	34.382	37.652	41.566	44.314	52.620
26	12.198	13.409	15.379	17.292	19.820	21.792	25.336	29.246	31.795	35.563	38.885	42.856	45.642	54.052
27	12.879	14.125	16.151	18.114	20.703	22.719	26.336	30.319	32.912	36.741	40.113	44.140	46.963	55.476
28	13.565	14.847	16.928	18.939	21.588	23.647	27.336	31.391	34.027	37.916	41.337	45.419	48.278	56.893
29	14.256	15.574	17.708	19.768	22.475	24.577	28.336	32.461	35.139	39.087	42.557	46.693	49.588	58.302
30	14.953	16.306	18.493	20.599	23.364	25.508	29.336	33.530	36.250	40.256	43.773	47.962	50.892	59.703

TABLE V   TABLE OF RANDOM NUMBERS

Using a Random Number Table

You use a random number table by selecting numbers that have the number of digits that correspond to the number of digits in the population size. For example, a population size of 500 has three digits. Therefore, three-digit random numbers are selected to draw the random sample. The first random number may be selected from anywhere in the table. The three-digit number may be made up of the three digits starting on the left side of a column, the three digits ending on the right side of a column, or the three digits in the middle of a column. After the first number is selected, proceed to move in a systematic vertical (up or down), horizontal (left or right), or diagonal pattern and select numbers that fall in the range of 001 to 500 until the desired sample size is reached. The decision of where to start and what direction to proceed in is an arbitrary one. Random numbers that are larger than 500 (the population size) are skipped, and care should be taken to ensure that no number is selected more than once.

The random numbers on the following pages can be used to select random samples.

26203	95922	34009	69651	01356	64264	61445	26597	04005	38318
75437	58382	36108	44359	98592	33148	41686	63480	84801	64312
73126	65038	02219	80983	66429	26432	92263	24923	72437	04278
22732	98009	62337	35191	44256	97591	31050	02342	30141	75975
85893	00162	29357	03746	70544	45658	43214	09614	32926	52149
13774	55916	86636	60615	20977	97863	19044	94411	61029	15045
88188	67131	39604	16544	53367	12097	85278	97970	37989	73168
06781	68222	29334	46018	06793	64226	47956	40942	67801	94233
95685	15658	90989	46006	60094	24631	39331	66466	98200	57210
95483	11390	79500	95929	21018	80234	11967	02100	15249	75466
98447	86088	38236	52711	97289	05929	34306	41298	20159	16429
86732	24965	57529	65692	45102	94170	72991	34499	25469	88295
00017	14428	13950	27867	96012	90020	05657	36040	32013	73593
19577	23379	32314	88972	80943	00810	24438	02910	26327	11837
99949	02938	04327	68140	96504	90920	43025	42032	59946	39301
07888	07495	49523	62903	72418	67769	73333	50603	40895	79813
71122	74229	02785	51996	17100	75967	17346	28091	15781	12987
66431	12160	32367	29420	02365	41955	78345	64987	69707	19315
07508	74254	15399	78034	41472	74756	36962	91117	24407	87084
08235	04811	09261	23772	48732	68675	23262	05142	21310	52588

Used by permission of RAND Corporation.

99576	03093	87527	35848	71876	21027	42002	67787	17981	67468
87429	81377	22996	43586	44303	98724	85239	86036	92063	25693
69704	95249	20426	55681	48290	56229	51269	93367	13304	62412
58287	91145	74044	73706	43089	43285	52871	20600	15172	63205
44543	06981	64923	94700	18579	34495	92207	46201	83687	45565
51345	82679	85959	58707	74177	73530	44421	72805	72445	77638
60805	54760	49291	35370	31358	53728	48837	22398	78577	34699
94709	77225	49119	59636	32374	29280	14821	72847	37038	97215
40692	55578	31932	31631	99065	59480	11434	94820	33320	48576
85772	87197	77476	86304	21054	27750	54141	47031	91362	46553
64109	17486	07580	90241	25288	67441	63958	26040	72928	58371
44130	68856	84927	08921	16351	34826	81753	13036	68664	55103
47570	64977	11839	81049	14859	45800	93519	56783	26678	95403
71505	97496	44242	62072	02427	67070	61558	77425	33061	28573
33130	39631	56393	41573	90914	28526	40997	43082	84646	00789
64943	12781	40642	46853	12205	35390	29999	58113	87978	44549
11636	25414	07362	35505	53651	23549	59229	02636	94269	67293
10140	13163	92380	98525	55559	43111	43137	64856	78413	73472
86815	46792	68828	32135	09493	95685	40409	47342	21559	81035
02601	84804	30947	70588	31510	36512	86046	92035	80971	78461
84167	05822	78593	71579	71522	17517	34760	26696	68553	63587
71741	48249	03605	81257	52236	59017	81071	02322	93910	51656
20901	53017	63203	17806	46713	33609	28888	39065	45852	41570
15574	07082	19542	60725	97056	66901	32613	53817	63856	85991
49319	56431	40655	18391	61770	46077	35487	25332	03194	16694

72195	68767	60846	08353	57475	15280	52887	51368	15713	20758
44052	49228	15868	07676	14994	39430	71803	79499	34989	51312
43646	55384	76359	07399	60317	42285	52859	30206	00584	51279
78899	85420	93118	33521	11608	50190	09894	77582	90196	22745
50201	89343	95604	32522	55549	33205	58427	86504	79224	85404
53664	24220	82877	11621	35505	32810	59665	42479	75120	42638
21884	09397	95109	51780	35828	34928	42561	23413	87256	96098
60576	79805	24509	92685	75800	57765	08333	81168	50606	36877
27642	32199	80919	80059	48973	19362	48226	64877	06207	08396
40917	46217	04820	20523	24956	43686	40304	01939	26727	90083
89658	80329	02180	54181	83692	53855	97220	64569	93510	54849
83426	65760	00098	29270	54332	33983	08605	52378	97373	23578
01837	82029	98140	60385	34759	38317	96270	14697	55137	91876
00997	61617	06272	00283	67396	91682	15334	73062	04327	58763
22529	54432	50704	00393	90650	11412	19933	86194	97585	31679
05078	55974	42408	34593	59319	84423	15322	92885	53548	71959
89729	54175	98683	72919	53001	99886	54586	86866	30767	60654
15565	90647	55917	05217	11039	86111	26083	49670	60226	09534
25500	60560	61431	52963	93685	74015	93275	16247	57468	87710
17339	53708	34099	75573	86717	02524	19945	79265	02488	79953

Continued

80302	89644	46540	16807	46562	61799	22816	88015	46304	13336
56452	13100	23947	31330	97352	12165	01178	98728	13430	64012
35392	18601	48424	38352	98377	11871	45511	07625	50878	92715
52728	68665	57473	88285	23203	22955	22663	49092	42908	33008
57726	68825	61025	59688	46649	45254	48217	66220	46873	11208

11767	41715	96921	39440	91713	01252	95477	90091	74570	47814
10209	39469	04395	96949	68306	59930	43058	74922	84796	25716
88035	86619	10325	12403	59223	80176	03721	42071	86811	58308
01488	22623	75963	52672	08033	94360	23673	80897	68904	98109
85453	72323	32385	04738	68076	97592	19285	41760	42244	51078
94870	60073	79608	75998	05122	18855	98943	26426	84879	74388
92793	48899	87556	46924	20939	72246	53768	14024	09495	40912
02048	90603	58746	02696	73115	25929	51870	61184	65085	78295
99402	91657	18017	77315	39059	24381	21328	36197	89852	69923
52804	36184	32274	65204	35397	44192	06055	60314	10940	34627
74967	53533	93594	69969	16216	97183	95154	37719	90074	06928
15360	86221	06240	68606	05993	28257	80451	90422	20624	31777
53092	10820	71341	56926	48072	70936	33884	63004	81011	90241
78293	43707	65260	46559	21593	61172	05802	48592	96801	88425
24698	22898	26339	77971	47433	41759	74193	54506	04385	71026
36341	31972	45946	23649	94999	27633	01609	19345	83854	65117
70032	05924	91583	26358	42395	85283	36548	48571	90295	65056
58505	19927	12491	29716	88554	84748	75150	20811	92332	52934
73594	99247	47006	04316	15214	68184	50502	00906	58323	81340
76445	56970	29913	49436	49418	89565	90371	02911	18781	49995

E

CPS Questionnaire

Bowling Green-Warren County Community Preference Survey

1) Telephone # __ - _____   Record Number _____

2) Interviewer Code _____

Introduction

3) We would like to begin by asking you how you feel about Warren County as a place to live. Do you consider it to be a good, fair, or poor place to live?

1 good   2 fair   3 poor   4 DK   NA

4) Is your residence inside the city limits of Bowling Green?

1 Bowling Green   2 Warren County   3 DK   NA

5) Were you born in Warren County?

1 Yes   2 No   3 DK   NA

6) IF YES, ASK: Have you lived here all your life?

1 Yes   2 No   3 DK   NA

7) IF NO, ASK: How many years have you lived in Warren County?

_____ years   99 DK   NA

8) IF R HAS LIVED HERE OVER 5 YEARS, ASK: Over the past 5 years would you say that Warren County has become a better place to live, a worse place, or stayed about the same?

1 Better   2 Worse   3 Stayed Same   4 DK   NA

9) Over the next 5 years do you think Warren County will become better, worse, or stay the same?

1 Better   2 Worse   3 Stay Same   4 DK   NA

Favor or Oppose

Right now there are several local issues, some of which have received a lot of attention and discussion in this community. We would like to know your opinions on them. Now I would like to ask you about some of these issues.

Are you in favor of, opposed to, or uncertain about . . .

10) .. The proposal to merge the city and county governments into one urban or metropolitan government?

1 favor   2 oppose   3 uncertain   NA

11) .. Combining the city and county school systems?

1 favor   2 oppose   3 uncertain   NA

12) .. The city ordinance that bans nude dancing where liquor is served?

1 favor   2 oppose   3 uncertain   NA

13) .. Establishing a commuter airline service to Nashville and Louisville?

1 favor   2 oppose   3 uncertain   NA

14) .. Building a convention center?

1 favor   2 oppose   3 uncertain   NA

15) .. Measured telephone service?

1 favor   2 oppose   3 uncertain   NA

16) .. Mandatory drug testing for all employees?

1 favor   2 oppose   3 uncertain   NA

17) .. Mandatory drug testing for athletes starting at the high school level?

1 favor   2 oppose   3 uncertain   NA

18) . . Mandatory seat belt use?

     1 favor   2 oppose   3 uncertain   NA

19) . . Having smoking and nonsmoking areas in work places?

     1 favor   2 oppose   3 uncertain   NA

20) . . A ban on building new shopping centers until vacant buildings are used?

     1 favor   2 oppose   3 uncertain   NA

21) . . A leash law for dogs in the city limits?

     1 favor   2 oppose   3 uncertain   NA

22) . . Sex education in schools?

     1 favor   2 oppose   3 uncertain   NA

     23) IF YES, ASK: At what grade level should it begin?

     _____ grade level   99 DK   NA

24) . . Drug education in schools?

     1 favor   2 oppose   3 uncertain   NA

     25) IF YES, ASK: At what grade level should it begin?

     _____ grade level   99 DK   NA

Rate the Quality of BG/WC

Students are often given grades of A for excellent, B for good, C for average, D for poor, and F for failure to describe the quality of their work. Now, I am going to ask you to grade some aspects of our community. If conditions in Bowling Green–Warren County were graded in the same way what grade (A, B, C, D or F) would you give the . . .

26) . . City Government

     1 A   2 B   3 C   4 D   5 F   6 DK   NA

27) . . County Government

     1 A   2 B   3 C   4 D   5 F   6 DK   NA

28) . . Police Protection where you live

     1 A   2 B   3 C   4 D   5 F   6 DK   NA

29) . . Fire Protection where you live

     1 A   2 B   3 C   4 D   5 F   6 DK   NA

30) . . Bowling Green city public schools

     1 A   2 B   3 C   4 D   5 F   6 DK   NA

31) . . Warren County public schools

     1 A   2 B   3 C   4 D   5 F   6 DK   NA

32) . . Western Kentucky University

     1 A   2 B   3 C   4 D   5 F   6 DK   NA

33) . . Medical Facilities

     1 A   2 B   3 C   4 D   5 F   6 DK   NA

34) . . Shopping Facilities

     1 A   2 B   3 C   4 D   5 F   6 DK   NA

35) . . Cultural Opportunities

     1 A   2 B   3 C   4 D   5 F   6 DK   NA

36) . . Park City Daily Newspaper

     1 A   2 B   3 C   4 D   5 F   6 DK   NA

37) . . WBKO TV Channel 13

     1 A   2 B   3 C   4 D   5 F   6 DK   NA

38) . . The Chamber of Commerce

     1 A   2 B   3 C   4 D   5 F   6 DK   NA

39) . . The Planning and Zoning Commission

     1 A   2 B   3 C   4 D   5 F   6 DK   NA

40) . . Parks and Recreational Facilities

     1 A   2 B   3 C   4 D   5 F   6 DK   NA

Seriousness

Next we would like to get your opinions on some aspects of life in this community. In your opinion is there a serious problem, a slight problem, or no problem at all in this community with . . .

41) . . Crime?

     1 serious   2 slight   3 No problem   4 DK   NA

42) . . Underage drinking?

     1 serious   2 slight   3 No problem   4 DK   NA

43) . . Smoking among youth under 18?

    1 serious   2 slight   3 No problem   4 DK   NA

44) . . Drug use among elementary students?

    1 serious   2 slight   3 No problem   4 DK   NA

45) . . Drug use among high school students?

    1 serious   2 slight   3 No problem   4 DK   NA

46) . . Drug use among college students?

    1 serious   2 slight   3 No problem   4 DK   NA

47) . . Drug use among adults?

    1 serious   2 slight   3 No problem   4 DK   NA

48) . . Racial discrimination?

    1 serious   2 slight   3 No problem   4 DK   NA

49) . . Sexual discrimination?

    1 serious   2 slight   3 No problem   4 DK   NA

50) . . Water pollution?

    1 serious   2 slight   3 No problem   4 DK   NA

51) . . Pollution from bird roosts?

    1 serious   2 slight   3 No problem   4 DK   NA

52) . . Illiteracy?

    1 serious   2 slight   3 No problem   4 DK   NA

53) . . Pornography?

    1 serious   2 slight   3 No problem   4 DK   NA

54) . . Road conditions?

    1 serious   2 slight   3 No problem   4 DK   NA

55) . . Unemployment?

    1 serious   2 slight   3 No problem   4 DK   NA

56) . . Poverty?

    1 serious   2 slight   3 No problem   4 DK   NA

Needs

Now I'm going to ask you about a number of community projects which would require public funding. All of these questions can be answered yes or no. In your opinion, do we need to . . .

57) . . Expand rape crisis services?

    1 Yes   2 No   3 DK   NA

58) . . Provide more child abuse prevention service?

    1 Yes   2 No   3 DK   NA

59) . . Provide services to the homeless?

    1 Yes   2 No   3 DK   NA

60) . . Provide drug rehabilitation services?

    1 Yes   2 No   3 DK   NA

61) . . Attract new industry to Bowling Green?

    1 Yes   2 No   3 DK   NA

62) . . Provide public day care facilities for working parents?

    1 Yes   2 No   3 DK   NA

63) . . Revitalize the downtown district?

    1 Yes   2 No   3 DK   NA

64) . . Build a new public swimming pool?

    1 Yes   2 No   3 DK   NA

65) . . Build a new public 18-hole golf course?

    1 Yes   2 No   3 DK   NA

66) . . Provide a community center for the elderly?

    1 Yes   2 No   3 DK   NA

67) . . Build an I-65 interchange at Cemetery Road?

    1 Yes   2 No   3 DK   NA

68) . . Build a traffic loop around Bowling Green?

    1 Yes   2 No   3 DK   NA

69) . . Start a city bus system in Bowling Green?

    1 Yes   2 No   3 DK   NA

70) Is there a need for a community college at WKU?

    1 Yes   2 No   3 DK   NA

Taxes

Next, I would like your opinion about local taxes.

71) Are the city taxes . . .

    1 too high   2 about right   3 too low   4 DK   NA

72) Are the county taxes . . .

    1 too high   2 about right   3 too low   4 DK   NA

73) Would you be willing to support a tax or fee to pay for community improvement?

    1 yes   2 no   3 DK   NA

Background Variables

We are almost finished but there are several bits of background information we would like to ask:

74) DO NOT ASK BUT RECORD RESPONDENT'S SEX HERE.

    1 Male   2 Female

75) What was your age at your last birthday?

    _____ years   99 DK   NA

76) What is your marital status?

    1 Married   2 Single, never married
    3 Divorced   4 Widowed
    5 Separated   6 Cohabiting
    9 Don't know   NA

77) How many people live in your household including yourself?

    _____ people   99 DK   NA

78) How many of these are under age 18?

    _____ people < 18 years   99 DK   NA

79) What was the last grade level that you completed in any school?

    _____ grade   99 DK   NA

80) IF NOT CLEAR, ASK: What is your highest diploma or degree?

1 Not HS graduate
2 HS Graduate
3 Some college or trade or business school
4 College graduate or beyond
5 DK   NA

81)   Do you own or rent the place you live in?

1 Own   2 Rent   3 DK   NA

82)   What race do you consider yourself?

1 White   2 Black   3 Other   4 DK   NA

83)   Are you employed?

1 Yes   2 No   3 DK   NA

84) IF YES, ASK: What is your occupation?

specify _____   NA

85)   Into which of the following categories would you say that your total family income would fall?

Less than $10,000 1
Between $10,000 and $20,000 2
Between $20,000 and $30,000 3
Between $30,000 and $40,000 4
Between $40,000 and $50,000 5
Over $50,000 6
Don't know 9   NA

86)   Generally speaking, do you consider yourself a Republican, Democrat, Independent, or what?

1 Republican   2 Democrat   3 Independent

4 Other, specify _____   NA

87)   Are you registered to vote in the precinct where you live?

1 Yes   2 No   3 DK   NA

88)   What area of the city or county do you live in?

specify _____   NA

F

Answers to Selected Exercises

Answers are provided to selected odd-numbered computational problems and noncomputer exercises.

INTRODUCTION
Exercise A: Math Review Quiz

1. -13
3. 13.42
5. 243
7. 97.48
9. 54
11. 2.24
13. $c - a$
15. $5/2(x - 7)$
17. 88.44
19. 26
21. 384

SECTION 2
Exercise 2A

Table 2.14   Frequency Distribution of Marital Status

Marital Status	f	%	cum%
Never married	5	25.0	25.0
Married	7	35.0	60.0
Widowed	3	15.0	75.0
Divorced	4	20.0	95.0
Separated	1	5.0	100.0
Totals	20	100.0	

SECTION 3
Exercise 3A

1a. .70, or 70 per 100
1b. 41.24 percent
1c. .59

Exercise 3C

1. no mode
3. 67.2
5. 75
7. 201.6—it is multiplied by 3
9. $\sigma^2 = 441.96$
   $s^2 = 491.07$

Exercise 3D

1. $21,000
3. $26,000
5. $38,000
7. $\sigma^2 = \$133,200,000$
   $s^2 = \$140,210,520$

Exercise 3E

1. $10,000 ($9,750 rounded to nearest thousandth)
3. 21.19 (if interval is 14,000–23,000)
5. 30.17
7. $\sigma = \$11,779.22$
   $s = \$12,085.22$

Exercise 3F

1. 35.5 (interval 31–40)
3. 29.0
5. $\sigma^2 = 190.25$
   $s^2 = 192.66$

SECTION 4
Exercise 4A

1. .64
3. critical chi-square = 3.84, fail to reject H_0
5. C = .176

Exercise 4B

1. 4.10
3. critical chi-square, at $\alpha = .05$, = 3.84
   critical chi-square, at $\alpha = .01$ = 6.64
   results not significant at .01
5. Somer's d = .434

SECTION 10
Exercise 10A

1. .4251
3. .6270
5. .2260
7. .9699
9. .0301

Exercise 10B

1a. .1179
1c. .6179
1e. .2234
1g. $.0287 < 31$
    $.9731 < 69$
3. 33.55

Exercise 10C

1. .0030
3. widen

Exercise 10D

1a. $.53 < P < .61$
1c. $.51 < P < .63$
3. widen

Exercise 10E

1a. 12.963
1c. .135
3a. $12.698 < \mu < 13.228$

Exercise 10F

1a. .857
3a. .028
5. 1,849 (if $P = .5$)
   906.4 (if $P = .857$)

SECTION 11
Exercise 11A

1. $H_1: P_s < P_\mu$
   $Z = -2.437$; Reject H_0
3. $H_1: X \neq \mu$
   $t = -2.46$; Fail to reject H_0
5. $H_1: P_1 > P_2$
   $Z = 1.78$; Reject H_0
7. $H_1: d > 0$
   $t = 2.14$; Reject H_0

Exercise 11B

1. $H_1: P_1 > P_2$
 $Z = .55$; Fail to reject H_0
3. H_1: Means are not all equal
 $F = 4.64$, Reject H_0
5. $H_1: d > 0$
 $t = 2.01$; Fail to reject H_0
7. $H_1: \sigma_1^2 > \sigma_2^2$
 $F = 2.25$; Reject H_0

Exercise 11C

1. $F = 11.10$; Reject H_0

Exercise 11D

1. $H_1: \mu_1 > \mu_2$
 $t = 2.10$; Fail to reject H_0
3. $H_1: P_s > P_\mu$
 $Z = 8.08$; Reject H_0
5. $H_1: P_1 > P_2$
 $Z = 1.50$; Fail to reject H_0
7. $H_1: \mu_1 \neq \mu_2$
 $t = -2.77$; Reject H_0
9. $H_1: P_s > P_\mu$
 $Z = 3.54$; Reject H_0
11. $H_1: P_1 < P_2$
 $Z = -1.92$; Fail to reject H_0

Exercise 11E

1. $F = 1.45$; Fail to reject H_0

SECTION 12
Exercise 12A

1. $r_s = .91$

Exercise 12C

1a. $\chi^2 = 4.9$; Fail to reject H_0

Exercise 12E

1. $Z = -1.22$; Fail to reject H_0

Exercise 12G

1. $Z = -.777$; Fail to reject H_0

Exercise 12H

1. $H = 11.20$; Reject H_0

SECTION 13
Exercise 13A

1. $Y' = 2.57 + .358(X)$
3. 22.23
5. $r = .61$
7. the proportion of the variation in Y explained by X

Exercise 13B

1. $Y' = 4.13 - .21(X)$
3. .05
5. $r = -.98$

Exercise 13C

1. $Y' = 4.806 - .081(X)$
3. 6.16
5. $r = -.10$

Exercise 13D

1. $Y' = 3.886 - .208(X)$ for GRADEDR
 $Y' = 5.166 - .011(X)$ for GRADESEX
5. $r = -.09$ for GRADEDR
 $r = -.005$ for GRADESEX

Exercise 13E

1. $Y' = 16.54 - .075(X)$
5. $r = -.274$

SECTION 14
Exercise 14F

1. The original bivariate table would be:

Table Income by Sex

Income	Sex	
	Women	Men
$30,000 or more	30.3	58.3
Less than $30,000	69.7	41.7
	100.0%	100.0%

3. The diagram is:
   Sex ----------> Type of Occupation ----------> Income

Exercise 14H

1. The original bivariate table reporting the INCOME BY DIPLOMA relationship
   is:

Table CPS Respondents' Total 1986 Family Income by Highest Diploma

	Highest Diploma		
Total 1986 Family Income	Some College or Less	College Degree or More	Total
More than $30,000	26.4	60.1	34.8
$30,000 or Less	73.6	39.9	65.2
Total	100.0%	100.0%	100.0%
(N)	(416)	(138)	(554)

chi-square (corrected) = 50.38, p < .01, d.f. = 1
Somer's $d = +.30$, tau $b = +.31$, gamma $= +.62$

5. The diagram is:

DIPLOMA ------->MEN --------- +.34 -----> INCOME
DIPLOMA ------->WOMEN ------- +.27 -----> INCOME

SECTION 15
Exercise 15A

1. Stepwise $R = .62$
   Enter $R = .6286$

3.

	Beta Weights	
	Stepwise	Enter
GRADEDR	.558	.539
GRADE	−.173	−.170
SEX	.116	.128

5. Stepwise $R^2 = .385$
   Enter $R^2 = .395$

Index